Compliments of

MERI☀N
WEALTH PARTNERS, LLC
www.merionwealth.com

We hope you find this to be an educational resource.
Please consult with the appropriate professional advisors
before considering any financial plan or implementation.

The Power of Leveraging the Charitable Remainder Trust

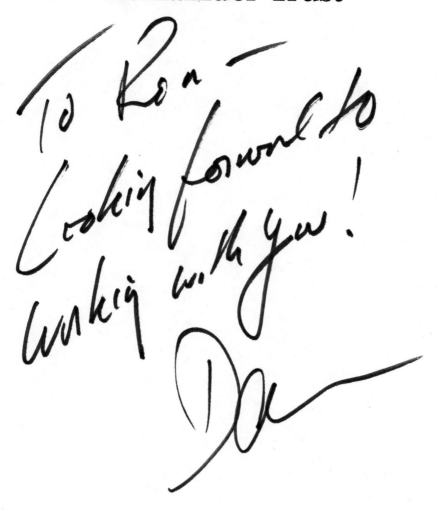

To Ron –
Looking forward to
working with you!

D

The Power of Leveraging the Charitable Remainder Trust

YOUR SECRET WEAPON AGAINST THE WAR ON WEALTH

Daniel G. Nigito

WILEY

John Wiley & Sons, Inc.

Published by John Wiley & Sons, Inc., Hoboken, New Jersey.
Published simultaneously in Canada.

No part of this publication may be reproduced, stored in a retrieval system, or transmitted
in any form or by any means, electronic, mechanical, photocopying, recording, scanning,
or otherwise, except as permitted under Section 107 or 108 of the 1976 United States
Copyright Act, without either the prior written permission of the Publisher, or authorization
through payment of the appropriate per-copy fee to the Copyright Clearance Center, Inc.,
222 Rosewood Drive, Danvers, MA 01923, (978) 750–8400, fax (978) 646–8600, or on the
web at www.copyright.com. Requests to the Publisher for permission should be addressed to
the Permissions Department, John Wiley & Sons, Inc., 111 River Street, Hoboken, NJ 07030,
(201) 748–6011, fax (201) 748–6008, or online at http://www.wiley
.com/go/permissions.

Limit of Liability/Disclaimer of Warranty: While the publisher and author have used their
best efforts in preparing this book, they make no representations or warranties with respect
to the accuracy or completeness of the contents of this book and specifically disclaim any
implied warranties of merchantability or fitness for a particular purpose. No warranty may
be created or extended by sales representatives or written sales materials. The advice and
strategies contained herein may not be suitable for your situation. You should consult with a
professional where appropriate. Neither the publisher nor author shall be liable for any loss
of profit or any other commercial damages, including but not limited to special, incidental,
consequential, or other damages.

For general information on our other products and services or for technical support, please
contact our Customer Care Department within the United States at (800) 762–2974, outside
the United States at (317) 572–3993 or fax (317) 572–4002.

Wiley also publishes its books in a variety of electronic formats. Some content that appears in
print may not be available in electronic books. For more information about Wiley products,
visit our web site at www.wiley.com.

Library of Congress Cataloging-in-Publication Data:

Nigito, Daniel G.
    The power of leveraging the charitable remainder trust: your secret weapon against the
war on wealth/Daniel Nigito.
        p. cm.
    Includes index.
    ISBN 978-0-470-54112-8
    1. Endowments—United States.   2. Charitable uses, trusts, and foundations—United
States.   3. Tax planning—United States.   I. Title.
    HV35.N54 2009
    336.2'06—dc22
                                                                            2009021633

Printed in the United States of America
10 9 8 7 6 5 4 3 2 1

For my wife, Shelley.
Just being in your presence elevates my game.

Contents

Acknowledgments

No one can whistle a symphony. It takes a whole orchestra to play it.
—H.E. Luccock

I have been blessed in my life to be supported along the way by people who allow me to do the "job" that I love—teaching folks how to add meaning to their money. I want to mention a few of them here. At the heart of our team at Market Street Financial Advisors, in Bethlehem Pa is David Weikert. Dave handles all the day to day "stuff" that keeps our business running, while I'm off writing books and giving lectures. He's been with me for over ten years and I could not do what I do without him.

In the "What good is family if you can't get them to help you?" department, I want to thank my cousin, Jennifer LaBracio. In addition to being gorgeous and talented in her own right, Jen opened the door to my new publisher, John Wiley and Sons, Inc. It has proved to be a great fit for me. At Wiley, I have enjoyed working with David Pugh, Senior Editor, and Todd Tedesco, Senior Production Editor. They are professional, responsive, and have a great sense of humor. I also want to add a special thank you to Kelly O'Connor, Development Editor, for her thoughtful comments and changes to the original manuscript. It is a welcome experience to work with people who actually "get it."

None of this would be possible without my wife, Shelley. She is simply the finest person I've ever met. She also has the best business sense of anyone I know. Her impact on our community through her leadership as the CEO of the State Theatre, Center of the Arts in

Easton, Pa is the stuff legacies are built on. She set the standard for integrity.

Finally, I must thank our kids—in order of their appearance, Courtney, Tim, Natalie, Dominic, and Vince. They range in age from 30ish to 20ish and I have cherished every single year. I love my family (even our bulldog, Gracie), and I can't put it any simpler than that. I thank God for them every day. Speaking of God, this book may be mine, but the glory is His.

Disclaimer

This publication is designed to provide accurate authoritative information in regard to the subject matter covered. It is distributed with the understanding that the publisher is not engaged in rendering legal, accounting, or other professional service. If legal advice or other expertise is required, the services of a competent professional should be sought. From: *A Declaration of Principles* jointly adopted by a committee of the American Bar Association and a Committee of Publishers.

IRS Circular 230 disclosure: In order to comply with requirements imposed by the IRS, please be advised that any tax advice contained in this communication (including attachments) is not intended or written to be used, and cannot be used, for the purpose of (i) avoiding tax-related penalties under the Internal Revenue Code or (ii) promoting, marketing, or recommending to another party any transaction or tax-related matter(s) addressed herein.

INTRODUCTION

Is this the Change
You Can Believe In?

*If you put the federal government in charge of the Sahara Desert, in
five years there'd be a shortage of sand.*

—Milton Friedman

Well, here we are. Just about everything we earned over the
last 12 years is gone. But it is not enough. If you played by the
rules, paid your taxes, paid your bills (mortgage, too), put a few
dollars away, and invested in the United States—or the world for
that matter, you lost. We lost. But it is not enough. The revolution
came and went, without a shot fired, without blood spilled. We are
now ruled by a congress and president determined to redistribute the wealth at all costs—even if it costs all. America, this is your
wake-up call: *This is not a congress or administration that cares about
getting it right, it is about getting even.*

In a nutshell, your government feels that they can spend your
money better than you can, that they can *manage* your money better
than you can. They determine who gets what and how much; which
causes are worthwhile and which are not. And, they do it with *your*
money. But, not to worry, they can be trusted to be the stewards of
your tax dollars, right? How's that been working out so far?

This book is about one simple strategy that we can use to help
us take back control of our money and how it's spent. There are

many strategies—this is only one, *but it is effective.* It's about wiping the blood from our collective nose, taking the standing eight-count, and staggering back into the ring. Okay, maybe I'm getting a little carried away with the athletic analogies—but you get my point, *fight back!*

Wake Up and Smell the Reality

- If you earn more than $150,000 per year (not the $250,000 you've heard about), you're the enemy.
- If someday you plan on taking more than $150,000 out of your retirement plan, or plan on transferring what's left of it to your kids when you die, you're the enemy.
- If you own your own business—even if you're the only employee—you're the enemy.
- If you own any investment that will someday be sold for a gain (which is the whole point), you're the enemy. I know that seems like a reach after the market beat-down, but gains do still exist and will return.
- And if you spent your life building your assets to where they exceed $3,500,000, you are really the enemy.

Notice that nowhere in the list above did I mention Wall Street moguls making $20 million bonuses. Nowhere above did I mention the "titans" of industry who amassed vast amounts of wealth while running their companies into the ground. This book is not about them, it is about us. They make great headlines and make us furious. But they are thieves and thugs, they are not us. Unfortunately, they have provided a great excuse for the current administration to wage a war on wealth and on those who actually believe in capitalism and the creation of wealth. What used to be called "the American dream."

Look in the mirror, look at you paycheck, look at your assets—that's us, you are us. We are the 10 percent who pay 71 percent of all the income taxes. We are the 5 percent who pay 89 percent of all the capital gains taxes. We are the 2 percent that pay 100 percent of all the gift and estate taxes. We are a targeted class of *accidental philanthropists.* That is, we don't have the choice of who we give our money to, or how much we give them. The government takes, the government decides—who and how much.

Until now.

There is a way to fight back. There is a way to take control of your tax dollars and how they are spent. The best way to avoid the redistribution of wealth through taxation is by avoiding the taxation in the first place—legally. The best way to avoid becoming an accidental philanthropist is by becoming an *active* one by using the specific strategy detailed in this book. *The best way to fight back is by unleashing the power of charitable leverage.*

Stay with me and I will teach you this strategy in words of one syllable or less. I'll use plain New Jersey English and lots of step-by-step charts. Stay with me and I will show you the real magic of this strategy, that when you use charitable leverage you take the power away from congress and keep it for yourself. Better still, in the process you will provide more wealth for you and your family.

It's your money. Shouldn't you be the one to decide what happens to it?

The Power of Charitable Leverage

> *We have the right as individuals to give away as much of our own money as we please in charity; but as members of Congress we have no right to appropriate a dollar of the public money.*
>
> —Davy Crockett

Before we go any further, I want to be very clear on this strategy I call *charitable leverage*. I want you to become a philanthropist instead of a dope. Is that clear enough? The current state of our tax system penalizes those among us who work the hardest, take the risks, and actually buy into capitalism and free markets. And it is going to get worse. The key to a charitably leveraged plan is that *dollars you would normally lose to taxes are rerouted to causes you actually care about—to be used exactly the way you want.*

Throughout the nonprofit world a battle has raged forever among development officers and professional fundraisers about the role tax incentives play in charitable giving. This strategy takes place outside of that debate. The use of a charitably leveraged strategy is not about whether you have it in your heart to give, but whether you have it in your stomach to let the government give it for you.

Charitable leverage offers a new type of wealth management—one that allows you to become a *partner with charity* to gain control over your tax destiny and to provide for you and your family in the bargain. In short, it allows you to add meaning to your money. This is not about some new tax loophole I discovered. It is completely the opposite. This strategy uses two financial instruments that are rooted in the tax code and have been hiding in front of us for decades.

This may not be the right approach for you. For you to fully benefit from the programs I present in this book, you first must fit into one of the accidental philanthropist targeted categories that we cover in the next chapter; and *you do need to have a desire to create a charitable legacy.*

So here's how we're going to do this.

- First, I show you how you are exposed to accidental philanthropy by virtue of the current tax structure and redistribution of wealth.
- Next, I explain the mechanics of charitable leverage. I break it down so that you see clearly how it works. There are only two moving parts so it's pretty simple to understand.
- When, we're done with that, I show you how you can apply a charitably leveraged strategy in specific everyday financial planning scenarios.
- Finally, I follow each planning strategy with a case study that plugs in real numbers and then compares it with its traditional and "accidentally philanthropic" alternative.

When we're done you'll be in a position to judge for yourself whether this is the right plan for you. Imagine that, you—in control—of your money.

PART

I

WELCOME TO THE WAR ON WEALTH

1

The Weapons of Mass Destruction in the War on Wealth

Government's view of the economy could be summed up in a few short phrases: If it moves, tax it. If it keeps moving, regulate it. And if it stops moving, subsidize it.

—Ronald Reagan

Taxes are the weapons of choice used by the government in its War on Wealth. Income tax, dividend tax, capital gains tax, estate tax, and income tax again on retirement plans are the new WMD. They may not be Weapons of Mass Destruction, but they are Weapons of Mass re-Distribution. Further, it impacts a hell of a lot more than 5 percent of U.S. taxpayers. *You are the target.*

This chapter poses a simple question, "Just how many times can you tax the same damn dollar?" I tell you in advance that you're not going to like the answer, but you need to know what you're up against. We work under the brunt of a tax system that can impose different types of tax on the same dollar up to *three or four separate times*. With every tax dollar you pay you move farther along the road to accidental philanthropy. Let's take a look at each tax, when it is applied, and just who pays it. If you have any antidepressants or antacids lying around the house, you may want to take them *all* now. Put the laxatives away—you're not going to need 'em.

Tax #1: The Federal Income Tax—Negative Impact 28 Percent to 35 Percent. Going to 36 Percent to 40 Percent

Before I get into what the income tax rate is now and what it will be when the Bush tax cuts expire in 2011 (as proposed under President Obama's budget), let's take a look at who *actually pays this tax* and how much we pay.

Table 1.1 shows that, according to the latest IRS statistics (based on 2006 Adjusted Gross Income, AGI), the top 5 percent of the highest earning Americans, pay more than 60 percent of all the income taxes paid. But here is the stunning part of that statistic—to be in that category you only need income over $153,000! To be in the top 10 percent, who pay 71 percent of all the taxes, your earnings only need to exceed, $108,000. If you want to be in the rare air of the 1 percent who pays 40 percent of all the income taxes, you only need adjusted gross income greater than $389,000. The bottom 50 percent pays less than 3 percent of the tax burden.

The takeaway from Table 1.1 is that while everyone seems focused on the evil top wage earner making more than $250,000 per year, the reality is that if you're earning more than $150,000 you're bearing the brunt of taxes as well. How much are we talking about? Take a look at Table 1.2.

We may not like it, but it is the simplest to understand. For every new dollar we earn, we give away currently 33 cents to 35 cents. When the Bush tax cuts expire at the end of 2010, that number increases to 36 cents to 40 cents. Not great, but if that was the only time that dollar was taxed I don't think many of us would complain. I'm not saying we'd be throwing a party, but we wouldn't be miserable either. The problem is that if you play by the rules and save some of your money instead of spending it all, the government repays you by continually taxing that same dollar. How? Read on.

Table 1.1   Income Taxes Paid by Catagory

Percentage Ranked by AGI	AGI Threshold on Percentages	Percentage of Federal Income Tax Paid
Top 1%	$388,806	39.89
Top 5%	$153,542	60.14
Top 10%	$108,904	70.79
Top 25%	$64,702	86.27
Top 50%	$31,987	97.01
Bottom 50%	<$31,987	2.99

Source: IRS Statistics via Kiplinger.com, July 25, 2008, "What's Your Share of the Nation's Tax Bill?" by Kevin McCormally.

Table 1.2   Current and Proposed Income Tax Rates.

2009 Tax Bracket	AGI Range for Married Couples	AGI Range for Singles	Proposed Increase in 2011
28%	$137,050–$208,850	$82,850–$171,550	28%
33%	$208,850–$372,950	$171,550–$372,950	36%
35%	<$372,950	<$372,950	39.6%

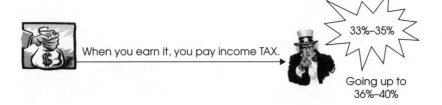

When you earn it, you pay income TAX.

33%–35%

Going up to 36%–40%

Tax #2: Investment Income Tax—Negative Impact: 15 Percent to 35 Percent. Going up to 20 Percent to 40 Percent

After you have paid income tax on your earnings, you have a choice as to what to do with what's left. You can spend it, you can save it, or you can do a combination. Remember, we're talking about your after-tax earnings, not your 401(k), or other pretax retirement plan (we cover those later). You probably spend some, save some in an effort to accumulate a nest egg for whatever the future holds. You would think that a country with one of low-est savings rates in world would provide an incentive to save, we don't. In fact, we do the opposite; we tax the crap out it.

If you invest that after-tax dollar into corporate America (you know, the stuff capitalists do to make money and help the country grow) you'll pay a tax on your earnings. If you buy corporate bonds the annual bond income is taxed at your ordinary income tax rate. If you buy a stock that pays a dividend, you'll pay tax at the cur-rent dividend tax rate of 15 percent. Both rates are scheduled to increase under the proposed budget.

If you choose to invest some of your savings into other programs like real estate or more exotic funds, you will not escape an addi-tional tax on your investment earnings. Municipal bonds are the only income-producing investment that is tax-free. Have you looked at those returns lately?

There's no need to beat this to death, I have far more disturb-ing stuff to get to. I just want you to be aware of tax #2. A lot of peo-ple skip over it like it's not a big deal. It is.

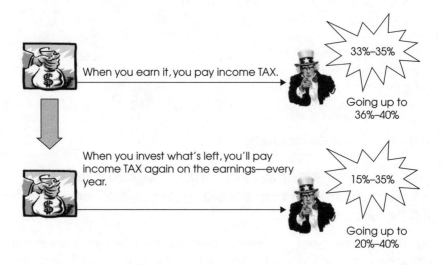

Tax #3: Capital Gains Tax—Negative Impact: 15 Percent Going to 20 Percent

In my view there is nothing quite as harmful as the tax on capital gains. It is a pure penalty imposed on the capitalist for investing in something that works. For the U.S. business owner, it is the ultimate slap in the face for his or her success. It is like the government saying, "Our way of thanking you for building this country is to tax you on the profits you made on the money we've already taxed, after taxing you on all the income that you produced." Does that make any sense to you, or is it just me?

Like the federal income tax, the sweet spot for capital gains tax is the top 5 percent of income earners. People earning more than $154,000 per year account for 89 percent of all the capital gains tax paid! That is a stunning number. Even more stunning is the fact that the tax rate, currently 15 percent will increase under the proposed budget to 20 percent in 2011. That ought to stimulate the economy, right? Table 1.3 shows the stats on who pays the capital gains tax. For example, if you are a taxpayer in the top 10 percent of wage earners, your group accounts for more than 94 percent of all the capital gains taxes.

So, if you're keeping score, first you pay 40 percent tax on the income you earn. Then, you take some of that remaining income and invest it for the future, and you pay 20 percent to 40 percent on the income that it generates each year. Then, if you're lucky enough to invest in something that appreciates in value over time, you pay tax again when you sell it; to the tune of another 20 percent! And, that's just the injury; we haven't gotten to the insults yet.

Table 1.3   Who Pays Capital Gains Tax?

Percentage Ranked by AGI	AGI Range in Dollars	Percentage of Capital Gains Tax Paid in Range
Top 1%	>$396,000	72.6%
Top 5%	$154,000–$396,000	16.9%
Top 10%	$110,000–$154,000	4.8%
Top 20%	$77,000–$110,000	3.2%
Bottom 80%	<$77,000	2.5%

Source: IRS Statistics of Income, 2006; Institute on Taxation and Economic Policy, March 2006.

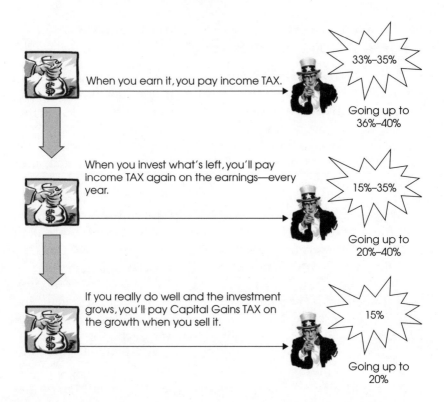

When you earn it, you pay income TAX.

33%–35%

Going up to
36%–40%

When you invest what's left, you'll pay
income TAX again on the earnings—every
year.

15%–35%

Going up to
20%–40%

If you really do well and the investment
grows, you'll pay Capital Gains TAX on
the growth when you sell it.

15%

Going up to
20%

Tax #4: Federal Estate Tax—Negative Impact:
45 Percent on Transfers at Death Over $3,500,000

And then, you die. Imagine that after paying tax all along the way
during your life, you get one more parting shot when you die and
try to transfer what's left to your kids. The message behind this tax
is very clear; it is redistribution of the wealth in its purest form. It is
the government standing between you and your children. It is that
simple.

Federal estate tax impacts less than 2 percent of Americans
each year, but accounts for more than $22 billion in tax revenue.
We all receive a tax credit on the transfer up to $3,500,000 at death.
Estate tax kicks in after that to the tune of 45 percent. Here's the
part you need to understand. Unlike the other three taxes you pay
along the way, the federal estate tax is not a tax on new income or
new growth. It is not a tax related to cash flow at all. *It is a tax on all
your stuff*!

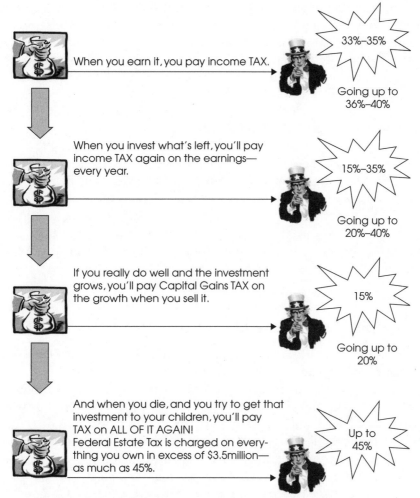

When you earn it, you pay income TAX.

33%–35%

Going up to
36%–40%

When you invest what's left, you'll pay income TAX again on the earnings— every year.

15%–35%

Going up to
20%–40%

If you really do well and the investment grows, you'll pay Capital Gains TAX on the growth when you sell it.

15%

Going up to
20%

And when you die, and you try to get that investment to your children, you'll pay TAX on ALL OF IT AGAIN!
Federal Estate Tax is charged on everything you own in excess of $3.5million— as much as 45%.

Up to
45%

And don't think you can do something clever like give it to your kids before you die, because you'll pay Federal GIFT TAX on all gifts in excess of $1,million at the same 45% rate! And gifts to grandchildren in excess of $3.5 million get hit with an additional 46% tax on top of the Gift TAX. *Yes, it is possible to pay more tax than you actually gifted!*

Everything, your house, your car, your rugs, your collectibles, your jewelry, your investments, your *retirement plan* (I get into more detail on that in a minute), your business, your investment real estate, your insurance, your furniture, everything you own is subject to estate tax. Even stuff you inherited from other family members— that you already paid tax on—is subject to tax.

And here's the cruelest rub of all, though your assets are valued at current market prices, even if they are illiquid, the government wants cash—in nine months. Can you imagine forcing a sale of a home in the current real estate market? Do you think you'd get what the home is worth, especially if the buyers knew there was a government clock ticking?

Estate taxes can be devastating because it sucks out all of the cash first, and leaves the family with illiquid assets. The net result to the family can be far worse than the 45 percent price tag.

Don't think that you can fool the IRS by gifting your assets to your children before you die. You can't beat 'em, in fact the tax could be worse. The gift tax rates are the same as the estate tax rates with one major difference, the free pass ($3,500,000 at death) is only $1,000,000 for gifts. Skip the kids and go directly to the grandkids and you face an *additional* generation-skipping transfer tax of 46 percent on transfers more than $3,500,000.

But Wait, There's One More Tax

Do you have any idea what happens to your IRA when you die? You better grab a bucket; you're going to need it.

The war on wealth takes place on many fronts; the bloodiest of these is the battle over control of the destiny of your retirement plan. Retirement plans come in many types: IRA, 401(k), SEP, SIMPLE, TSA, or 403(b). They are lumped together as "qualified retirement plans." To keep things simple I refer to all qualified plans as IRAs. They are savings vehicles that the government allows you to fund on a before-tax basis. Of course, the amount you can deposit each year is capped because we wouldn't want to encourage you to save too much. Your deposits are invested, and the whole thing grows without tax until you begin to draw on it in retirement. The theory is that when you reach retirement age you're in a lower tax bracket. How's that been working out for you?

But what happens when you die? Where does the remaining balance of your IRA or other qualified plan account go? If you're like most people, you designate your spouse as the beneficiary. That works, until she or he dies. Then it becomes a tax orgasm for Uncle Sam, and that is not a pretty sight for the following reasons:

- The entire value of your IRA is included in your estate for federal estate tax purposes. Although the value IRA itself may not exceed the $3,500,000 threshold, it is added to other assets, pushing up the value of your taxable estate. The amount that the IRA exceeds the unified credit is subject to federal estate tax.
- With or without the federal estate tax, the full value of the IRA must be declared as ordinary income because it is distributed to the next generation. This special income tax, imposed on *Income in Respect of a Decedent* (IRD), will place the IRA squarely in the highest income tax bracket.
- Finally, if you intend to skip your kids and give your IRA directly to your grandkids, the generation-skipping transfer tax (46 percent) is added to the estate and income taxes.

So, what I'm saying is that the least amount of tax you'll pay on your IRA distribution is 35 percent to 40 percent, and, if your estate is large enough, you could pay 63 percent to 70 percent! In Table 1.4 I show what happens to a $1,000,000 IRA in three different taxable estates.

Let's start with the easy stuff. If your IRA is worth $1,000,000 in an estate that is less than $3.5 million total, the tax is $350,000 (35 percent) and that becomes 40 percent or $400,000 in 2011. When is the last time you wrote a tax check that large? And, that's as good as it gets!

When we factor in the estate tax, let's just say the result is not very pretty. If the estate size grows to $4 million, of which $1,000,000 is IRA assets, you pay income tax plus estate tax. The estate tax is $225,000 and the income tax on the balance of the IRA that is not used to pay the estate tax is $271,250. The combined

Table 1.4 $1,000,000 IRA

IRA Value	Taxable Estate	Estate Tax	Income Tax	Total Lost to Tax	Net to Family	Percentage Lost
$1,000,000	Under $3,500,000	$0	$350,000	$350,000	$650,000	35%
$1,000,000	$4,000,000	$225,000	$271,250	$496,250	$503,750	50%
$1,000,000	$5,000,000	$450,000	$192,250	$642,500	$357,750	64%

Source: "Capital Punishment by Confiscation" software, Number Cruncher, Stephen R. Leimberg and Robert T. LaClair, March 2009.

taxes are $496,250 and the family receives $503,750. Your tax on the IRA just became 50 percent!

If the estate crosses the $5 million level, with a $1,000,000 IRA, you now enter the *64 percent* tax rate! The estate tax is $450,000 and the income tax adds another $192,500 for a total liability of $642,500. Your kids now only receive $357,500. Look at this: *the government actually gets more from your IRA than your kids do*! Imagine building a retirement account just for congress to play with.

Don't shoot the messenger.

How Many Times Can You Tax the Same Damn Dollar?

The same dollar is subject to tax three or possibly four times. The increases in income tax rates, dividend tax rates, and capital gains tax rates as proposed in the 2009 budget stand as road blocks on the road to wealth accumulation. However, the attack on capitalism reaches its pinnacle when you die; when all the past taxes are coupled with the insane taxation on retirement plans and estates at death. Talk about an Axis of Evil! Table 1.5 illustrates my point.

The table shows you four different asset value views of a poor shmoe who bought into the same American dream as the rest of us (the one where you work hard, depend on yourself, build your fortune, pass it on to your kids) only to have the rug pulled out from underneath him by his elected representatives who never worked a single day of their lives in the business world. Our man, we'll call him Mr. Schmooley, is a married business owner somewhere in his mid-sixties. He has spent his life building his business from nothing; hence, after deprecation, there is zero cost basis. He has a home, maybe a vacation property and some investments. His wife, the lovely Mrs. Schmooley, has had a long career in public education. Most of her savings has taken place in her Tax Sheltered Annuity (also known as a 403[b] or TSA). When coupled with Mr. Schmooley's retirement plan, they have about $1,500,000 of qualified retirement accounts. Lucky Mr. S. is about to sell his business and enjoy a life of leisure. It all sounded so good, he didn't know he was about to get nuked by the WMD in the war on wealth. His last words were, "funny, I didn't know I was wealthy . . ."

Table 1.5 The Four Faces of Mr. Schmooley

	Case #1		Case #2		Case #3		Case #4	
	Bus.:	$5,000,000 ($0 basis)	Bus.:	$5,000,000 ($0 basis)	Bus.:	$5,000,000 ($0 basis)	Bus.:	$3,000,000 ($0 basis)
	Inv./RE:	$3,000,000	Inv./RE:	$2,000,000	Inv./RE:	$1,000,000	Inv./RE:	$1,000,000
	IRA:	$1,500,000	IRA:	$1,500,000	IRA:	$1,500,000	IRA:	$1,500,000
	Estate:	$9,500,000	Estate:	$8,500,000	Estate:	$7,500,000	Estate:	$9,500,000
(1) Capital Gains Tax Loss at Sale of Business	$1,000,000		$1,000,000		$1,000,000		$600,000	
(2) Net Estate at 1st Spouse's Death	$8,500,000		$7,500,000		$6,500,000		$4,900,000	
(3) Free Pass Via Unified Credit	$3,500,000		$3,500,000		$3,500,000		$3,500,000	
(4) Net Estate at 2nd Spouse's Death (row 2 - row 3 = row 4)	$5,000,000		$4,000,000		$3,000,000		$1,400,000	
(5) Net Estate Tax	$675,000		$225,000		$0		$0	
(6) IRD (Income) Tax on IRA at Death	$330,000		$510,000		$600,000		$600,000	
(7) Total Estate Tax (5 + 6 = 7)	$1,005,000		$735,000		$600,000		$600,000	
(8) Total of All Tax (7 + 1 = 8)	$2,005,000		$1,735,000		$1,600,000		$1,200,000	
(9) Net to Family (gross estate – 8 = 9)	$7,495,000		$6,675,000		$5,906,000		$4,300,000	
(10) % of Total Lost Without Control	21%		21%		21%		22%	
(11) % of IRA Lost Without Control	67%		51%		40%		40%	

Case #1 shows Schmools at his most successful:
- Business value at $5,000,000 (all subject to capital gains)
- Investments and real estate valued at $3,000,000
- Combined IRAs at $1,500,000
- Total gross estate of $9,500,000

Case #2 shows the Schmoolster, still very successful, but not as fortunate in the investment world:
- Business value at $5,000,000
- Investments and real estate valued at *$2,000,000*
- Combined IRAs at $1,500,000
- Total gross estate of $8,500,000

Case #3 shows our hero with his brains beaten in by the stock market:
- Business value at $5,000,000
- Investments and real estate valued at *$1,000,000*
- Combined IRAs at $1,500,000
- Total gross estate of $7,500,000

Case #4 shows the Schmoolinator after a business downturn and market upchuck:
- Business value at *$3,000,000* (still, all subject to capital gains)
- Investments and real estate valued at $1,000,000
- Combined IRAs at $1,500,000
- Total gross estate of $6,500,000

Some Assumptions

Note, Table 1.5 assumes the President Obama tax increases (based on the 2009 proposed budget) are in effect (i.e., the top income rates increase to 40 percent and 36 percent—I know it's 39.4 percent, I'm rounding; capital gains tax rates increase to 20 percent; federal estate tax exemption held at $3,500,000 per person, excess taxed at 45 percent). Both Mr. and Mrs. S. take advantage of the combined unified estate tax credits totaling $7,000,000.

The first thing that smacks you in the face in the table is row 1, the tax loss resulting from the sale of the business. The folks who want to redistribute your wealth ask, "What are you complaining about, you got to keep $4,000,000?" The appropriate response is, "What the hell did *you* do for your $1,000,000?" I said appropriate response—not your first response—I don't use that kind of language. In Case #4, the lost dollar amount is reduced to $600,000 because the sale price has been reduced to $3,000,000. It's still 20 percent, and it still stinks, but the impact is greater since we're dealing with a smaller pot.

The rest of calculations occur at the death of the second spouse, when the estate is transferred to the Schmooley children. After taking into consideration the full use of the unified credit for both spouses, only the first two cases are subject to federal estate tax (row 5). Remember, that's paid in cash—in nine months.

Next, row 6 shows the Income in Respect of a Decedent (IRD) Tax on the IRA money that's supposed to go to the kids. Since they cannot roll it to their own IRAs, the result is a 40 percent tax on *all* of the IRA that has not been used to pay estate taxes. So, even in estates that pay no estate tax, redistribution takes place. What's interesting is that the largest estate (#1) pays about one half the IRD tax of the smallest estate (#4) on the same amount of IRA money.

Rows 7 and 8 show the total amounts of real dollars that are taken away from the Schmooley family and redistributed elsewhere via the tax code. The kids get what remains in row 9. While no one is going to need to hold a telethon to get by, that's really not the point is it? Or is it? Please put yourself in the Schmool's shoes and walk around for a moment. That was his and his wife's money. They worked for it, they earned it. His business generated jobs and income taxes for years. Why shouldn't they keep what they earned? Why shouldn't their kids benefit from it? Where's the incentive to take the risks needed to achieve something worthwhile? Where's the incentive to save?

The percentage of lost wealth without any control (row 10) is a staggering 21 percent across the board, and the impact on the retirement savings is mind-boggling (row 11). So I ask you, do you have appreciated assets like a business or real estate that you'd like to sell some day? Are you building wealth in a qualified retirement plan?

Our country was only 40 years old in 1816 when Thomas Jefferson said, "To take from one, because it is thought his own industry and that of his father's has acquired too much in order to spare to others who have not exercised equal industry and skill, is to violate arbitrarily the first principle of association, the guarantee to everyone the free exercise of his industry and the fruits acquired by it."

One hundred and ninety-two years later, in October 2008, Barack Obama stated in his now infamous confrontation with Joe the Plumber, "It's not that I want to punish your success, I just want to make sure that everybody who is behind you, that they've got a chance for success, too. My attitude is that if the economy's good for folks from the bottom up, it's gonna be good for everybody . . . *I think when you spread the wealth around, it's good for everybody.*"

Welcome to the change you can believe in. What you may not believe, however, is how those crazy cats in congress spend your money. If taxes are the injury, what they do with them is the insult.

2

Accidental Philanthropy— Adding Insult to Injury

A man goes to a psychiatrist. The doctor says, "You're crazy." The man says, "I want a second opinion!" The doctor says, "Okay, you're ugly too!"

—Henny Youngman

How does one become an *accidental* philanthropist? It might help by defining what a real philanthropist is. The textbook definition of a philanthropist is *a person who practices the voluntary activity of or disposition towards donating money, property, or services to the needy or for general social betterment.** In other words, it's a person who gives a lot of money away . . . willingly. And, everybody loves him or her for it. There's always lots of praise for the benefactor.

The accidental philanthropist, on the other hand, is the poor slob who also donates money to the needy or for social betterment, but does so unwittingly. Unlike the active philanthropist this person doesn't choose where the donations go. Further, there are no accolades or adulation for the money given because *nobody knows about it.*

**Source:* Ologies and Isms. The Gale Group, Inc, 2008.

And here's the rub, this person probably gives as much or more as the recognized philanthropist. You may know the accidental philanthropist by another name, "taxpayer!"

This chapter explores the insult to the injury. I show how you can become the accidental philanthropist by detailing what happens to your tax dollars after your buddies in Washington get a hold of 'em.

Where Do Your Taxes Go?

Tax distribution all begins with the federal budget allocations. Figure 2.1 shows a breakdown of the budget.

Just to provide a reference point, let's look at the top four budget items shown in Figure 2.1.

1. Military use: About 42 cents of every dollar is allocated for military use. Things like national defense, the Coast Guard, veterans' benefits, and even the military share of interest payments on the national debt, are included in this category. In 2008, that amount accounted for more than $874,000,000,000 out of a $2 trillion budget.
2. Health programs: Health programs accounted for another $458 billion, or 22 percent of the budget. That's mostly the federal funds going toward Medicare.
3. Interest payment on debt: The interest payment on the national debt is the third largest budget item! It is 10 percent of the entire budget (more than $212,000,000,000). I don't need to tell you how fast this item is growing.
4. Antipoverty programs: Weighing in at 9 percent or about $180,000,000,000 is the allocation for antipoverty programs. Items like food and nutrition assistance, cash assistance to the poor and elderly, temporary assistance to needy families are included in this category.

Interestingly, the budget allocation for education, training, and social services only accounts for 4 percent of the budget. Would you run a household where you spent 235 percent more on your debt service than you do on your own family? While we're at it, how long do you think you'd be able to run your business mounting huge deficits each year?

You give Congress control of your tax dollars.

Your tax dollars are distributed according to the Federal Budget allocations:

- 42% to past and current military
- 22% to health programs
- 10% to interest on nonmilitary Debt
- 9% to antipoverty programs
- 4% to education, training, and social services
- 4% to government and law enforcement
- 3% to environment, energy, and science
- 2% to agriculture, commerce, and transportation
- 1% to international relations

Figure 2.1   Budget Allocations

Source: National Priorites Priorities Project: Where Do Your Tax Dollars Go, 2008 Report.

The Other White Meat

This isn't even the insulting part. You may not agree with how your money is allocated in the budget, but at least you have some sense of where it's going. The real insult takes place *inside* each budget item. Accidental philanthropy occurs when Congress gets their hands on the budget allocations. That's when representatives and senators; Democrats and Republicans; liberals and conservatives, all take their best shot at some special project that will benefit their state or constituents. We the taxpayers wind up paying for the few people who benefit from these entitlements. You know this by its more popular name, "pork." Whatever you want to call it, it is out of control and it undermines our economy. Let's be clear, pork is not a Republican or Democrat issue, both parties do it and they support each other doing it. Let him or her who is without sin throw the first slab of bacon.

To illustrate the role pork plays in accidental philanthropy, I created Table 2.1 based on information I gleaned from a fantastic book that focuses on government waste, *The 2008 Congressional Pig Book*. It is both hailed and reviled by members of congress and it is a must read. (You can order it online at www.cagw.org.) Table 2.1 highlights just a few of the pork projects buried in the 2008 budget. I've listed the amount, the project, and the project's sponsor. A few bucks here and few bucks there added up to more than $17,000,000,000 divided among 11,610 projects!

In today's media saturation of the United States economic crisis, we have become desensitized to a number like a billion. Especially, since the government now speaks about spending trillions of dollars that we don't even have. But a billion dollars is a lot of money. To put it in perspective, a billion seconds ago, it was 1959. A billion minutes ago, Jesus was alive. A billion hours ago, our ancestors were living in the Stone Age. A billion months ago, the earth was ruled by dinosaurs. If you wanted to count from 1 to 1 billion, and counted 24 hours a day for 7 days a week, it would take you 95 years to complete your task!

Congress gave 17 times that amount away in 2008, and more is scheduled for this year. It is 17,000,000,000 of your taxpayer dollars! Please ponder what's going on here because this exercise becomes more valuable the more incensed you become. This is how the people *you* elect to represent *you* show stewardship over *your* money in the toughest economic climate of our lives. Also, consider that the list below is only the entitlements and special projects and *has nothing to do with any of the economic stimulus or bailout spending* (which is also on our nickel to the tune of $800,000,000,000).

Let's take a look at what happens when you insert the U.S.'s other white meat into the budget. (See Table 2.1.)

Table 2.1   Examples of Pork in the Budget

How Much	For What?	Sponsored By
$742,764	Olive fruit fly research	Mike Thompson (D-CA)
$1,117,125	Study of Mormon Crickets	Harry Reid (D-NV)
$1,950,000	The Charles B Rangel Center for Public Service	Charles B Rangel (D-NY)
$188,000	The Lobster Institute	Collins (R-ME), Snowe (R-ME), and Allen (D-ME)
$148,950	The Montana Sheep Institute	Max Baucus (D-MT) and John Tester (D-MT)
$625,000	The Congressional Cemetery, Washington	Jerry Lewis (R-CA)
Totals: $17,000,000	11,610 projects	Congress—your representatives

To add a little more insult to the insult, of the $743,764 spent on olive fruit fly research, $211,509 is to be spent in Paris, France. Perhaps the greatest insult of all, however, is that the sponsor of the Charles B. Rangel Center for Public Service is the same Charlie Rangel who is currently fighting charges that he failed to pay *his own taxes* (see "Sorry, Charlie—Rangel Makes More Excuses for His Failure to Pay Taxes" by Sam Dealey in *U.S. News and World Report,* September 15, 2008).

Additionally, beer and wine drinkers may like to know that the government spent more than $7,500,000 for grape and wine research, and $460,762 on hops research. Senator Richard Shelby (R-AL), the ranking member of the Commerce, Justice, and Science Appropriations Subcommittee is the guy you see most often on TV opposing the bailouts and lecturing us about fiscal responsibility. Yet, he managed to squeeze in $470,000 for a National Oceanic and Atmospheric Administration (NOAA) Maritime Museum. Where, you ask? Mobile, Alabama. Did I mention he was the senator from Alabama?

If this wasn't so sad it'd be funny. But it's not. Look, I'm not about to debate whether any of the projects above are worthwhile, let's assume all 11,610 are. The point is that you and I never had a say. We never got a vote. Is that how you want your tax dollars used? This isn't about economic class, or race, or politics, it is about the redistribution of wealth into pet projects that benefit the few. *This is accidental philanthropy.* Hell, this is forced philanthropy.

The good news is that you have now received your wake-up call. Couple accidental philanthropy with the reckless spending of myriad bailout plans, and you have created the environment for the defining moment of *your* life. The point where the insult is so real and so painful that you actually decide to get off your ass and do something about it.

PART II

THE ROAD TO WEALTH IS PAVED WITH CHARITABLE INTENTIONS

3

How to Fight Back Against the War on Wealth

All war is deception.

—Sun Tzu

Things do not need to be complicated to work great. The strategy we use to fight back in the war on wealth is simple, and effective. All I ask is that you hear me out and don't strain yourself by looking for the complexity; you're not going to find any.

Before I use some common sense to lay the groundwork for my battle plan, let's review the key points in this administration's war on wealth:

- The government's objective of the war is to redistribute your dollars to the people and programs that are of importance to them—not necessarily you.
- The way they effect redistribution is through a WMD known as taxation.
- That taxation takes place at four or five different levels
  1. Income tax
  2. Dividend tax

3. Capital gains tax
4. Estate (and/or) gift tax
5. IRD tax (income tax) on retirement accounts
- The net impact of redistribution is that you lose all control over how your tax dollars are spent, turning you into an accidental philanthropist.
- The real result is less money for you and your family.

I'm not saying that all taxation can or should be avoided, but I am saying that there are ways around the type of taxation that unfairly targets the country's successful taxpayers by penalizing them for doing well. *So, pay attention*: this is the part where I give you the secret for winning the war! The way to avoid being killed in the battle is to not show up for it. The way to avoid being taxed into oblivion is to not participate, *legally*. The way to avoid becoming an accidental philanthropist is by becoming an active one. Perhaps a little illumination in the form of one of my amusing sports analogies might help to illustrate my point.

Walking Barry Bonds

There was a time, not so long ago, that the game of baseball was dominated by the greatest home run hitter of all time, Barry Bonds*. The asterisk is here because you'd have to be living in hole not to know the steroid accusations surrounding his accomplishments. However, this is not a debate about whether he used steroids to help him hit those blasts. The only thing that matters about this story and its relevance to our strategy, is that nobody *knew then* if he was juiced, just that he hit the baseball farther than anyone else and with more frequency than anyone else.

Barry Bonds was the most feared man in the game. He smacked 98 mile an hour aspirin-sized fastballs thrown by professional pitchers over the wall and often into the watery grave outside the stadium where the San Francisco Giants played. When he hit those homers, the fans went wild.

Dream with me for a minute:

> *How do you think you'd do against Barry Bonds if you were asked to pitch against him in his heyday? Assuming you could reach the plate, what do you think he'd do to one of your 20 mph hummers? I'd venture*

a guess that you'd hear a lot of the fans going wild as the ball landed in McCovey Cove.

Let me spell it out for you, in this dream/nightmare, Barry Bonds represents the Internal Revenue Service. He's there to enforce the tax code. You are you, and the ball you are trying to throw past him represents the portion of your assets that is subject to all those taxes the IRS employs in the War on Wealth. The fans in the stadium are the U.S. Congress, cheering on their man as he smacks another one out of the park and into the appropriations subcommittees.

What in the world would make you think you could strike out Barry Bonds? What would make you think you could beat the IRS? You've got about as much chance of sneaking one by the IRS as you do of striking out Mr. Bonds. Yet, folks try to do just that all the time, and their family pays the price, as the stadium goes wild.

Let's get back to our dream sequence; I'm starting to like this.

Here's the situation. Barry Bonds, looking particularly ginormous, strides to plate with the game on the line. The fans are cheering, "Baa-ree, Baa-ree!" Suddenly, the crowd is hushed as the game stops and you are summoned to come in from the bull pen. After you get done changing your pants, you are pushed on to the field feeling very much like an over-matched gladiator facing the lions. You reach the mound just as the chants from Congress—I mean the fans—starts again, "Baa-ree, Baa-ree!" You look in to the catcher, get your sign, and tiny little tears begin to form in the corners of your eyes. "Time Out!" shouts the manager, and a chubby little guy from Jersey struts out to give you a pep talk. It's me! I'm the manager! What are the odds that I'd show up in your dream?

"Skip," you say, when I finally reach the mound. I love it when you call me Skip, and you know it.

"Skip, I don't think I can do this. That guy's gonna take my business and tax the crap out of it. He's going to take my IRA and confiscate it, he's going to plunder my life's work and send it to other people and give what's left to my kids—and I can't do a thing about it."

Before you start to sob again, I whisper something into your ear. I pat you on the butt, because that's what managers do, and anyway you like that, and I return to the dugout.

The tears stop. If I'm not mistaken, I believe a smile works its way across your face and you return to the mound. "Baa-ree, Baa-ree!" Let them chant, you say to yourself, for you are about to employ the only legal method that guarantees that Barry Bonds will not hit the ball out of the park. It's a solution so simple it's scary, and it works every time. You walk him. You throw four simple pitches far outside where he can't reach 'em, and he walks to first base—powerless. Your assets are safe, and the fans hiss and boo—loud and long. Beautiful music.

Barry Bonds holds the record for hitting more home runs than anyone else in the history of the game. He also holds another record. He received more intentional walks than anyone *ever*, 688. That's more than twice the number of intentional walks (299) over the guy's who is number two on the list. A nice man by the name of Hank Aaron.

The Planning Equivalent of Walking Barry Bonds

The strategy that I am about to teach you to fight against accidental philanthropy is called Charitable Leverage. The tax planning equivalent of walking Barry Bonds is a specially designed trust that we will employ as the heart of our strategy. Congress actually created it as part of the tax code in 1969! The trust is called a Charitable Remainder Trust (CRT). Just like the intentional walk keeps the baseball in the park, so does the CRT keep your assets safe from tax loss. Once assets are placed into it, they cannot be touched by Uncle Sam (or anyone else for that matter). That's called real asset protection. When the CRT is coupled with the second part of our strategy, a cash value insurance policy, the results look like this:

- Dollars you would normally lose to taxes are *self-directed* to causes and organizations you actually care about.
- You can even direct those formerly lost dollars to your own Private Family Foundation or Donor Advised Fund, creating a perpetual charitable legacy.
- The *same dollars* will be used to generate more personal wealth for you (that's the leverage part).
- Ultimately, those *same dollars* will be used to provide your family with *more* after tax future wealth (that's even more leverage).

If it sounds like a win-win scenario, it is. The only ones who are left out in the cold are the people who were counting on your money to fulfill their political promises. Their hisses and boos will be your beautiful music.

When you unleash the power of charitable leverage, you stop accidental philanthropy dead in its tracks. The technique you are about to explore will do much more than just protect your assets, it can save America's soul.

Unleashing the Power of Charitable Leverage

Simplicity is the ultimate sophistication.

—Leonardo da Vinci

I t's time to dig into *The Power of Charitable Leverage*. As I walk you through this process step by step, a light bulb is going to turn on in your head and you'll start to apply this strategy to your personal situation. The key to this program, and the key to your success using it, is that it is simple. It is simple to understand and simple to use. When we're done with this chapter, you're going to know the meaning of the term. In the following two chapters I discuss the components of the plan.

How Do You Define Charitable Leverage?

Take a deep breath, and let it out. If you thought that I was going to discuss "leverage" in financial terms, you can relax. I'm not that smart, and it's way too complicated. The term "leverage" that I use in the phrase "charitable leverage" has *nothing at all* to do with the financial kind. There is no borrowing of money, or using option strategies, or margin accounts, or anything else that is remotely sophisticated or advanced. We are not going to use anyone else's money but yours. To understand the term "leverage" as I use it, you need only to have a grasp on the concept of *physical* leverage. Since that's a topic usually covered in grammar school, this should be pretty easy.

Leverage = Power

The thing I like the best about the definition of physical "leverage" is that it's easy to understand and easy to explain to someone else. If you've ever used a screwdriver or a wrench, you know what I mean, it's pretty simple stuff. If you look up "leverage" the dictionary, you'll find the following definition:

1. The action of a lever
2. The increased force resulting from the use of a lever
3. Increased means of accomplishing some purpose*

My definition: *It's the ability to do superhuman things using simple tools—with fantastic results.* Remember this; it will come in handy later.

I give to you, Exhibit A: The Screwdriver. Did you ever try to twist a screw into wood with just your fingers? You don't get very far. However, with a long piece of steel that fits into the groove on the screw, and a handle that allows you to grip the steel with your hand, and the force created when you twist your wrist (which is attached to your hand), that screw is going to tighten rapidly and securely. You can accomplish this task in a few seconds with great results. Is that simple enough for you?

Need more examples? I could use a basic wrench as another perfect example of leverage, and the force that it creates on a nut as you try to tighten or loosen it. Either action cannot be done successfully without this simple tool. How about a hammer? Did you ever try to drive a nail with your fist? Not very effective, and it hurts!

---

*Source: Webster's New World College Dictionary, John Wiley & Sons, 2005.

To Understand Charitable Leverage,
You Need to Understand Physical Leverage.

Simple tools used to perform superhuman feats.

Figure 4.1   This Is Not Rocket Science

My point is that you do not require any greater level of sophistication than a basic understanding of how the simplest of tools can be used as levers to accomplish superhuman feats of strength. The lever (screwdriver, wrench, and hammer) provides maximum power with minimum effort on the object (screw, nut, nail, respectively) with great results. (See Figure 4.1.) That's leverage, pure and simple. You need to get this in order to move forward. If you don't get it, you need to repeat the fourth grade.

Charitable Leverage = Financial Power

Using the same principle as physical leverage, charitable leverage uses a simple financial tool exerting maximum power with minimum effort on a financial object, resulting in magnificent results. In our case, the desired result is the avoidance of accidental philanthropy.

The "lever" in charitable leverage is a simplified version of an oldie but goodie in the fund-raising world, *The Charitable Remainder Trust (CRT)*. The object that it acts upon, the nail to the hammer if you will, is another old financial warhorse, a *Cash Value Life Insurance Policy* (CVLI). Like the CRT in this strategy, the type of insurance policy we use is a specific design that I discuss in detail later.

Charitable remainder trusts and cash value insurance policies have been used independent of each other for years. (See Figure 4.2.) It's when they are combined in the formula that you will learn here, when they become the lever and the object working together that we tap into each one's unique tax characteristics to produce some or all of absolutely amazing benefits listed below:

- Avoid capital gains tax on sales of appreciated property.
- Increase your current income while paying less tax on it.
- Generate substantial income tax deductions.
- Create millions of tax-free dollars for future generations.
- Reduce and even eliminate federal and state estate taxes.
- Slash the taxes on retirement plan distributions.
- Sell or transfer the family business without tax—on a tax deductible basis.
- Use potentially wasted tax dollars to create a philanthropic legacy.
- Use the same potentially wasted tax dollars to create a tax sheltered grandparent gifting program.
- Provide real asset protection with the blessing of Uncle Sam without moving your money off-shore or by using complicated and often questionable tax schemes.
- Build a personal tax deductible retirement account that does not interfere with other retirement plans.
- Add meaning to your money.
- Never, ever, lose control of your assets.

Charitable Leverage

Simple financial tools used to perform superfinancial feats.

Figure 4.2   The Basic Concept of Charitable Leverage

That's It?

That's it. Charitable Remainder Trust (CRT)—Cash Value Life Insurance (CVLI). Hammer-nail; wrench-bolt. Simple to use, simple to understand, and very effective.

The two components of charitable leverage are no strangers to financial advisors because they have both been around forever, and have even worked together before. So what makes this strategy so unique? The answer is that we are going to completely *invert* how these two tools are normally used to create something new and exciting. Prepare yourself for a major paradigm shift.

I present this process in four steps. First, I cover the features and benefits of *all* CRTs and *all* CVLIs. I admit upfront that this discussion is about as interesting as oatmeal. But, a lot of people eat oatmeal because they know it's good for them. Likewise, knowing how the components of a charitably leveraged plan work is good for you. I, however, hate oatmeal and therefore, don't eat it. You may feel the same way about a basic knowledge of CRTs and insurance. If you want to skip ahead to the next section, I will be not offended. If you get confused, you can always come back here. I'll be waiting with your oatmeal.

After we cover the basics, I focus on the features and benefits of the specific types of CRTs and CVLI politics that we use in our charitable leverage program. With that information in hand, we move to the third step where I show you how CRTs and CVLIs have been used in the traditional way (the existing paradigm). In our final step I show the new paradigm using our unique formula.

So grab yourself some raisins and sugar and whatever else you need to dress up your oatmeal, because I'm about to shovel a whole lot your way.

The First Component to Charitable Leverage—The Charitable Remainder Trust

May your charity increase as much as your wealth.

—Proverb

If there was ever a near perfect tool designed to create and preserve your wealth and legacy, the charitable remainder trust has to be it. It is loaded with tax benefits, not loopholes, which are provided to people who are willing to help America's nonprofits as a part of their personal financial plans. There's a lot to this powerful tool approved by the IRS in 1969 and we cover the dynamics here. It is the perfect choice as "the lever" in our charitable leverage strategy.

The Ground Rules

Before we begin, however, I think it might be a good idea if we establish some ground rules to make your effort in reading this thing more productive.

1. Don't get bogged down in technicalities—yet. You will have a far more enjoyable experience and get more out of this book if you *relax* and just read it. With that in mind, I will paint the picture of charitable leverage in broad strokes so that you stay awake long enough to see how you can apply it to your personal situation.
2. The technical stuff is important though, and it keeps you on the right side of the IRS. Not to worry though. I have provided tax references at the end of this book so you know that I'm not making this stuff up. More importantly, you can go to my web site: www.nigito.com where you will find a guide for your professional advisors (tax and legal) that contains all of the stuff they love and even some prototype documents.
3. This is not a "do it yourself" project. Get the concept, fall in love with the strategies, and then get thee to a professional advisor to put your plan into action. I'll show you later how to pick the right advisors or evaluate the ones you already use. The bottom line is that there is too much at stake for you to use an amateur.
4. The key to avoiding accidental philanthropy is to practice active philanthropy through the CRT I designed in this program. That requires a commitment on your part. Since the CRT is irrevocable, you need to *want* to do something for charity. It's called *charitable intent* and it is essential to the success of this program.
5. *This is important: A CRT is not a tax dodge, tax shelter, or tax avoidance scheme.* Rather, it is powerful exercise of your freedom of choice that is rooted in the tax code. It allows you to redirect the dollars that would normally be lost to taxes to the charitable organizations that are important to you. It also gives you the opportunity to specify exactly how they are to be used. You need to possess the heart to *give* as well as *get* or this program will not work. I call it adding meaning to your money.

The Lever: The Charitable Remainder Trust

I am not trying to insult your intelligence but I have found that if I keep my explanations on a fourth grade level, even I can follow them. So, here goes. To borrow a phrase from a certain almost president, Charitable Remainder Trusts (CRTs) are "lock boxes" that

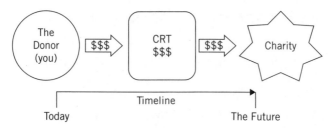

Figure 5.1 The Basic Concept of Charitable Leverage—overview

hold the title to assets like securities or real estate that are transferred into it by "the donor" (you) (see Figure 5.1). At some point in the future, the CRT will be transferred to any qualified charity or charities that you choose. It is all of the positive things that happen between the time that you donate assets to your CRT and the day it passes to charity that make it such a valuable tool.

The CRT is an *irrevocable* trust. That is to say that once you transfer an asset to the lock-box, you cannot remove it. That's not necessarily a bad thing because you can manipulate the hell out of it while it's in the box. More importantly, because the CRT is irrevocable your assets are creditor-proof. I'll go in more detail on that later.

The other basic feature of the CRT is that, from the time you donate your assets to it, to the date it transfers to charity, you receive income, or as I prefer to call it, cash flow from it. We are going to have all kinds of fun with the CRT cash flow.

Simple enough? You, as the donor, transfer an asset(s) to your CRT. Someday the CRT will pass on to charity. Between now and that date in the future when the CRT ends, it will distribute cash flow either back to you or someone you choose. (See Figure 5.2.)

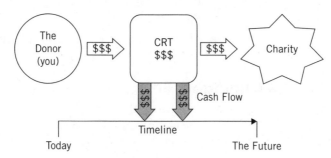

Figure 5.2 The Basic Concept of Charitable Leverage—Cash Flow

The Shared Features of All CRTs

CRTs come in two flavors; *Annuity* Trusts (CRATs) and Unitrusts (CRUTs). The major difference between the two types of trusts centers on how they pay the cash flow back to the income recipient (you or someone you choose). Annuity Trusts pay a *fixed dollar amount* each year regardless of how the CRT principal is invested. Unitrusts allow you to participate in the investment returns of the CRT (positive and negative) by paying a *fixed percentage of the fair market value* of the trust each year. All CRATs and CRUTs share the same six impressive features:

1. Clear IRS guidance and support
2. Shelter from capital gains tax
3. Current income tax deduction
4. Increased cash flow with favorable tax treatment
5. A meaningful charitable legacy instead of meaningless taxes
6. Asset protection

Clear IRS Guidance

I know it's not exactly a "feature," but you can't beat a program where there are no questions as to its validity. There aren't even any gray areas. I have given hundreds of presentations about CRTs and invariably there is always someone who just can't believe that I'm not exploiting some loophole in the tax code. I'm not. The tax code was expanded in 1969 to create rules for the use of split interest charitable remainder trusts. The rules can be found under IRC§664. Suffice it to say that everything I talk about hereafter can be traced specifically to the tax code. There is nothing that makes a tax advisor feel more secure than honest-to-God tax code. This is right up there with a wooly blanket.

Even the documents that are used to create different the types of CRTs have been provided by the IRS in recent rulings. Don't take that as an invitation for you to act as your own attorney, but when the very documents that allow you to do all the fantastic things a CRT does are already approved and provided by the tax entity that watches over them, I'd say you could move ahead with a fair degree of confidence.

Shelter from Capital Gains Tax

Earlier I said that the tax code allows you to transfer the title to assets like stocks, bonds, and real estate to a CRT "lock-box" that will someday go to charity.

When the asset that you donate to your CRT is one that has appreciated in value, and the trustee of your CRT (which, by the way, can be you), subsequently sells the asset, the CRT pays *no capital gains tax!* I kid you not. *The CRT is the only financial tool with the IRS blessing that allows you to sell an appreciated asset and avoid the tax on capital gain.*

This remarkable feature of the CRT is perhaps the single best example of choosing voluntary philanthropy to avoid the accidental kind and reaping a personal benefit by doing so. Some of the more technical advisors say that a CRT only defers the capital gains tax until the income is withdrawn. But that statement simply isn't correct. When you sell an appreciated asset inside a CRT there is no capital gains tax due—period. If you don't lose any money to taxes, then you have more money to invest—immediately. That seems pretty simple and clear to me.

Table 5.1 illustrates my point. Suppose you sold a position in a stock with a gain of $250,000. Which column would you rather have; C or E? Or put another way, if your future income was based on the remaining money you had *after the asset was sold* (investment returns being equal), which column would give you more income? I call this the principle of More = More. The more money I have remaining after the sale will yield more income to me for the rest of my life. For example, $200,000 (column E) will generate $12,000/year income at 6 percent. In column E, $250,000 will generate $15,000/year earning the same 6 percent. I think we would agree that we'd rather have column E. Three thousand dollars per year more for you. Thirty thousand dollars more in only 10 years. More = More.

Table 5.1   The Impact of Capital Gains Tax

(A) Profit	(B) Lost to Capital Gain Tax at 20%	(C) Net to Reinvest	(D) Profit Lost if Sold by CRT	(E) Net to Reinvest
$100,000	$20,000	$80,000	$0	$100,000
$250,000	$50,000	$200,000	$0	$250,000
$500,000	$100,000	$400,000	$0	$500,000
$1,000,000	$200,000	$800,000	$0	$1,000,000

Table 5.1 is a great example of how we use a CRT to avoid accidental philanthropy. Once you lose that $50,000 in Column B to taxes, it is gone. It is never coming back and you can't control where it goes. Later, when I put charitable leverage in place, you're going to give it away and get it back again! For now, just remember More = More. (See Figure 5.3.)

Generate a Current Income Tax Deduction

Your transfer of assets to a CRT generates a current income tax deduction scoring another victory in our battle against accidental philanthropy. The Internal Revenue Code allows you to take a charitable income tax deduction *today* for the gift you plan to give to charity in the *future*. The tax deduction is not for the full value of today's transfer, but rather for the "present value of the future gift," and it usually averages about 25 percent to 35 percent of your contribution. In most cases, the tax deduction can be taken against 30 percent of your adjusted gross income (AGI)—as opposed to current and cash contributions that can be taken against 50 percent of your AGI. If the charitable beneficiary is a Private Family Foundation, the deduction can be used against 20 percent of your AGI. In all cases, you can take the deduction against the maximum income allowed this year and then carry the balance forward against next year's income. You carry it forward for five additional years. (See Figure 5.4.)

Calculation of the tax deduction can be a little tricky, so let's take a closer look at the three major factors used in the calculation. As we work through them you'll see that it is all pretty logical.

> Tax Deduction Calculation Question #1: How much income do you plan on taking out of the CRT each year? A few pages ago, when I was covering the basics, I said that between the time you fund the CRT and the time it goes to charity, it

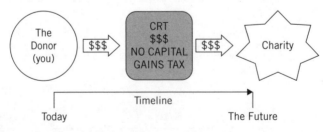

Figure 5.3   The Basic Concept of Charitable Leverage—No Capital Gains Tax

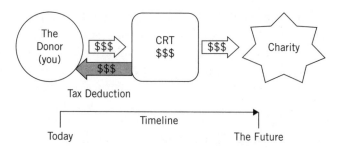

Figure 5.4 The CRT Generates an Income Tax Deduction

spins off income to you. This is often referred to as the *distribution rate* or cash-flow rate. I'm going to go into detail on the CRT cash flow in the next feature. But for now, the rule to remember is: The greater the distribution rate, the more income you will take from the CRT, therefore, the lesser the tax deduction you will receive. Makes sense, because the more you take, the less will remain for charity.

Tax Deduction Calculation Question #2: How long will the CRT generate income to you *before* it passes to charity, or put another way, *How long will the CRT last?* CRTs can run for as long as a lifetime or as short as a few years. You decide how long you want that cash flow to last when you establish the trust. Again applying common sense, the longer the time between CRT creation and its transfer to charity, the less the tax deduction. Obviously, if you're getting a tax deduction *today* for a *future gift* to charity, the farther off the future is, the less valuable the gift today. In a lifetime CRT, age becomes a factor. The older you are, the greater the tax deduction. For example, if the CRT will pay income for life, then the older donor would receive a greater deduction than the younger one because statistically her life expectancy is shorter and the charity will get the assets sooner. I'm actually going to spend more space on this in the next feature. But you get my drift.

Tax Deduction Calculation Question #3: What could you reasonably expect to earn on your money if you invested it in a government midterm investment *instead* of the CRT? This last factor is kind of a moving target. It is based on an IRS table that is published monthly that projects what you could earn in a government-backed medium term investment. This rate is called the Applicable Federal Rate (AFR) and it really is the only funky part of the CRT experience, equaling 120 percent of the federal midterm rate. The premise is that the earnings based on the AFR are what you give up by giving the money to charity. Therefore, the greater the AFR, the larger your tax deduction. Since the rate changes each month, you are allowed to choose the highest rate over the last three months to gain the largest tax deduction at the time you fund your CRT. Historically, the AFR has been in the 5 percent or higher range. With the collapse of interest rates following the financial tsunami of 2008, however, AFR rates began to plummet. At one point (February 2009) rates actually hit an all time low of 2 percent. A drop like that suppresses the tax deduction. For planning purposes we use a more stable rate of 4 percent to 5 percent range. In reality, a movement up or down in the AFR of a point or so does not have a significant impact on your overall deduction.

Tax Deduction Example.   Table 5.2 gives a quick view of how the tax deduction can vary based on the answers to the three questions above. It may seem a little fuzzy at first, but once you read the next section on cash flow, it will come into clearer focus. Also, this is only one example of many combinations. You can go to my web site www.nigito.com and plug in your own variables for a more specific example with current AFRs, or you can call your CPA or financial advisor for a quick calculation. The software for such things is readily available.

Table 5.2 is based on a life expectancy of 15 years. That could be a 15-year term trust or a lifetime trust where the income recipient's age would generate a life expectancy of about 15 years (single life age 65ish or joint lives of 74/66ish). Across the top of the table are the cash-flow or distribution rates increasing by 1 percent increments. The far left column shows what happens to the

Table 5.2   CRUT with 15-Year Life Expectancy

AFR	Cash Flow at 5%	Cash Flow at 6%	Cash Flow at 7%	Cash Flow at 8%	Cash Flow at 9%	Cash Flow at 10%
4%	.47	.40	.35	.30	.25	.21
5%	.47	.41	.36	.31	.26	.22

AFRs at 4 percent and 5 percent. At first blush we can make two observations:

1. The major impact on your tax deduction, after the term of the trust, is your distribution rate. The greater the cash-flow rate to you, the lesser your tax deduction will be.
2. The AFR doesn't have anywhere near the impact that the distribution rate or length of trust term has on your tax deduction.

For example, a $100,000 transfer to a CRT with a 5 percent AFR and 6 percent distribution rate will generate a tax deduction of $41,000 dollars (41 percent). If the AFR dropped a full percentage point to 4 percent, the tax deduction would only be reduced to $40,000 (40 percent). Not a big deal. Compare that to the same transfer to a CRT with a 5 percent AFR, and a one percentage point greater distribution rate of 7 percent. The result is a tax deduction of around $35,000 (35 percent). It is still a good deal and my point is that you should not get hung up on the AFR.

One final note, the combination of the distribution rate and the term of the trust life cannot result in a tax deduction of less than 10 percent of whatever the donor contributes. In other words, if the donor contributes $100,000 the tax deduction must be at least $10,000 based on the all the factors in this section and expanded on in the next.

The tax deduction feature of a charitable remainder trust is a strong weapon in our fight against the war on wealth. Every dollar we save using this technique goes directly in our pocket.

Increased Cash Flow

This will come as no surprise since I've been blabbering about this feature throughout the previous section. All CRTs are designed to provide the donor (or someone the donor designates) with a stream of income from the day he or she establishes the trust, to the day it ends and passes to charity. I prefer to use the term "cash flow" instead of "income" because the CRT can distribute far more than the income it earns. (See Figure 5.5.)

It is at this point that the trust can be highly customized. Remember, the CRT will act as our *lever* in the charitable leverage

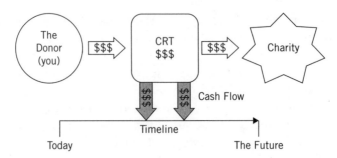

Figure 5.5   The CRT Distributes Cash Flow

plans in the next section, so paying attention here will help you understand the strategy later. God, I sound like a school teacher.

There are three things you should know about cash flow, before we design your personal plan:

1. The difference between *Annuity Trust* income versus *Unitrust* income
2. How the annual cash flow is *taxed*
3. How to select the proper *duration* of the CRT (how long the CRT will generate income before it goes to charity)

Annuity Trust versus Unitrust.   There is a basic difference between a Charitable Remainder Annuity Trust (CRAT) and a Charitable Remainder Unitrust (CRUT) and it can have a major impact on your income stream (See Figure 5.6.)

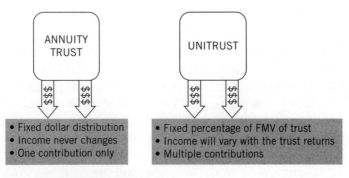

Figure 5.6   CRAT versus CRUT

CRAT: A CRAT pays a *fixed dollar* payment to you each year based on your initial contribution. That's what an "annuity" means. No matter what happens to the CRT investments, your cash flow remains the same. The *minimum distribution* rate a CRAT can select is 5 percent.

In the following example we assume that you are both the donor and income recipient of a CRAT. That's not much of a stretch since most CRTs work exactly that way. If you fund a 6 percent CRAT with a contribution of $100,000, it will distribute $6,000 each year. If the $100,000 CRAT balance grows to $120,000 or shrinks to $80,000, the *$6,000 distribution remains the same.* I love CRATs because they're simple and effective. The only downside is that you cannot make additional contributions to your CRAT. The annual distribution is fixed based on the original contribution, so additional deposits are not allowed.

CRUT: A CRUT pays a *fixed percentage* of the fair market value of the trust account to you each year. If the trust account grows, so does the annual distribution. Likewise, if the account decreases, so does your income. Like the CRAT, the *minimum distribution* rate a CRUT can select is 5 percent.

All CRUT distributions are determined based on the CRUT account value on the last business day of the tax year. That account value or *fair market value* on that day is then multiplied by the distribution rate. The result is the income to be distributed for the following year.

If you select to fund a 6 percent CRUT with a contribution of $100,000, it will also distribute $6,000 in the first year similar to a CRAT. However, if the account value grows to $120,000 by the end of that first year, the distribution would increase to $7,200 (6 percent of $120,000) for the following year. The reverse is also true. If the trust account dropped to $80,000, then the distribution would decrease to $4,800 (6 percent of $80,000).

The other distinction from a CRAT is that CRUTs do allow for additional contributions. Your annual distribution is based on whatever the trust is worth at the end of the year, so additional contributions just get added to the account. You (as the income beneficiary) receive a piece of the pie each year, for better or worse. As you can imagine, since the distributions in 2009 were based on the CRUT balances at the close of business on the last trading day of 2008, the income distributions were down—way down. Better or worse, was worse.

There are minimum and maximum restrictions on distribution percentages, which are shared by both the CRAT and the CRUT.

- The minimum distribution percentage must be 5 percent.
- The maximum distribution percentage cannot be greater than 50 percent.
- The combination of the distribution rate, the length of the trust life, and AFR cannot result in a tax deduction of less than 10 percent of what the donor contributes.
- An additional restriction on the CRAT is that it must pass what's called the "5 percent probability test." Based on the trust AFR, if there is a 5 percent or greater probability that the donors will live long enough for the trust to be exhausted, then the charitable deduction will be denied. Remember the AFR is an assumed earnings rate, so the 5 percent probability test is meant to ensure that you could not pull out so much cash flow that there might not be anything remaining for charity at the end.

How the Annual Cash Flow Is Taxed

Now things start getting interesting. CRT income is taxed under a unique method called "four-tier accounting." Generally speaking, it is a very good deal. It is taxed on worst to best case scenario; therefore the underlying investment in the CRT really matters. When cash flow is distributed from the CRT, the income recipients pay tax as follows:

1. Ordinary income tax to the extent that the underlying investment earned ordinary income (CDs, treasuries, rental income, etc.)
2. Qualified dividend income is taxed at the qualified dividend rate if it still exists (15 percent in 2008, going up to 20 percent based on the Obama Administration's proposed budget)
3. Capital gain income to the extent that the underlying investment earned capital gain income

4. Tax-free income to the extent that the underlying investment earned tax-free income (like municipal bonds)
5. Return of principal if the underlying investment did not earn enough in the above categories to pay the required distribution

I know that the list depicted in Figure 5.7 is actually five tiers. That's because the separate tax on dividend income was created during President Bush's administration. Before that, it was considered all tier one, ordinary income.

Let's stick with our $100,000 example we were just using. Say you fund your CRT with $100,000 of stock with a $5,000 basis and you take a 7 percent distribution ($7,000). You know from Feature 2 that when the stock is sold *inside the CRT* you will avoid the tax on capital gains. If you (acting as your own trustee) then invest the proceeds of the sale into investments that earn either ordinary or capital gain income, you pay tax on that $7,000 as follows:

- If all of the $7,000 was ordinary income, the tax is charged at your ordinary income tax rate (tier 1).
- If some of that $7,000 was qualified dividends, the distribution relative to the dividends is taxed at the qualified dividend rate (15 percent going to 20 percent)

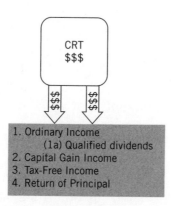

Figure 5.7   CRT Distributions Are Subject to Four-Tier Accounting

- If all of the $7,000 was capital gain income, the tax on the distribution is taxed at the capital gain rate (tier 2)—a substantial savings over tier 1.
- If the $7,000 was a combination of tiers 1 and tier 2, your tax on the income is a combination in the same proportion.
- *Be careful!* You cannot get to tier 3 (tax-free income) until you have exhausted all of the capital gains you avoided when you sold it in the first place. In other words, if you or your trustee invested the sale proceeds in tax-free municipal bonds, the distribution to you is taxed at the capital gains rate. This is an important pitfall to avoid and it is the only way you can screw up the capital gains shelter that is provided by the CRT.
- Ditto for tier 4, return of principal. This is a bigger issue in an annuity trust. It is possible that your distributions could be far in excess of the trust earnings, requiring your trustee to dip into principal each year to pay you. Under normal circumstances, the return of principal would not be taxed. However, if you have not exhausted all of the capital gains you avoided in the original sale, you could pay tax here as well. It is a rare situation, but one you need to know about so you can avoid it.

The Duration of the CRT

This is an absolutely key design point. CRTs run for one life (typically the donor's), two lives (the donor and spouse), or for a term of years (which cannot exceed 20 years). You would think that most CRTs would be of the lifetime variety, either single or joint, and you'd be correct. But there are significant advantages to a *term of years* trust as well, especially for older donors. (See Figure 5.8.) Also, if a business is the donor and income beneficiary, then a term of years trust is the only type allowed by the IRS.

Let's look at the differences in selecting your CRT duration.

Lifetime Trusts

- The upside:
  - The CRAT or CRUT income runs over the life spans of one or two lives, which can be a pretty long time.
  - Long life(s) = a lot of income.

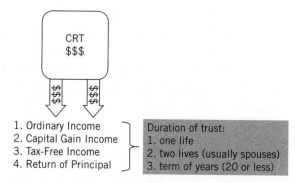

Figure 5.8   The Donor Determines the Duration of the CRT

- The downside:
  - A shorter than expected life may end the trust prematurely. Remember, CRTs are irrevocable so there can be no changes.
  - The tax deduction calculation can get really messy due to life expectancies. In fact, at young ages, like 40ish, you may not be able to do a CRT at all because it may not generate the required 10 percent tax deduction.

Term of Years Trusts

- The upside:
  - Simple design.
  - Everybody at every age gets the same tax deduction because we know exactly when the CRT will end.
  - If the first income beneficiary does not live out the term of the CRT, the trust will continue to pay out to successor beneficiaries until the end of the term. Very useful at advanced ages.
- The downside:
  - Maximum term is 20 years.
  - Lifetime trusts could generate more cumulative income if the income beneficiaries live beyond 20 years.

Time Out to Show an Example of the Benefits of the First Four Features

The most often used version of a CRT is a two-life, or joint-life *uni-trust* (CRUT). I call it the traditional approach. Typically, a husband and wife will transfer appreciated stocks or other property to their CRUT. The CRUT trustee (which, as I've stated previously, can be the donors themselves) sells the stocks and reinvests the proceeds. The donors then choose a conservative distribution rate for consistent future income. At the end of the surviving donor's life, the balance of the CRUT is transferred to their designated charities. That is the subject of the next feature. While this traditional approach is *not* the one I use later, when I show you charitable leverage, it is the most popular use of the CRT. It is also a great example of how personal wealth is enhanced when you avoid accidental philanthropy.

Remember Mr. Schmooley and the lovely Mrs. Schmooley from Chapter 1? They own shares of XYZ stock valued at $1,000,000. Their original cost basis is $100,000. The capital gains tax rate is assumed to be 20 percent. The stock pays a dividend of 3 percent or $30,000 per year (taxed at the projected 20 percent dividend tax rate). Their projected income tax bracket is 40 percent.

Where They Are Now:

- Value of stock = $1,000,000
- Basis of stock = $100,000
- Annual dividend income = $30,000
- Tax on income = ($6,000)
- Net after tax income = $24,000
- Total projected income over a 20-year life expectancy = $480,000

All Mr. S. really wants is to catch a break. He and the Mrs. would like to generate more income while reducing their risk. They would like to move their asset to an investment yielding 6 percent, but the problem is that if they sell the appreciated stock, they'll get hammered with capital gains tax.

If They Sell the Stock and Reinvest at 6 Percent:

- They would pay capital gains tax of ($180,000)
- Net amount to reinvest after tax = $820,000
- Annual income at 6 percent = $49,200
- Tax on income (20 percent) = ($9,840)
- Net annual income = $39,360
- Total income over a 20-year life expectancy = $787,000

Selling the stock and reinvesting at a higher fixed rate looks pretty good on paper, but it also involves a lot of accidental philanthropy. In fact, $180,000 is lost right off the bat.

However, if they choose a traditional joint-life CRUT, the financial principle of More = More takes over.

If They Transfer the Stock to Two-Life CRUT with a 6 Percent Distribution Rate:

- They would pay capital gains tax of $0!
- Net amount to reinvest after tax = $1,000,000
- Annual income at 6 percent = $60,000
- Tax on income (20 percent) = ($12,000)
- Net annual income = $48,000
- Total income over a 20-year life expectancy = $960,000
- *Plus* they get a tax deduction of $295,000, which in their tax bracket is like putting an extra $118,000 in their pocket

Often, the tax deduction is mentioned and then forgotten. But I want to emphasize the power of this feature by showing its impact on reducing taxes today and the potential for growth over the long haul. The tax deduction represents $118,000 that is not leaving the Schmooley's control through taxation. Think about that. What other program do you know that can do that? Further, if that $118,000 of tax savings—real money—was invested at the same 6 percent rate over the same 20-year period, it would build to more than $378,000. The moral of Schmooley story is tax dollars saved from accidental philanthropy can become major money for you and your family.

Creating a Meaningful Charitable Legacy: Voluntary Philanthropy Triumphs Over Accidental Philanthropy

The fifth feature of all CRTs is that it will eventually create your personal charitable legacy. When the CRT reaches the end of its term, the remaining balance (i.e., the charitable remainder) is distributed to the qualified charitable organizations designated by you, the donor.

In the battle against the redistribution of wealth, the best part of voluntary philanthropy is that you get to reroute the dollars normally lost to taxes directly to the charitable organizations that *you* support, instead of the ones that are chosen for you by Congress.

Table 5.3   Financial Impact of a Traditional CRUT

	Hold Current Position	Sell	2-life CRUT at 6%
Current Value	$1,000,000	$1,000,000	$1,000,000
Gain if Sold	$900,000	$900,000	$0
Capital Gains Tax	N/A-not selling	$180,000	$0
Net After Tax	N/A-not selling	$820,000	$1,000,000
Income	$30,000	$49,200	$60,000
Tax on Income	$6,000	$9,840	$12,000
Net a/t Income	$24,000	$39,360	$48,000
Total income over 20 years	$240,000	$787,000	$960,000
CRUT Tax Deduction	$0	$0	$295,000
Tax Savings	$0	$0	$118,000
Tax Savings 20 years growth at 6%	$0	$0	$378,440
20-year Grand Total	$240,000	$787,000	$1,338,440

You can name any number of charities, there are no limits. The next best part comes when you get to choose *exactly how those funds will be used.* An added bonus is that you enjoy the constant control you have over the eventual distribution. If the charitable organizations that you designate do something to fall out of your favor, you can change to another organization. (See Figure 5.9.) Of course, you can always add or delete charities along the way. What an incredible sense of empowerment when you turn the tables on taxes!

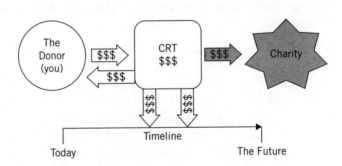

Figure 5.9   The CRT Creates Your Charitable Legacy

From the moment we are born (if you consider that most of us are born in a hospital) our lives have been touched and shaped by nonprofit organizations that count heavily on private donations to keep their doors open. Nonprofits are found in the fields of medicine, medical research, hospice, religion, education, performing and visual arts, community outreach, humanitarian aid, and on it goes. Imagine a world where the organizations that are important to us could focus their efforts on what they do best instead of fundraising. We have that ability to create that world for them— one charity at a time. When we choose voluntary philanthropy over the involuntary kind, we add control and direction to our money, we take the hands of congress out of our pockets. We can literally affect change on our terms. You can further enhance your charitable legacy by choosing one of two methods for charitable distribution; direct gifts or legacy gifts. (See Figure 5.10.) We're going to take a closer look at both.

Direct Gifts.   The simplest of all the charitable beneficiary designations, a direct gift occurs at the end of CRT term. You choose which charities you wish to endow, select the percentage of the CRT you want each charity to receive, and even establish how you want the funds used. You maintain the right to change the charitable beneficiary up until the CRT actually ends. That's an important little nugget that keeps your selected charities on their collective toes. I like to call it "holding the hammer."

It goes without saying that it is very important that the charitable beneficiaries you select actually qualify under the Internal

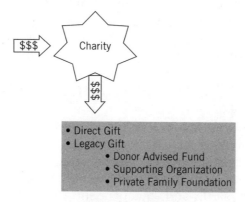

Figure 5.10   You Choose the Type of Legacy

Revenue Code as honest to God charities. Most of the time this is not a problem at all, but just to make sure, the charity (or non-profit) must qualify under IRC§170(c). A simple phone call to the charity's development department to verify will do the trick.

A sample direct gift designation would read something like this:

> Upon the end of the trust term, the remaining balance of the trust will be distributed as follows:
> - 40 percent to XYZ Hospital, for the Cardiac Care Center,
> - 40 percent to ABC University, for merit-based scholarships,
> - 20 percent to the ABC Center of the Performing Arts, for the endowment fund.
>
> If any of the charitable beneficiaries I have named is no longer qualified as a charity under IRC§170(c), my trustee may select other qualified charities for final distribution at his or her discretion.

Direct gifts are straightforward and simple. Don't overlook the power you have in designating exactly how your funds are to be used. In addition, you should always maintain the right to change the charity. If there is one thing I've seen in more than 30 years of doing this kind of work, it's that organizations can change—and when they do, it's usually not for the better.

Legacy Gifts.   A Legacy Gift is my term for a popular method of giving that can provide ongoing gifting from the charitable remainder. The direct gift to charity is clean, simple, and effective. Unfortunately, it is also a one-shot deal. Legacy Gifts by design keep you and your family in the philanthropy game for as long as you want—even through multiple generations. Legacy Gifts come in three varieties:

1. *Donor Advised Funds:* Donor Advised Funds (DAF) were originally developed by Community Foundations across the country as a way to provide a low-cost alternative to Private Family Foundations for donors who wanted to create a meaningful perpetual giving program but didn't want to commit huge sums of money. Today, thanks to commercial sponsors like Fidelity and Vanguard, and independent charitable organizations like the Giving Back Fund, the Heritage Foundation, and the

American Endowment Foundation, DAFs are the fastest growing charitable giving vehicle in the United States with more than $17 billion in assets.

In essence, a DAF falls under the umbrella of a public charity (i.e., your local Community Foundation). This allows you to gain the maximum tax deductions *without* the restrictions and costs of a Private Family Foundation. You get to use that organization's administrative staff and legal team to cut your operating costs to about zero. In exchange, the fund takes over complete control of the assets and you retain *advisory* status. Your choices of investments are restricted to those offered by the umbrella foundation. You *recommend* to the fund what grants you wish to make to other public charities each year. The fund will do the due diligence on the charity you wish to support and will almost always follow your recommendation—unless the charity does not qualify or falls on some restricted list.

For CRTs where the remainder balance will be less than $1,000,000, or if you just don't want to be bothered by administrative headaches and costs of a Private Family Foundation, the Donor Advised Fund is ideal. You do give up some control, but you gain the long-term impact at far less expense.

2. *Supporting Organizations:* Without a magnifying glass it is hard to tell the difference between a DAF and a Supporting Organization. They look and sound identical except that the Supporting Organization has a *direct relationship* with one or more parent charities. Colleges, hospitals, and religious organizations typically use Supporting Organizations to allow donors to establish perpetual giving programs without the costs and restrictions of private foundations. A Donor Advised Fund at a Community Foundation can also be designated as a beneficiary of a Supporting Organization. For a donor who wishes to name two or three specific charitable organizations as beneficiaries, but doesn't want you give an outright gift, or like the idea of establishing a perpetual gift, the Supporting Organization may be the ticket.

3. *Private Family Foundations:* Private Family Foundations (PFF) offer the donor the most controlled situation for ongoing philanthropy. In fact, a PFF itself is qualified as a charity

under IRS§501(c3). As such, any contributions you make to it are as tax deductible as they would be to any other charity. As a qualified charity, the PFF is also allowed to receive the proceeds from your CRT (though the use of your tax deduction is limited to 20 percent of your adjusted gross income with a five-year carryforward). The foundation must distribute a minimum of 5 percent of its asset value each year, net of expenses to other charitable organizations, or in grants or scholarships—and no, you cannot give scholarships to your own family.

If you can afford the ongoing administrative costs, a Private Family Foundation is about the coolest thing you can do with the CRT beneficiary. Think of a PFF as your private charitable company. You can name your own board of trustees, set your mission, manage the investments, and decide who gets how much. It is all about total control. As you might imagine, there are a ton of rules in the Internal Revenue Code that must be followed by the PFF in order to maintain its qualified status. In addition, there is an excise tax on investment income of 1 percent to 2 percent each year. But if you follow the rules, you can't beat it for the ultimate control and flexibility for your ongoing philanthropy.

Control and flexibility has its price. Private foundations are far more expensive to create and maintain than either the Donor Advised Funds or Supporting Organizations. Therefore you should probably not consider using them for amounts much less than $1,000,000.

I don't want to turn this into a Private Family Foundation discussion. I just wanted to give you a taste of the PFF as the alternative. The reason we're even talking about Private Family Foundations, or any of the other gifting alternatives, is because we need someplace for our charitable remainder trusts to go when they end.

There are plenty of good sources to learn much more about Private Family Foundations, Donor Advised Funds, and Supporting Organizations. Google any of the phrases and you'll be overwhelmed by the volume of information that's available on the Web. In addition, I've included some additional sources on my web site. In the meantime, I've provided Table 5.4 to help you differentiate among the three legacy gifts. The bottom line is that legacy gifts

Table 5.4   A Comparison of Legacy Gifts

	Donor Advised Funds	Supporting Organizations	Private Family Foundations
Deduction limit for cash contributions	50% of AGI	50% of AGI	30% of AGI
Deduction limit for appreciated assets (i.e., securities)	30% of AGI at current fair market values	30% of AGI at current fair market values	20% of AGI at current fair market values
Okay as CRT charitable beneficiary?	Yes	Yes	Yes
Excise tax on investment income	0%	0%	1%–2%
Control over investment selections	Donor usually selects from a menu of options	No control, but may recommend a strategy	Complete control over investments and advisors
Required annual distributions	None	None	5% of fair market value annually
Control over grants	Donor recommends grant recipients	Donor designates other charitable beneficiaries	Complete control (but not family members)
Costs	Minimal to zero	Minimal to zero	Substantial
IRS Reporting	Handled by the umbrella foundations (i.e., Community Foundation)	Shared by the Supported Organizations	IRS Form 990-PF must be filed annually. All reporting is the responsibility of the foundation
Lifespan	Perpetuity	Perpetuity	Perpetuity

provide us with a method of control over where our CRT dollars go. More importantly, they take congress out of the loop and keep you in the driver's seat.

Asset Protection

An added bonus to the CRT is asset protection. The CRT is an irrevocable trust, therefore you no longer "own" the property in it. If you don't *own* it, no one can take it away from you or force you to break it. Of course, if you created the CRT just for the purpose of sheltering assets from an impending lawsuit, all bets are off (and you'll probably face charges of fraud). Play by the rules, though, and you will add this valuable feature to an already great tool.

The CRT from Start to Finish

The charitable remainder trust (CRT) is an IRS-sanctioned tool that acts as the *lever* in our charitable leverage strategies. In the five point review below, each numbered item corresponds to its mate on Figure 5.11.

1. Assuming that you are the *donor*, you transfer cash, securities, or some other asset to a charitable remainder trust. The trust is a "split interest trust" with noncharitable income recipients and a charitable beneficiary. The lifespan of the CRT can be for one life (i.e., your life), two lives (you and your spouse), or for a term of years (not to exceed 20). When a business is the donor, a "term of years trust" is the only kind that can be used.

2. You are allowed to act as your own trustee. Once the appreciated assets have been transferred to the CRT, the trustee can sell them *in the trust* and *avoid the tax on capital gains*. The net proceeds can be invested in just about anything—but not aggressively stupid.

3. The CRT generates an *income tax deduction* today for the future gift to charity. The deduction can be used against 30 percent of your adjusted gross income (20 percent if the charitable beneficiary is a private foundation) and carried forward for five additional years.

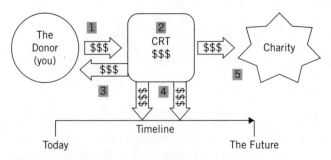

Figure 5.11   The CRT from Start to Finish

4. During the term of the trust, the income beneficiary (you or someone you designate) will receive a distribution from the trust based on either a *fixed dollar annuity payment* (CRAT) or as a *fixed percentage of the assets* in the trust as revalued each year (CRUT). In addition, the distributed income will be taxed under the highly favorable "four-tier" accounting rules.

5. When the trust ends, either at the death of the measuring life or at the end of the trust term, the remaining balance in the trust (*charitable remainder*) will be distributed to the *specific charities you select* or through your own legacy gift like a Private Family Foundation, Donor Advised Fund, or Supporting Organization.

I've covered the highlights in broad strokes here. As you might expect, over the years some unscrupulous types have tried to manipulate this wonderful tool to create a pure tax shelter without any charitable benefit. As a result, there are plenty of regulations in place that deal with items such as "self-dealing" or "unrelated business income." The rules are important but beyond the scope of this section. I've covered them in more detail in the professional advisors guide on my website. A word of caution, CRTs are incredibly powerful financial tools that offer a host of benefits, please don't screw it up by trying to "do it yourself." Get the help of a professional advisor.

The charitable remainder trust is the active application of voluntary philanthropy to defeat accidental philanthropy. It counters forced redistribution with selective donations. When coupled with its partner, the cash value insurance contract, it becomes the ultimate defense in the war on wealth.

CHAPTER 6

The Second Component to Charitable Leverage—The Cash Value Life Insurance Contract

There are worse things in life than death. Have you ever spent an evening with an insurance salesman?

—Woody Allen

I know what you're thinking, "you've got to be kidding me, life insurance?" I guarantee you that by the time you're finished with this chapter, you'll be dying to get some. Okay, that may have been an unfortunate choice of words, but of all the financial tools we use, I don't think there is a more valuable and misunderstood one than life insurance. *There is simply no other existing financial instrument that can do all of the things that a properly designed cash value insurance policy can do.* There is a reason I emphasize "properly designed." Unfortunately, cash value life insurance has had its reputation sullied by slick talking (usually part-time) salespeople, looking to make an extra buck by selling high commission products to an unsophisticated public. As a result, an alarming number of financial advisors, especially those in the financial media, lump all the products together, and in group-speak, repeat the following mantra, "only buy term insurance, only buy term insurance . . ." While term insurance does play an important role in providing huge amounts of death benefit for people with large obligations, it cannot create the living benefit of tax sheltered liquid capital that a *properly designed* cash value policy can do.

To prove that point and, more importantly, to support the bold statement I made in my opening, I'm going to spend some time here defining and describing just what a properly designed cash value life insurance policy looks like and what it can do—using real numbers from real companies. When I'm done with that, I show you how it becomes the pivotal player in our charitably leveraged strategy.

More Ground Rules

Like we did for the charitable remainder trust, let's lay down the ground rules to help you through this section.

1. Advisors who use sweeping generalities generally do not know what they're talking about. In other words, be wary of the advisor who says that term insurance is the only insurance to buy—they either have an agenda or have limited expertise.
2. Keep an open mind. Check your preconceived notions at the door. What we're going to discuss here is *not your father's life insurance.*
3. Some very smart folks buy cash value insurance. For example:
   • The Office of the Controller of the Currency (OCC) reports that more than 90 percent of the largest banks in the United States' own cash value insurance to provide benefits to key employees and provide a competitive return to the bank. In addition, 60 percent of mid-size regional banks and more than 40 percent of small community banks own cash value insurance, to provide benefits to key employees and provide a competitive return to their banks. What do you think they know that the financial pundits don't?
      ◆ In reference to the above, insurance cash value is booked as "Tier One" capital, which is considered the safest assets

of the bank. In the time of TARP, banks love their cash value insurance policies and they ought to since they have more than $110 billion *safely* stored there.

- Corporations thrive on cash value insurance, too. In a recent Clark Consulting nonqualified benefit survey of Fortune 1000 companies:
  - 90 percent have deferred compensation plans for key executives, of which 70 percent are funded using cash value insurance
  - 65 percent have Supplemental Executive Retirement Plans (SERPs), of which 74 percent are financed through corporate-owned cash value life insurance

    These are pretty savvy guys. Do you think they know the value of a quality cash value insurance product?

4. The key to making cash value insurance work for you is to know what type to buy. You want to use the kind the best and brightest use (referenced in the bullet points in item 3 above). I will show how to find the right type because there's a lot of crap out there. You can make a pile of tax sheltered money with an investment quality life insurance product that is purchased properly.

5. There *is* a place for term insurance, and it's a very large place, it just isn't here. The appropriate use for term insurance is for:
- Young folks with limited savings, or limited cash flow, who need to provide for their family (living expenses, mortgage, debts, college) in case they should die before the kids are raised and the debts are paid.
- Businesspeople who need to cover a bank note or similar time-sensitive loan.
- Folks whose financial situation makes them unsuitable for the charitable leverage plans I discuss in this book.

The Object—Cash Value Insurance

There are two types of cash value insurance—the kind you *die with* and the kind you *live with*. Both play important roles in our charitable leverage strategies. You need to know which to use when, just like you need to know when to use a CRAT or a CRUT. So, let's start with the basics and then we'll differentiate from there.

It Is All About Time and Money

Cash value insurance builds tax-sheltered *money* and provides a hedge against the *time* it takes to build it. The Internal Revenue Code specifically allows cash value life insurance that meets certain guidelines to build cash in a tax-sheltered manner. If you do it right (and I will show you how) *you will never pay tax on your cash.* So, given enough *time*, you'll build a nice little nest egg. But what if you don't live long enough to reach your accumulation goals? The life insurance policy is the only vehicle that will complete your savings goal with a pile of tax-free cash for your beneficiaries.

Imagine going to your bank and telling the president, "I'm going to open a savings account at your bank and deposit enough money into it each month so that at prevailing interest rates, I will accumulate $1,000,000 in 20 years. But, if I don't live that long, you have to pay the full $1,000,000 *immediately* to my beneficiaries—tax free, even if I die this year!" The bank president would laugh you out the door. However, that is *exactly* the unilateral contract that is made by the insurance company. Just chew on that for a second before you read on.

The Five Key Components and What Can Ruin Them

There are five key components to a cash value insurance policy (see Figure 6.1).

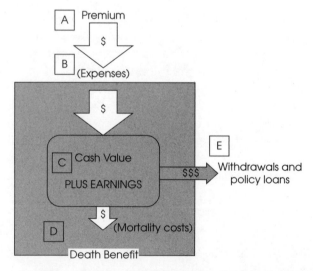

Figure 6.1   The Basic Design of a Cash Value Insurance Policy

1. What you put in it. This is called your *premium* payment.
2. Where the premium is stored. This is referred to as *cash value.*
3. How your money (cash value) earns more money. There are few different methods to crediting earnings to the cash value. We'll cover them all.
4. What your beneficiary gets if you die. Obviously, this is the called the *death benefit.*
5. What you get if you live. This is referred to as the *living benefit.*

The only things that can ruin a cash value insurance policy are:

• Out of line costs and administrative expenses. If the expenses associated with maintaining the policy are too high, you will not be able to earn enough on your cash value to make it worth your while. In this section, I will show what a "low-load" policy looks like and what questions to ask your advisor to make sure you get one.

• Lousy health. Life insurance companies don't like to issue polices on people who are bad risks due to health, lifestyle, or occupation. When you get into the area known as "substandard risk" the actual cost of the death benefit could increase to the point of absurdity. Again, if the costs are too high, the plan won't work. The good news is that in a charitably leveraged program you can always *borrow a life* from someone else. More on that later.

• Choosing the wrong type of insurance for the job. This is an absolutely crucial area. If you try to use a screwdriver to hammer a nail, you're going to have disappointing results. We need to choose the right tool for the job. There are a lot of different types of cash value insurance products out there. Most of them will never give you the chance to make money. We need to use only the ones that will.

Insurance Professionals Earn Commissions—Get Over It.   The good stuff cannot be purchased over the Internet or by mail order. Professional quality cash value life insurance can only be purchased through licensed insurance agents. Much like an investment professional, they earn commissions on the products you buy. Here's your tip for the day, *get over it!* You need a full-time *professional* to design the policies I use in this book. These professionals are paid through a percentage of the premium you pay for the policy, called commissions. For some reason the financial media has turned this into a dirty word. It is not. Great polices pay fair and reasonable commissions. Look, there are bad people who sell lousy products and take advantage of consumers in all consumer areas. Work with a professional, get references, do your homework and move on.

Removing the Mystique: A Cash Value Policy Explained

You will be stunned at how easy a cash value policy is to understand. Let's take it in baby steps.

Step # 1—Premium

You start by paying a *premium.* That may sound easy, and it is. You can choose from policies that have fixed annual premiums or flexible ones. At the risk of getting ahead of myself, note that the premiums are what drive the policy. The more you can put in against the fixed costs to maintain it, the more money will build in the following steps.

Step #2—Policy Expense

The next item is by far the most dangerous. It's called the *policy expense,* which is charged against the premium payment. Policy expenses include:

- Front-end loads or commission charges expressed as a percentage of the premium payment. They can be as low as 0 percent and range much higher (like 8 percent to 12 percent). Sometimes the loads are reduced after the first policy year. I bet you knew intuitively that the greater the load, the less your chance for making money. You're right, of course, and you're starting to see that if we break the insurance policy into pieces, you're going to know what questions to ask to make a better purchase.
- Administrative charges and policy fees are usually expressed as a flat dollar amount. These amounts reflect what the insurance

company charges for processing. It is important to note that while these charges are not prohibitive, they are debited each month or year, whether you actually pay a premium or not.

Step #3—Cash Value Account

After the expenses have been deducted, the remaining premium is deposited into your *cash value* account. (See Figure 6.2.) The beauty of the cash value account is that it "technically" grows tax deferred, but unless you really screw it up, it should be tax free. I bet now you're getting a clue as to why corporations and banks buy so much of it (hint: tax-free cash). Cash value will grow in one of four ways.

1. The most popular pays a *fixed interest return* declared by the insurance company; these policies are called Universal Life (UL).
2. Others pay interest based on *an outside index* like the S&P 500. Not surprisingly these are referred to as equity indexed universal life or Indexed Universal Life (IUL).
3. The oldest form of cash value insurance is known as whole life. The cash value in a whole life policy builds each year based on a declared *"dividend."* The word "dividend" in life insurance is not used the same as what you know as a dividend paid on a stock. The dividend is actually derived from a formula based on earnings and company expense savings

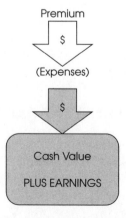

Figure 6.2   The Net Premium Becomes "Cash Value"

and is declared annually. Although whole life has enjoyed resurgence of late due to a turbulent economy, it is hard to unbundle the benefits from the costs like the more consumer-friendly UL or IUL contracts do. Therefore, my diagrams on how cash value insurance policies work should apply only to the UL, IUL, and VUL varieties.

4. The most active and potentially aggressive type of cash value life insurance is called Variable Universal Life (VUL). A VUL policy allows the owner to *invest* the cash value into mutual funds, or use fund managers selected by the insurance company. The mutual funds are clone funds that look exactly like the ones any consumer could buy on the open market. We're talking about big time fund managers like Fidelity, MFS, PIMCO, American Funds, American Century, Vanguard, and many more have their funds represented in these policies. As you might imagine, *these policies are regulated as securities* so it's serious stuff and should only be used by the prepared investor. More importantly, they should only be purchased after you have actually *read* the prospectus.

   • That's right, unlike the other types of policies mentioned here, variable universal life must be accompanied by a prospectus.

   • Since VUL policy cash values are invested in mutual funds they carry with them additional expenses charged internally by the funds themselves. These expenses will have a negative impact on the net performance of the fund. They can range anywhere from 0.5 percent to 1.5 percent per fund—so reading the prospectus is important. Fund expenses are an accepted course of doing business in the investment world but you do need to know that they exist, especially in down markets.

   VUL policies were the all the rage prior to 2009 because they provided an investor with a way to participate in the financial markets without paying tax, while providing his or her family with insurance protection. Then the bottom fell out of the market and VUL sales plummeted. I'm not going to comment *yet* on whether they are good or bad. For now, I just want you to know what they are, and that they are a part of the cash value life insurance family. In this family, the VULs drive the hottest cars, have the coolest lives—but you know they have a dark side.

A Word About Cash Value versus Surrender Value.   This is an important point to cover before we move on. *Cash value* is what your account is actually worth and it is the money upon which you earn interest, dividends, or investment returns. *Surrender value* is what you walk away with should you "cash out" of your policy. It is a way that the insurance company covers its costs and payment of agent commissions. Surrender charges are imposed for a period of years ranging anywhere from 0 to 20 and are all over the ballpark. It is imperative that you understand how much the surrender charges are and how many years they are in force, because they will vary both among insurance companies, and within the different policies sold by the same company. I don't get too hung up on the surrender value in our charitable leverage plans because it is a long term program that should far exceed the surrender years.

Step #4—Death Benefit

Ultimately all life insurance provides a *death benefit.* As you can visualize using the Figure 6.3, your cash value account is "wrapped" by a much larger tax-free insurance benefit. The life insurance death benefit is paid to your named beneficiaries free of income tax, probate fees, and state death taxes (in most states). If you stop to think about it, that's pretty remarkable. The cost of the insurance

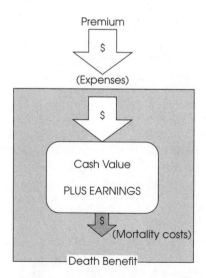

Figure 6.3   The Death Benefit "Wraps Around" the Cash Value

wrapper works like term insurance in that it reflects the pure "mortality" expense based on the insured's age and health rating. Each month, money is deducted from the cash value to pay for that month's mortality charge.

The insurance amount must be substantially greater than the cash value in order for the policy to qualify as "life insurance" under IRC§101a. The older the insured, the less amount of insurance is needed. This is referred to as the insurance to cash value corridor.

You can choose to have the insurance death benefit paid *inclusive* of the cash value. This is the most typical approach and amounts to actually buying less coverage as you get older. For example, a $1,000,000 death benefit will be a $1 million death benefit if your cash value is $2 or $200,000. The other choice is to have the death benefit paid *in addition to* the cash value. The same $1,000,000 policy with a $200,000 cash value will pay out $1,200,000 to the beneficiary. It's simple math. A policy with a $200,000 cash value that pays out a flat $1,000,000 actually provides $800,000 of real mortality coverage. Therefore, the cost to maintain this policy will be cheaper than one that always provides a flat $1,000,000 plus cash value.

A valuable feature of the indexed, variable, and fixed UL polices is that the face amount is adjustable. That means that you can increase or decrease the insurance amount in the same policy.

Step #5—Living Benefits

The *living benefits* of a life insurance policy center on your ability to tap the cash value. In a nutshell, you can access the cash value of your policy at any time, for any reason, without government penalty. The way to do it is through *policy withdrawals and/or loans*. (See Figure 6.4.) This is an important feature that takes advantage of the very favorable tax laws pertaining to all life insurance policies. It is in these "living benefits" that our charitably leveraged strategies flourish. In addition to providing a tax-free death benefit, a policy that is properly funded in compliance with IRC§7702 provides an approved method to grab your accumulated cash without paying tax on it—ever. Here's how:

- *Withdrawals are taxed under the First In, First Out (FIFO) accounting rule.* Cash value life insurance is the only remaining financial tool that is allowed this significant tax advantage.

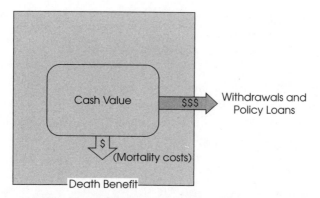

Figure 6.4 The Owner Has Access to the Cash Value Through Withdrawals and Loans

What this means is that you don't pay any tax until you have withdrawn all of your original deposits. Hence, the first money that went in is the first money to come out. FIFO accounting provides the maximum tax deferral because earnings come out only after *all* the principal has been withdrawn.

Every other tax-deferred investment is taxed on a LIFO basis (Last In, First Out). Tax deferred annuities are great examples of these types of instruments. Financial products subject to LIFO accounting offer the least amount of tax deferral since *all* of the earnings must be withdrawn and taxed first, followed by the principal.

If all the "First In" money is withdrawn "first out" in a life insurance policy, then logically the next dollars that are withdrawn are subject to tax. That is a correct statement unless you move on to the next item then you won't need to pay tax at all!

- You, as the policy owner may "borrow" against the remaining cash value of your policy in what is known as a *policy loan.* Policy loans are not taxed because they are considered the same as any other commercial or personal loan. Loans from the policy are charged nominal interest (like zero to 0.5 percent). Further, there are no restrictions or repayment schedule. The annual interest can actually be rolled into the loan each year so that no out-of-pocket payment is required.

    How is this possible? Policy loans are technically borrowed against the death benefit of the policy. If the loan is outstanding at the time of death, the balance is deducted from the tax-free death benefit. How's that for simple. Loans are loans and are not a taxable event.

Don't Take All of the Money Out!   You must be aware of potential disaster regarding taking money out of an insurance policy. If the policy is surrendered, or if it lapses because there is not enough cash value or premium payments to keep it in force, *then all of the past gains become taxable as ordinary income* in the year of the lapse or surrender.

On the other hand, if you die with the insurance policy still in force—no matter how small the remaining death benefit, all loans will be cleared against it and there is no tax on anything! So, what have we learned here? *Keep the damn thing in force!*

For example, let's say Mr. X purchases a policy with a $1,000,000 death benefit. Over time he paid $100,000 into his policy and his cash value had grown to $300,000. After reviewing his financial needs, he decides he wants to take $250,000.

If he surrenders the policy, he will pay income tax on the $200,000 total earnings (he must take the full $300,000 on surrender) and his family will receive no insurance benefit.

If he withdraws up to the $100,000 basis (first in) and then borrows another $150,000 via a policy loan, he will pay no tax. He will need to keep the policy in force, maintaining the family's death benefit.

If at any time in the future the policy lapses—even if that date is 20 years later, Mr. X will receive a 1099 for all of the gains in the policy (which will be at least the $150,000 he borrowed—maybe more). Not good.

However, if he dies while the policy is still in force with the loan outstanding, then he pays no tax on the earnings because the loan and any accumulated interest is "netted" against the death benefit. Mr. X's family will receive the remaining death benefit, tax-free. That's a pretty darn good deal.

Obviously, the key is to keep the policy in force so that it results in a death benefit, even if that death benefit is a very little, teeny-tiny one. A policy in force at the time of death avoids tax—period. Fortunately, many of the major the insurance companies have addressed this need by providing what are called "Lapse Protection Provisions" or "Over-loan Provisions." These features are built into their policies to protect the policy from a lapse disaster. In short, the contractual provision states that if a qualifying policy reaches a point where it is about to lapse, it will automatically convert into a reduced face amount, paid-up policy. Remember, a policy in force at the time of death avoids tax—period. It is simple and effective. Be careful, not all policies carry this valuable feature. Never, never, never buy one without it.

Recap of the Basics

A properly designed cash value life insurance policy provides the following benefits (See Figure 6.5.)

- Builds a source of tax-deferred cash. If you have a brain, even a small one like mine, you can turn tax-deferred cash into tax-free cash.
- Allows access to your cash at any time for any reason without government restrictions or penalty. It's your money, so take it when you want it.
- Provides your beneficiary with a lump sum tax-free death benefit. It is the only financial vehicle that completes your financial goals for your family if you die.

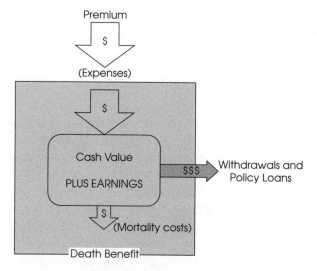

Figure 6.5   Recap of a Cash Value Insurance Policy

There are Two Types of Policies: The Kind You Die With and the Kind You Live With

In the next chapter, I'm going to show you how to combine the right CRT with the right cash value insurance policy to achieve charitable leverage. To make that transition possible we need to start here as we differentiate between the two different uses for life insurance. As we just discovered, not all cash value life insurance policies are built the same. I like to break them into two general categories:

1. The kind you die with: Focuses on the *death benefit* and is used for asset replacement at death; cash accumulation is not an issue.
2. The kind you live with: Concentrates on the *living benefits* such as the accumulation of cash value. It uses the death benefit as a necessary requirement to achieve the tax benefits on growth and income.

Each one has its place in the planning world, but care must be taken in selecting the right type of policy for the right situation. The nice part is that it's really simple to tell them apart and even easier to apply.

The Kind of Insurance You Die With

The most common use for life insurance is to provide a large lump-sum of tax-free cash in the event of death. That cash is normally used to pay the expenses, settlement fees, and taxes associated with your demise. The goal is to provide enough liquid capital so that your family will not suffer financial hardship due to your very bad luck.

In the estate planning arena, it is a widely accepted and excellent planning strategy to use life insurance to pay the estate settlement taxes and costs. This approach allows investments and real estate to remain intact, while the insurance proceeds are used to pay the bills. Imagine how important that strategy is now, following the financial tsunami of 2008.

For the purposes of this book, we're going to look at insurance as it relates to planning with a charitable remainder trust. In a traditional plan, the life insurance death benefit may be used to actually replace the value of the CRT that passes to charity. At death, when the CRT moves on to the charitable beneficiaries, the tax-free death benefit is paid to the heirs. When the insurance proceeds are equal to, or greater than the value of the CRT, this becomes a pretty slick estate planning device. Throughout the charitable giving world, this technique is often referred to as "wealth replacement."

Whether the death benefit of the insurance policy is used to pay estate settlement costs or for wealth replacement, the two key requirements shared by both techniques are:

1. The policy needs to be in force when you die: To be absolutely sure that the death benefit will be there when you die, the coverage must be permanent. Since you don't know when the unfortunate event will occur, term insurance just will not work. A universal life or whole life policy targeted to age 100 and up is the proper selection. Most policies of this nature are designed to stay in force well over age 100. Some companies issue their guaranteed death benefit to run from 110 to 120, you should live so long. The point is, when the death benefit is the key to the success of the plan, a guaranteed permanent approach is the only acceptable option.

2. You must pay the absolute minimum guaranteed premiums for the policy. Cash value is not the issue here, death benefit is. Therefore, the accumulation of a large amount of cash savings is not important. The only thing that matters is that we want to buy the *most* amount of coverage for the *least* amount of guaranteed annual premium. In that regard the longer you can stretch the premium out the better. A premium structured to be paid every year until age 100 will provide the lowest overall cost approach. Even though in the final years of the policy you may not know what day of the week it is, someone else will be there to pay the premium for you. Especially if that someone is the ultimate insurance beneficiary.

With the above in mind, the only types of policy that will work are Universal Life with guaranteed premiums, and Whole Life with guaranteed premiums. Variable Universal Life is the worst choice you could make, and an indexed product is not far behind.

In situations where a Joint-life CRUT is used to generate income to both spouses, the CRUT balance will be distributed to charity at the death of the second spouse. The perfect wealth replacement insurance policy matches it with what's called "second-to-die" insurance. The policy design averages the ages and health ratings of both spouses and pays the face amount at the death of the second spouse. As with the other policies in this area, only the guaranteed premium UL and Whole Life varieties are acceptable.

The Kind of Insurance You Live With

At the opposite end of the life insurance spectrum lives the types of policies that focus on the accumulation of cash with an eye toward future income. As a secondary feature, these policies provide an element of financial security through the tax-free death benefit. Variable Universal Life and Equity Index Universal Life are great choices for a wealth accumulation policy. I love these policies, but *only* for the potential they have for tax sheltered growth and income. They should *never* be purchased for pure death benefit coverage. Never!

As I shared with you earlier, VUL policies allow you to *invest* the cash value in mutual funds inside the tax-free protection of the insurance policy. Each insurance company's VUL plan is a little different, but in general, they all provide "clone funds" of the U.S.'s most well-known mutual funds from the best fund families. The sponsoring insurance company will provide you with a list of their particular fund choices, but you can count on names like Vanguard, Fidelity, Pimco, American Funds, MFS, and so on, being included. You won't see things like Bob's International Mid-Cap Fund (though I doubt he could have done much worse than the big boys in 2008). The wide selection of funds covers the complete spectrum of risk and reward. In addition, most companies provide asset allocation or lifestyle models that provide automatic management in the style of investing that best suits your particular investment suitability profile ranging from conservative to moderate to aggressive. Most provide automatic portfolio rebalancing. If this sounds a lot like a typical 401(k) plan, then you get the picture.

Unlike the traditional fixed cash value policies above, VUL policies are considered *investments* and subject to the compliance rules and scrutiny of the Securities and Exchange Commission (SEC). The policies are sold by prospectus and *you could lose all of your investment.* You could also accumulate a boatload of tax-free cash if you know what you are doing and *have the time and temperament required to play the investment game.* If we learned anything from the debacle of 2008, it is that folks with short-term investment horizons and weak stomachs should not be in the stock market, only those with the time to recover should participate.

The downside on VUL policies is that they have varying expense charges for the policy itself and for each fund you select. Coupled with the insurance costs, the downside exposure is substantial. You must work with an advisor who can look at the policy prospectus and educate you on *all* of the costs. In addition, you'll want your advisor to run illustrations from three of four companies. It is always a good idea to run illustrations at conservative rates of return. I like to use the 6 percent to 6.5 percent range. I've heard all the stories about how the stock market has been a 10 percent performer over the last 50 years. But if the numbers work for at 6.5 percent, they'll kick ass at 10 percent. Wouldn't you rather be happily surprised?

Equity Indexed Universal Life policies are an excellent alternative to VULs and work beautifully in the cash accumulation approach that we use later in our charitable leverage strategies. These types of policies allow the owner to "participate" in the upside potential of the securities markets without the downside risk of capital loss. In fact, most indexed policies offer guaranteed floor rates of interest should the market lose ground. The trade-off is that the upside is usually capped to a maximum predetermined growth rate.

Unlike a VUL policy, an indexed policy is not considered an investment since the cash value is not actually participating in the securities market. The cash value of the policy earns interest that is based on the growth of a definable index. The S&P 500 is the most often used index, but as more insurance companies get into the game, we are seeing other choices tied to both foreign and domestic indexes. This is an attempt to set companies apart from each other as well as diversify risk. How the growth rate is credited can vary among companies as well, and can have a major impact on your success. For example, some companies use what called a one-year "point-to-point" measure starting with the day you fund the policy and ending the same date, one year later. If the S&P 500 index has moved up *during that time,* you receive the corresponding percentage gain on your cash value (usually subject to a cap of 10 percent to 12 percent, or even greater). Other companies reset the rate monthly, while still others offer a multiyear point to point adjustment. It's a pretty competitive market and that's usually good news for the consumer.

They may be not as sexy as their VUL cousins, but index products are a good choice for someone who wants their money to be in a position to grow with the market and is willing to sacrifice some of the upside, to reduce the risk of capital loss. For example, let's say your indexed policy follows a one-year "point-to-point" based on the S&P 500 Index subject to a 12 percent cap on the gain. If the S&P 500 grew 8 percent from point-to point, that rate is credited to your cash value account. If the S&P 500 grew 18 percent from point-to point, the capped rate of 12 percent is credited to your cash value account. While you don't get the full 18 percent, it's not such a bad trade-off because if the S&P 500 stayed even or dropped in value during that same period you don't lose any money (though your account value will probably dropped a little due to insurance charges). You may even receive some guaranteed floor interest rate like 2 percent. It's like being in the market without actually subjecting yourself to loss of capital due to nonperforming investments. As you can imagine, the folks who had money in indexed annuities and insurance policies in 2008 did not make any money—but they didn't lose any either. In case you didn't hear that, I'll write louder, *they didn't lose any either!*

Like the VUL contract, your advisor becomes the key interpreter of the product offerings. When evaluating an index product he or she should answer these questions:

- What is the cash value indexed to?
- How is the index calculated?
- What is my rate cap?
- What is my guaranteed floor rate of interest?
- Does the policy offer a fixed account in addition to the indexed one?
- Can I blend my cash value between fixed and index?
- How often can I change the blend?
- What are the internal charges, loads, and carrying costs, and surrender charges?

I have personally found these cash value building contracts to be among the most competitively priced, but look at a couple of choices before jumping. Each has their own little twist that makes them unique. And remember, never buy a cash value building policy that does not offer some form of lapse protection rider or "over-loan" provision.

So, how do we play the living benefit/cash value growth game? The key to success is to purchase the *minimum amount of insurance death benefit possible as allowed under IRC§7702*. I mentioned this important code section earlier because it established the minimum death benefit required, relative to the cash value that allows the policy to enjoy the favorable tax treatment afforded only to *life insurance policies*. Simply put, you must always maintain substantially more death benefit than cash value.

When you are young, the ratio must be at least 250 percent or 2½ times more death benefit than cash value. As you get older, the ratio narrows to as low as 110 percent. These rules came about by way of the Technical and Miscellaneous Revenue Act of 1988 (TAMRA) and are known as the *TAMRA guidelines*. Remember that term.

Follow the logic; if we pump a lot of cash into one of these policies and keep to the minimum insurance as allowed by the TAMRA guidelines, then we will achieve the lowest possible overall cost for that policy, while assuring that

- The cash value will not be taxed
- The death benefit will not be taxed
- Withdrawals will qualify under the FIFO accounting rules
- Loans will not be taxed (that's why you *must* include a lapse protection feature)

In other words, you will create a huge source of tax-sheltered cash with an insurance benefit as a secondary feature.

Comparing the Strategies

Getting its guidance from the Internal Revenue Code, cash value life insurance provides a permanent solution to building and preserving wealth by offering a tax-sheltered environment. A properly designed policy will fit into one of two financial strategies—the preservation of wealth, or the accumulation of wealth for future income. Lucky for us, insurance companies have responded to both scenarios by creating specific policies to meet specific needs. In Table 6.1, I have provided a comparison of two types of strategies.

Table 6.1   Insurance Comparison

Comparison Category	The Type You Die With	The Type You Live With
Type	Universal Life or Whole Life (Guaranteed products only!)	Variable Universal Life or Indexed Universal Life
Strategy	Focus on the Death Benefit as tax-free asset replacement	Focus on the Living Benefits for tax-sheltered cash accumulation with future income
Premium to Death Benefit Design	Maximum guaranteed death benefit for the minimum guaranteed level premium	Fund at the TAMRA guidelines: minimum death benefit for maximum premium
Payment Period	Stretch over lifetime	Shorten the payment to 7 to 20 years
Other Considerations	• Use 2nd to die for joint-life CRT replacement • Not an investment, it is pure insurance	• Individual policies work best • Registered investment product with investment-type risks and rewards Should not be used for pure insurance purposes

You Made it this Far, So Let's Measure Your Progress

You now know how to define charitable leverage. It's not the financial kind of leverage one would associate with borrowing or margin—and a lot of risk. Rather, it is the physical kind you'd associate with the most basic of tools like a screwdriver or wrench, where the tool is applied to an object to achieve superior results. A screw is the object of the leverage created by the screwdriver achieving a secure result. Charitable leverage then, is where we use a Charitable Remainder Trust (CRT) as the lever and a Cash Value Life Insurance Policy (CVLI) as the object of the lever's force. The result is the accumulation, preservation, and distribution of wealth for ourselves and our families without government interference. Further, the philanthropy created by charitable leverage—large or small—takes place on our terms and not at the whim of Congress.

We then learned about the basic characteristics of all CRTs and CVLIs. As promised, it was probably not the most stimulating reading you've done. But it was necessary to bring you to this point. With a basic knowledge of the two types of CRTs (annuity trusts and unitrusts), and a general understanding of the two types of CVLIs (the type you die with and the type you live with), you are now in a position to understand how we combine them to create superior financial results. You are now ready to see how using charitable leverage changes everything.

CHAPTER 7

Blowing Up the Paradigms

I came, I saw, I got blowed up.
—Ernest P. Worrell, from *Ernest Goes to Jail*

Charitable leverage planning reverses the traditional thinking about charitable remainder trusts, life insurance, and how the two work together. Traditional thinking is what people who are smarter than me call "paradigms." There is an existing paradigm for charitable remainder trusts. There is another one for life insurance. There is yet a third about how they work together, which is based on the first two paradigms. Webster's New World Dictionary defines the word "paradigm" as:

> An overall concept accepted by most people in an intellectual community because of its effectiveness in explaining a complex process, idea, or set of data.

That sounds to me a lot like what I heard my Dad saying when I was a kid, "It is the way I say it is because that's what I say it is." Who could ever fight against logic like that? Who would even dare?

The bottom line is that the existing paradigms are fine for traditional planning, but we're not talking about anything traditional.

Charitable leverage is designed to help you fight back in the war against your accumulation of wealth. There's nothing traditional about it. In this battle, we not going to just shift the paradigms, we're going to blow the damn things up!

The Exploding Paradigm #1: The Charitable Remainder Trust Is a Planned Giving Tool That Results in a Gift to Charity

The process that transforms the way we use charitable remainder trusts begins with another round of applause for the features that make it so powerful.

- Solid tax authority under IRC§664 and the subsections thereunder
- Capital gains bypass
- Increased income generation
- Favorable four-tier accounting
- Income tax deduction
- Charitable legacy
- Asset protection

If you missed any of these features, you may need to return to Chapter 5 where they are discussed in detail. The important point concerning the list above is that both Charitable Remainder *Annuity* Trusts and Charitable Remainder *Unitrusts* enjoy the same major benefits.

We also know that the "operating system" of CRUTs and CRATs revolve around the same five steps (see Figure 7.1).

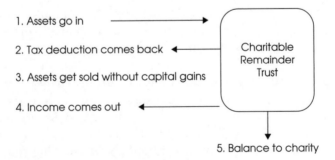

1. Assets go in

2. Tax deduction comes back

3. Assets get sold without capital gains

4. Income comes out

Charitable Remainder Trust

5. Balance to charity

Figure 7.1 The CRT Operating System

1. Assets are transferred in by the donor.
2. A tax deduction comes back to the donor.
3. Appreciated assets may be sold inside the Charitable Remainder Trust (CRT) without capital gains tax.
4. Income (or cash flow) comes out of the trust.
5. When the trust ends, the balance goes to charity.

The traditional use of a charitable remainder trust is to provide a donor's favorite charity with a substantial "deferred" or "planned" gift. That kind of thinking lends itself naturally as a technique used in the estate plans of older and wealthier donors. So here's the existing paradigm:

> As an estate planning technique a charitable remainder *unitrust* is used to provide a donor (or joint donors) with income for life resulting in a substantial deferred gift to charity at death.

Blow it Up!

Let's light the fuse on this stick of dynamite by suggesting that in the new paradigm, you don't actually *give away* anything, you're just rerouting tax dollars. Instead of giving a gift *to* charity you become a partner *with* charity to achieve your desired results. I know that sounds a little like "that depends on what your definition of 'is' is," but the concept of a partnership with charity is a key element to understanding this plan. If you want, you can even become the charity that you're going to build the partnership with by creating your own private family foundation or donor advised fund.

Unitrusts have long been the CRT of choice for the conventional plan, but the partnership with charity is best created by selecting a Charitable Remainder *Annuity* Trust as the lever in the charitably leveraged plan. You recall that the major difference between a CRUT and a CRAT is how the income is distributed. CRUTs pay a fixed percentage of the fair market value of the trust account each year. CRATs pay a fixed dollar payment based upon the original trust value.

With a CRUT, it's all about the investment performance of the account value each year. The performance of the investments directly impacts your income. If it grows, your income grows. If it makes less, so do you. The charitable beneficiary sits on the side-lines and collects what remains at the end. That's your gift. You bear the brunt of the pain or gain of the investment returns. That's not much of a partnership.

The CRAT, on the other hand, is going to pay you that fixed dollar amount without regard to the underlying investment per-formance. The charity bears *all* of the financial risk. If the trust performs well, the charity may receive more than what you put in. If it performs badly, or suffers from a couple of down years, they may get less. But *you* always get the same income. There is no stress, no guesswork, just cash flow. Do you give up the opportunity for increasing cash flow in rising markets? Yes. But really, how's that been working out for you? In a long-term positive market, the CRUT will outperform the CRAT in terms of income (distribution percentage being equal). One or two bad years, however, can have serious long-term negative impact.

In our planning structure we do not need to take on that kind of investment risk because we won't benefit from it. Don't lose focus, the CRAT is not the part of the plan where you make your money; it is the part of plan where you leverage your money. Now, that's what I mean by a partnership with charity.

Another change to conventional planning is that *you're not going to be in the CRAT for that long.* Traditional charitable trust planning is almost always focused on wealth transfer or estate planning. While a charitably leveraged plan will have a positive impact on your estate taxes, its primary purpose is for the *accumulation of wealth with an eye toward generating future tax-sheltered income* for yourself, or a member of your family (child/grandchild), or key employee. It is more of a retirement or deferred income plan than an estate plan.

If a traditional plan is centered on estate planning, then logi-cally the CRUT will transfer to charity when the last spouse dies and the estate settlement process takes place. In a charitably lever-aged plan, we only need the CRAT to act as a funding tool for your deferred income account (that comes later). Therefore, *the CRAT runs for a fixed term of years and then distributes what remains to your partner charities at the end of the term.*

When the smoke clears from the exploding paradigm, here's what you see. *The CRT we use for every charitable leverage strategy is the same.* It is a 10-year term CRAT with an annuity rate of 8 percent to 10 percent. Remember, an annuity rate is not what the trust earns, it is the fixed dollar amount based on the original deposit. For example, if you transferred $1,000,000 into a 10-year CRAT with a 10 percent annuity rate, your annual payment would be $100,000 per year for 10 years. At the end of the term, the remaining balance in the trust moves on to your designated charities. If you selected an 8 percent annuity for 10 years, you'd receive $80,000 whether the market went up, down, or sideways.

Before I compare the simplicity of a "term of years" CRAT to the complexity of a joint-life or single life CRUT, I'll state for the record that I am not anti-CRUT; I use them all the time in estate planning situations. I even wrote a book about them. However, as we fight against accidental philanthropy through the charitable leverage programs covered in this book, you'll love the simplicity and predictability of the term of years CRAT.

Look at the tax deduction calculation as an example of CRAT simplicity. The lifetime CRUT has so many moving parts and variables that it is impossible to tell you, the reader, what your tax deduction percentage will be. As much as I'd love to know you personally, I don't. How old are you? How old is your spouse? Is there a spouse? What distribution percentage rate did you choose? These are but some of the variables considered for the tax deduction calculation. However, a term of years CRAT with an 8 percent annuity rate, will give you, and every other reader, of any age, the same tax deduction (31 percent with a 3 percent Applicable Federal Rate [AFR], 34 percent with 4 percent AFR). We removed life expectancy from the equation. We know exactly when the trust will end.

Let's compare income streams over the next 10 years. How much income will you get each year from an 8 percent CRUT funded with $1,000,000? You don't know. It depends on how well the underlying investments do. I know this, if you funded a CRUT in 2007 and invested it in anything other than cash, it's worth a hell of lot less now. Therefore, your income is going to be a lot less. How much income will you get each year from an 8 percent CRAT funded with $1,000,000? That's right, $80,000 every year. I know this, if you funded a CRAT in 2007 and invested it in anything other than cash, it's also worth a hell of lot less now, *but that doesn't matter*, your income is still $80,000! Your partner, the charitable beneficiary might not be getting as much though. (See Figure 7.2 for a summary of how to blow up the CRT paradigm.)

All Charitable Remainder Trust Provide:
- ✓ Solid tax authority under IRC§664
- ✓ Capital gains bypass
- ✓ Increased income generation
- ✓ Favorable four-tier accounting
- ✓ Income tax deduction
- ✓ Charitable Legacy

Traditional Charitable Remainder Trust Design:
- ✓ Unitrust Design
- ✓ One or two lives
- ✓ Tax deduction primarily based on age and distribution %
- ✓ Income determined annually, could be more or less
- ✓ Lots of moving parts

Charitable Leverage Trust Design
- ✓ Annuity Trust
- ✓ 10-year term
- ✓ 8%–10% annuity rate
- ✓ Everybody, every age, gets the same tax deduction
- ✓ Income is fixed for the life of the trust
- ✓ No moving parts

Figure 7.2 Blowing up the CRT paradigm

A term of years charitable remainder annuity trust is simple to understand, simple to explain to others, yet provides enormous charitable leveraging power. Capito?

The Exploding Paradigm #2: A Life Insurance Policy Is Used to Provide a Permanent *Death* Benefit

The accepted financial wisdom says that a cash value life insurance policy is used to provide a large death benefit in the event of an untimely (or even timely) demise. While we're at it, everybody knows that life insurance is a lousy investment. Therefore, the rule is that when buying life insurance, get the most coverage you can get for the least amount of premium payment. But you already knew that from the previous chapters, right?

You also already know that there's more than one way to skin the insurance cat. So let's begin the cash value life insurance transformation by reaffirming what we know to be true about all cash value life insurance policies. They share the following common features:

- Solid tax authority under IRC§7702 and IRC§101a, keeps a life policy taxed under the favorable life insurance taxation rules.
- Tax-free death benefit.
- Tax-sheltered cash accumulations (tax deferred, but can be tax free).
- Tax-sheltered cash flow through FIFO withdrawals and policy loans (keeps the tax collector away from the insurance cash-flow).
- Early access to cash without government penalty.
- Flexibility of premium payments and death benefit adjustments.

If you're fuzzy on any the shared features, you may need to revisit the previous chapter, and this time try to stay awake. Just keep in mind that as long as you follow the rules as provided under the TAMRA guidelines, the features listed above will apply to your policy.

Cash value life insurance policies come in four tasty flavors: Whole Life, Universal Life, Variable Universal Life, and Equity Indexed Universal Life. Though each plan has unique characteristics, they all operate the same way (see Figure 7.3 for a graphical representation of how they operate):

- Premiums are paid by the owner, policy charges are deducted.
- Cash value accumulates without tax.
- Mortality costs are deducted to pay for the death benefit.
- Income comes out on demand (may be tax-free).
- Upon death, the tax-free death benefit is paid to named beneficiaries.

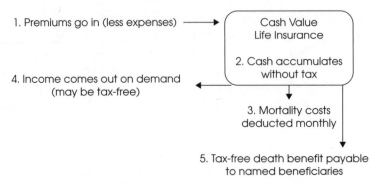

Figure 7.3   How a Cash Value Insurance Policy Works

I closed the previous chapter with an explanation of how life insurance can focus on either the death benefit or the living benefits. It's all a matter of adjusting the proportions to items 1 and 5 (premiums and death benefit) in Figure 7.3. Traditional life insurance planning, especially as it relates to conventional charitable trust planning, centers on the death benefit approach. Hence, the existing paradigm as it relates to life insurance policies is that:

> A life insurance policy is used to provide permanent death benefit. With that premise in mind, what follows naturally is that the owner of the policy desires to pay the least amount of premium for the maximum coverage without regard to cash value accumulation.

The fact is that if the policy accumulated no cash value at all, that would be just fine. The only two things that matter are that the policy be in force when the insured dies and that the premiums are reasonable. As you can see in Figure 7.4, the design parameters would create a policy that looks like this:

- A fixed rate Universal Life (UL) or Whole Life (WL) policy that is structured to provide maximum permanent coverage for a fixed annual premium.
  - We don't want to take any chances of the policy lapsing due to poor investment choices or market conditions, so we need a guaranteed fixed rate to plan properly.
  - We don't care about building cash value, so a Variable Universal Life (VUL) or Equity Indexed Universal Life (EIUL) policy is the wrong choice.

Traditional Design of the Insurance Contract

✓ Focus on Death Benefit, Wealth Replacement Trust Design
✓ Usually 2nd to die (matches the income term of the CRUT)
✓ Fixed rate UL or WL—based on guarantees
✓ Design premium to buy the *maximum death benefit*
✓ Pay for life

Figure 7.4 Traditional Life Insurance Policy

- The lowest possible premium schedule that would *guarantee* the death benefit for life.
  - Guarantee is the operative word. We want no risk of policy lapse.
  - We also want no surprises. If the policy is fixed at the guaranteed level, it cannot increase or run out of gas.
- Premium payments are payable every year for life.
  - The longer we can stretch out the premium, the less premium we'll need to pay each year.
- A second-to-die policy is the perfect fit if a joint-life CRUT is used.
  - It averages the ages and health histories on two lives to achieve the lowest overall cost against the maximum face amount of insurance. The death benefit is paid on the death of the second insured. This type of policy is almost always purchased on the joint lives of husband and wife.
  - With two healthy lives, this type of policy is the best overall value by far.

Blow it Up!

The existing paradigm is all about the death benefit. But, our new paradigm is not one built on death, it is built on life! We want to live, and prosper. It's a much happier approach. So we need to blow the old paradigm up. We do that by doing the *opposite* of everything in the box in Figure 7.4. We want to purchase the *least* amount of death benefit possible, while stuffing in the *most cash we can.* Later, when we combine the new insurance policy with the CRAT, I show you where all the *stuffing* comes from, but for now let's concentrate on this important change.

Our primary purpose is to use the unique tax rules regarding all cash value life insurance policies to accumulate a bucketful of tax-sheltered cash. At some point in the future we will convert the accumulated cash into tax-free income. Unfortunately, some of us might not make it to that date in time. If we die before we get there, then as secondary feature, the death benefit of the policy will complete our plans for our loved ones. The design parameters for this approach look like this:

1. Focus on the cash value accumulation through a VUL policy or EIUL policy.
   - VUL is more aggressive and is treated as an investment. The cash value participates directly in the securities markets and is subject to the vagaries of the market.
   - EIUL is not considered an investment. The cash value is indexed to a securities type measurement like the S&P 500, with minimum interest guarantees.
   - Either choice provides a better upside potential for the accumulation of cash than a low fixed rate UL or WL.
2. Maximum fund (maximum premium).
   - The insurance policy death benefit is targeted to the lowest amount allowed under the TAMRA guidelines relative to the premiums paid.
   - Qualifies for all the tax benefits allocated to life insurance policies.
3. Premium payments are paid over a relatively short period of time.
   - I use a 10-year premium payment schedule to match up with the 10-year term CRAT we discussed when we blew up Paradigm 1. More on this in the next section.
4. Single life insured.
   - The policy only needs to insure the life of the person who will be drawing the income from it. That may not necessarily be the policy owner. Unlike polices driven by death benefit, we can even "borrow" a healthy life to be the insured. The owner of the policy controls the benefits, not the insured.
   - Frankly, it doesn't matter if we use a single life policy or a second-to-die version, as long as we keep the death benefit as low as possible. We don't want to waste dollars on the mortality costs and other expenses.

5. Automatic lapse prevention feature is a must.
   - The policy will be used to generate income without tax. If the policy lapses, all the previous untaxed gain will be taxable in the year of the lapse. Therefore, the "over-loan" feature that converts a policy in danger of lapsing into a reduced paid-up policy is an essential element of this design.

The conversion to the new paradigm regarding life insurance is not about dying, it's about living. It is not about *replacing wealth*, it's about *accumulating* wealth. It is not about creating cash for our heirs as much as it is about creating cash flow for ourselves. It is the tax-sheltered greenhouse that grows the money you transplant from the clutches of congress. (See Figure 7.5 for a summary of how to blow up the life insurance paradigm.)

All Cash Value Insurance Contracts Provide
✓ Solid tax authority under IRC§7702 and IRC§101a
✓ Tax-free death benefit
✓ Tax-free cash accumulations
✓ Tax-free cash flow through withdrawals and policy loans
✓ Early access to cash without government penalty
✓ Flexibility

Traditional Design of the Insurance Contract
✓ Focus on Death Benefit, Wealth Replacement Trust Design
✓ Usually 2nd to die (matches the income term of the CRUT)
✓ Fixed rate UL or WL—based on guarantees
✓ Design premium to buy the *maximum death benefit*
✓ Pay for life

Charitable Leverage Insurance Design
✓ Focus on Living Benefits. Designed for cash accumulation and income
✓ Single life
✓ 10-pay premium
✓ Variable universal life or equity index to provide upside
✓ Maximum fund for the *least death benefit* (TAMRA guidelines)
✓ Automatic lapse prevention feature

Figure 7.5   Blowing Up the Life Insurance Paradigm

The Exploding Paradigm #3: The Marriage between the Charitable Remainder Trust and Life Insurance Is Based on Wealth Preservation

Once again, there is nothing at all wrong with thinking that the relationship between the CRT and the Cash Value Life Insurance Policy (CVLI) is based on wealth preservation *if you're developing a traditional use of a charitable remainder trust*. It's just that we're not going to be traditional.

As you read in Paradigm #1, the CRT of choice in conventional planning is usually a one- or two-life CRUT with an eventual gift to charity. This type of structure is an effective estate planning tool as assets transferred to charity will reduce the taxable estate. The downside of this type of plan is that when the CRUT is distributed to charity, it disinherits the heirs (usually the children). While the donor/parents may leave this world with a warm and fuzzy feeling about their philanthropic works, the kids may be feeling something entirely different.

The life insurance policy plays a vital role in fixing that problem. The death benefit–centered policy we learned about in Paradigm #2 acts as a wealth replacement tool when it is paid directly to heirs or to a trust for the heirs. In effect, when the CRUT is paid to the designated charity, a like amount in the form of tax-free insurance proceeds magically appears to replace it. Further, if the policy is owned by an Irrevocable Life Insurance Trust (ILIT), the proceeds will avoid federal estate and state inheritance taxes as well. (See Figure 7.6.)

The CRUT/Wealth Replacement paradigm is what most financial advisors think about when the topic of charitable remainder

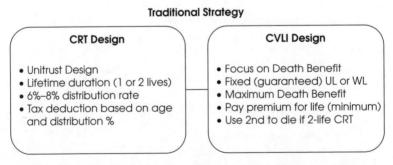

Traditional Strategy

CRT Design	CVLI Design
• Unitrust Design • Lifetime duration (1 or 2 lives) • 6%–8% distribution rate • Tax deduction based on age and distribution %	• Focus on Death Benefit • Fixed (guaranteed) UL or WL • Maximum Death Benefit • Pay premium for life (minimum) • Use 2nd to die if 2-life CRT

Figure 7.6   The Structure of a Traditional Charitable Trust Strategy

trust planning comes up. That's easy to understand since the client's interest in a CRT is usually driven by an estate planning issue or simply by a desire to leave a substantial planned gift to charity. It works beautifully in that capacity, especially when the CRUT uses a portion of its cash flow to pay for the wealth replacement insurance premium. The donor puts the balance of the cash in his or her pocket. In either case, it has always been viewed as a gifting and wealth preservation tool.

Blow it Up!

In the new paradigm we flip the whole deal around. The lifetime CRUT is replaced by the 10-year term CRAT. The income from the CRAT is fixed at 8 percent to 10 percent. At the end of the 10-year term, the CRAT moves on to the designated charities. The impact to charity can be pretty substantial since it will be receiving the trust remainder a lot sooner than it would with a lifetime trust.

The annual cash flow from the CRAT is pumped into the cash value insurance policy. You know already that this policy will be of the wealth-building variety. The premiums paid to the policy will be whatever the after-tax cash flow yields from the CRAT. At the end of the CRAT term, the premiums stop. Though the CRAT goes away, the fully funded policy stays invested until the owner starts taking his or her income from it. If the insured dies at any time along the way, the tax-free insurance proceeds are paid to the heirs. (See Figure 7.7 for a summary of the structure of a charitably leveraged strategy.)

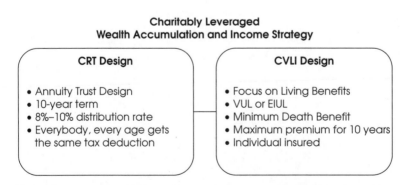

**Charitably Leveraged
Wealth Accumulation and Income Strategy**

CRT Design	CVLI Design
• Annuity Trust Design • 10-year term • 8%–10% distribution rate • Everybody, every age gets the same tax deduction	• Focus on Living Benefits • VUL or EIUL • Minimum Death Benefit • Maximum premium for 10 years • Individual insured

Figure 7.7 The Structure of a Charitably Leveraged Strategy

Summary

You learned in the previous chapter that the charitable leverage strategy uses the CRT as the lever and the CVLI policy as the object that the lever supercharges. *Now* you know that the CRT needs to be a CRAT designed in a specific manner and the CVLI needs to be the kind of insurance you *live* with. Put them together and you have a great way of doing well by doing good. Even better, you have the basis for your battle plan for fighting back for control of your money.

Your Battle Plan for Fighting Back Against the War on Wealth

A good battle plan that you act on today can be better than a perfect one tomorrow.

—General George S. Patton

With the new paradigm in place, let's take a closer look at how the process works. Don't overthink it. It is as simple as it looks. Always keep in mind the original concept of charitable leverage: The CRAT is the lever—it provides the power; the insurance policy is the object upon which the CRAT acts.

There are only four steps to every charitably leveraged plan.

Step 1: The Conversion from accidental philanthropist to active philanthropist

Step 2: Active philanthropy opens the door to charitable leverage

Step 3: Charitable leverage creates a philanthropic legacy

Step 4: Charitable leverage creates a financial legacy for you and your family

Every step will generate a couple of actions. Each action will have a direct impact on your financial life. Buckle up, this is the fun part.

Step 1: The Conversion from Accidental Philanthropist to Active Philanthropist

The conversion from accidental philanthropist to active philanthropist involves a series of three action steps.

The First Action

It all begins with your recognition that if you just sit there, accidental philanthropy will happen to you. So you take preemptive action by *creating your personal Charitable Remainder Annuity Trust (CRAT) and transferring cash or appreciated securities to it.* The CRAT follows the design criteria outlined according to our new paradigm: a 10-year term with a fixed annuity rate of 8 percent to 10 percent. The impact of this initial action strikes a huge blow in protecting your assets from the WMDs used war on wealth.

Remember the story of Walking Barry Bonds? You just did it. You completely neutered the government's attempt to reach into your assets by placing them in a lock box. The CRAT is an irrevocable trust and the stuff in it is no longer part of what you own. If it's not part of your estate, how could it be subject to federal or state death taxes or other settlement fees? It can't—it isn't.

The transfer to the CRAT has also sheltered your assets from creditor claims. True, you can't reach into the CRAT and pull your assets out, but neither can anyone else. The short-term nature of the 10-year CRAT does provide just about all of your money back over the term. In fact, if you chose a 10 percent annuity, you would get all of your money back.

The lever has landed! Once the CRAT is in place, every other part of your plan is funded. The CRAT is the lever that provides all of the up-front tax benefits, all of the future charitable benefits, and all of the fuel for your future tax-free accumulation and income benefits. All this is accomplished with one check (or one transfer), one time. *Wow!* (See Figure 8.1)

Important Planning Note: The Type of Assets Transferred to the CRAT. You may have noticed that I specifically stated that the

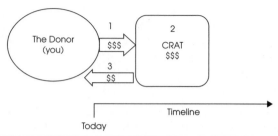

Item #	Action	Impact
1	You (or your company) transfet cash or appreciated securities into a 10-year term Charitable Remainder Annuity Trust (CRAT) with a fixed annuity rate of 8%–10%.	✓ Removes the assets from your taxable estate. ✓ Protects the assets from the claims of creditors.
2	If the CRAT sells the appreciated assets it pays no capital gains tax.	✓ Dollars that would be lost to tax remain in the CRAT to be reinvested for the charity.
3	The transfer to the CRAT creates an immediate income tax deductio for the present value of the future gift to charity. The tax deduction can be taken against 30% of adjusted gross income and carried forward for five years.	✓ Since the CRAT is for a fixed term with a fixed annuity rate, everyone at every age receives the same tax deduction. ✓ If a Sub. S corporation funds the CRAT, the tax deduction passes through to the shareholders.

Figure 8.1   Step 1—The Conversion from Accidental Philanthropist to Active Philanthropist

assets transferred to your new CRAT should be cash or appreciated securities. There is a reason for that, simplicity. Cash, cash equivalents, and publicly traded securities can be instantly and easily valued and reinvested. CRTs will accept all kinds of assets like public and private stocks, bonds, real estate, and collectibles. Assets other than cash and publicly traded securities, however, require more sophisticated (read expensive) trust planning. They often require outside appraisals and valuations, and possibly the use of an independent trustee to execute sales and avoid "self-dealing" issues (more on that later). Ultimately, a more complex CRT may be needed. I probably would not use the CRAT I suggest in this book for hard-to-value or hard-to-sell assets. I'm a simple guy with simple needs and simple thoughts. The charitably leveraged strategies covered in this and the next chapter all work because they are simple. We're going to stick with cash or publicly traded securities as the preferred assets to transfer. Trust me (I did a little pun there).

The Second Action

The second action taken in this first step is to sell the assets transferred into the CRAT and reinvest the proceeds. This action is executed by your appointed CRAT trustee. You may be the CRAT "donor," but the CRAT "trustee" calls the shots. The good news is that you can name yourself as trustee and other family members as successor trustees. I'm going to cover the role of the trustee in more detail after I'm done with this section. For now, let's assume that because you have a brain, you'll act as your own trustee and call your own shots.

I'm going to cover the CRAT cash flow in Step 2, but since the taxation of the cash flow is tied to the underlying investments of the CRAT, I do want you to see the connection here. If cash was transferred into the CRAT, the trustee could invest in just about anything, including tax-free municipal bonds or tax-free bond funds. Using the four-tier accounting method, all of the cash flow generated from the CRAT would be tax-free. If any or all of the transferred assets included appreciated securities, then a similar style investment would work better under the four-tier rules. The investment selection could include a portfolio of growth and income type securities or mutual funds. Exchange traded funds and indexed funds may be appropriate, but attention should be paid to risk. The trustee should lean to the conservative. This should not be construed as investment advice. It's more like common sense. The impact of this action can be enormous.

For instance, if appreciated securities are sold inside the CRAT, you have just avoided the most onerous weapon of mass redistribution—capital gains tax. The CRAT is not a taxpayer; therefore, it pays no capital gains tax. All of the sale proceeds remain intact to be reinvested instead of redeployed.

This avoidance of capital gains has a positive impact on you as well as the charity. In a CRAT, your income is what it is, so you might assume that any capital gains tax savings only benefits the charitable beneficiaries. That's mostly true, and it's all good. The driving motivation behind charitable leverage is the avoidance of forced or accidental philanthropy. So it is better that your charities receive the capital gains tax savings rather than letting Congress ride herd over your tax allocations. But you benefit as well, because all of that original value of your contribution to the CRAT is used to calculate your ultimate annuity payment. Further, it is used to qualify your

8 percent, 9 percent, or 10 percent trust annuity under the 5 percent probability test. It bears repeating, it's all good.

Important Planning Note: The Role of the Trustee.   As with all irrevocable trusts, the power rests with the trustee or trustees. The CRAT is the only irrevocable trust where naming yourself trustee does not destroy the trust. The bad news is that naming yourself trustee does expose you to the possibility of "self-dealing." As trustee, you simply cannot involve the CRAT in anything where the investment would benefit a family member (including extended family). The whole point of this book is to keep things simple. The CRAT design in our charitable leverage strategies is based on simple transfers of public securities or cash, followed by simple investments. Complex CRATs and CRUTs funded with private assets or real estate may work great but are beyond the scope of this book. Don't let that dissuade you from looking into them. Just be sure you work with an attorney or other financial advisor who has a specific knowledge of CRTs.

The Third Action

The third action created under Step 1 is actually a reaction to the first action, follow? What I'm trying to say in my clever way is that you get an income tax deduction based on the transfer to your CRAT. As you learned earlier, the tax deduction is based on the present value of the future gift to charity. It is calculated using the CRAT term, annuity distribution rate, and the highest monthly Applicable Federal Rate (AFR) over the last three months (counting the month you actually fund your CRAT). You may want to check back to Table 5.2 for an example. The tax deduction may be used against 30 percent of your adjusted gross income and carried forward for five more years. If you select a private family foundation as the charitable beneficiary, the deduction may be used against 20 percent of your Adjusted Gross Income (AGI), with the same five-year carryforward. The tax deduction amount is listed under the charitable contributions section of your itemized tax return. The power of the impact of the tax deduction is rooted in its simplicity.

- Everybody at every age will get the same tax deduction for the same type of CRAT purchased at the same AFR (see *the important planning note, following*). Because you know exactly when the trust will end (10 years) and exactly how much income you'll receive (your annuity rate), there's no guesswork or complicated calculations in determining the deduction. The only fuzzy part is the monthly AFR and that has a minor overall influence.

- If an LLC or Subchapter S corporation funds the CRAT, the tax deduction flows through to the shareholders. If you own your own business, keep that little nugget stored away for later—it's huge.
- The tax deduction strikes another blow against forced philanthropy by reducing the current income tax due on taxable events.
  - Use it against routine ordinary income.
  - Use it against distributions from a retirement plan (IRA, 401[k], etc.).
  - Use it against sales of appreciated property that is sold *outside* the CRAT.
  - Use it against any of the taxable income generated by the CRAT cash flow!

Important Planning Note: It's Easy to Calculate Your Tax Deduction and Its Real Value in the War on Wealth. Table 8.1 is not exact, but it will get you pretty damn close to calculating your tax deduction. The point is that using a Term of Years CRAT removes a lot of the confusion regarding income and deductions.

Let's check your math to be sure you're doing this right. If you transferred $1,000,000 into a 10-year term CRAT with an 8 percent distribution rate and a 3 percent AFR, your tax deduction would be about $310,000 or 31 percent. Your annual income would be $80,000. A 9 percent CRAT would distribute $90,000 each year for 10 years and under the same AFR would produce a $220,000

Table 8.1 Approximate Tax Deduction Schedule for a 10-Year Term CRAT at Various AFRs

Tax deductions assume quarterly payments starting the 4th month

AFA	8% CRAT	9% CRAT	10% CRAT
3%	.31	.22	.14
4%	.34	.26	.18
5%	.37	.29	.21

approximate tax deduction (22 percent). If the AFR moves to 4 percent, then the two CRATs would generate $340,000 (34 percent) and $260,000 (26 percent) respectively.

Take it one step further. What is the real value of that deduction as you fight back for control of your money? If your income tax bracket is 40 percent, or put another way, if you are a member of the targeted class, the tax savings from a $310,000 tax deduction is $124,000! That, my friend, is $124,000 that congress does not get their hands on and neither does anyone else. That money stays with you.

Charitable leverage is now in place and operational. This first step completely funds the others. Think about that for a moment. Everything that happens from this point on is fueled by the CRAT. Both your charitable legacy and your financial legacy can run on autopilot from here. If you become disabled or die, the plan still performs to your specifications. One check or one transfer, one time is all it takes to turn the tables on the boys from D.C.

Step 2: Active Philanthropy Opens the Door to Charitable Leverage

With the "lever" in hand, we can now use it to generate the force needed to create a superior financial result. Think about the impact a screwdriver has on a screw or a hammer has on a nail. That's what we're talking about here, simple and effective. Figure 8.2 is your snapshot of the second step in this four-step process. As I mentioned earlier, each step contains a couple of actions. To show you that this is a fluid, continuous process, I have continued numbering each action in sequence. The first action in Step 2 is the fourth action in the process, so I've numbered it accordingly.

The Fourth Action

The first action in second step is fueled by the CRAT. Each year for next 10 years the CRAT will distribute the fixed dollar annuity payment you selected. That income stream can be paid to you directly, or to someone else you name. It can also be paid to another trust. Most CRATs pay the income quarterly starting with the first quarter after the trust is funded.

You already know the next two parts of the cash-flow spiel. First, as the income recipient, you know exactly what your income will be every year, because it is based on the percentage of what you

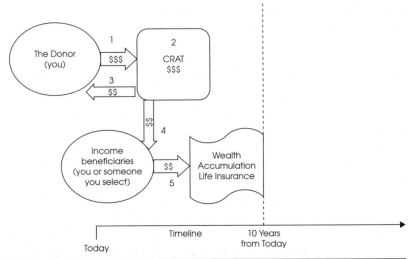

Item #	Action	Impact
4	Each year the CRAT distributes a fixed dollar annuity payment back to you or someone you select. You have absolute certainty about the income payments. Income is taxed under the favorable four-tier accounting rules.	✓ The investment performance of the CRAT impacts the *charity not your income.* ✓ The fixed payments continues for the full term of years—even if you don't.
5	After receiving the fixed annuity payment, the income beneficiary uses *all or most of* it to pay the premium on a minimum death benefit Wealth Accumulation policy (VUL or EIUL).	✓ Cash builds in the policy free from tax. ✓ Cash is available to the owner of the policy at any time, for any reason, without government penalty. ✓ The policy death benefit provides family financial security.

Figure 8.2   Active Philanthropy Opens the Door to Charitable Leverage

transferred into the CRAT. A $1,000,000, 8 percent CRAT will distribute $80,000 every year, fixed for the term of the trust. The second part is that the income distributed from the CRAT is subject to the four-tier accounting rules. I think I did a pretty good job covering that in Step 1, so let's not spend any more time on that. Let's look instead at the impact of that income.

1. You have absolute certainty that all the income you planned on will be paid. The "term of years" feature of your CRAT

means that the fixed payment you selected will be paid every year until the trust term ends. If you don't survive for the full 10-year term, the CRAT will continue to make payments to a contingent beneficiary. You'll see the full impact and importance of predictability when I put it to use in the strategies in Part III. For now, you should know about three general situations where this feature comes into play:

- The most common situation is in a personal plan where you are both the CRAT donor and income recipient. If something happens to you, the income from the CRAT can be paid to a contingent income recipient you name. You could even select another trust to receive the balance of the cash flow.
- In the case where the CRAT is used in business, the company that created the CRAT could redirect where the cash flow goes if the designated employee leaves. Talk about golden handcuffs.
- It also works in the case where the CRAT donor is old enough that his or her life expectancy may not be as long as the trust term, and that's pretty old. If the donor dies or becomes incapacitated physically or mentally, the trust just continues on making payments as scheduled to the next in line.

  In all three cases, the CRAT donor has the comfort of certainty that the plan will be completed. It is the comfort that only comes from knowing how much and how long.

2. The performance of the underlying trust account, positively or negatively, will not impact your income at all. This has huge implications for the impact on you and your designated charitable beneficiary. It is at the root of the first new paradigm that deals with being in partnership with your charity. The pressure of performance is on the shoulders of your selected charity, not you. That doesn't mean, screw the charity. It means you don't need to invest aggressively because it doesn't impact you. Your plan calls for income you can rely on. Your partner will get what's left. That's why it's called a charitable "remainder" trust.

Important Planning Note: Your CRAT Will Probably Decrease in Value During the Term of the Trust.   Don't worry, it's designed that way. At the substantial annuity rate the trust is paying, you must accept the fact that if the trust is conservatively managed, it almost certainly will not increase or even maintain its value over the 10-year term. But that's what the CRAT is supposed to do. It is okay for it to decrease in value, because if the money is not in the CRAT, it is in your hands! Voluntary philanthropy is supposed to redirect your *accidentally philanthropic* dollars, not *all* your dollars.

The Fifth Action

So, where does all that CRAT income go every year? That's right! It goes to the cash value insurance policy I was screaming about in the second exploding paradigm. That's the second action in Step 2. After paying whatever tax is due on the CRAT cash flow, the CRAT income recipient (let's just assume it's you, it be will far less confusing) uses all or most of it to pay the premium on a Wealth Accumulation Life Insurance policy. I use that term as a catchall to encapsulate any maximum funded, minimum death benefit Variable Universal Life (VUL) or Equity Indexed Universal Life (EIUL) contract that fits the design parameters I outlined in Paradigm 2.

You have control over the funding of the insurance policy. When the annuity payment is distributed from the CRAT, it comes to the income recipient first. It *does not go directly to the insurance policy.* This allows you to decide with every annuity payment just how much you will pay to the insurance policy and how much you will keep.

You may recall that I used the phrase "stuff all the money we can" into the insurance policy when I was describing the new insurance paradigm. I promised then that I'd show you where all that stuffing would come from. Here it is. The CRAT produces enormous cash flow that is pumped into the policy. Remember, one check, one time. The CRAT—the Lever—does all the work. The impact of the Wealth Accumulation Policy on your planning is outlined in the following list.

- The Wealth Accumulation Policy (VUL or EIUL) builds cash free from tax with little costs deducted for the death benefit.
- The cash is available to the policy owner at any time, for any use. There are no age restrictions or government penalties.

- The death benefit of the policy is large enough to completely replace the value originally transferred to the CRAT, tax-free. Throughout the program it provides a source of family financial security.

Important Planning Note: If You Fund the Policy Without the CRAT You Could Ruin Your Plan.   Charitable leverage is designed to use the CRAT cash flow to fund the policy. If you deposited a large lump sum of cash directly into an insurance policy, similar to the amount you'd transfer to the CRAT, you would violate the TAMRA guidelines. The policy would be deemed a "modified endowment contract" (MEC). The result would be an insurance policy that would be taxed like an annuity; withdrawals would be taxed on a Last-in, First-out (LIFO) basis rather than First-in, First out (FIFO). Loans or withdrawals prior to reaching age 59½ would be subject to a 10 percent penalty for early withdrawal, and the whole thing would just suck. By making the large deposit to the CRAT and letting it fund the policy over a 10-year period. You pick up all the tax and charitable benefits of the CRAT and maintain the tax sheltered nature of the insurance policy.

By now you are getting the sense of where this process is going. You have already struck a blow against the redistribution of wealth; now you're taking steps to protect future accumulations.

Step 3: Charitable Leverage Creates a Philanthropic Legacy

Time marches on and so does your CRAT. Step 2 plays out over it's the 10-year life span. During that time the cash flow continually funds the insurance policy, building the cash value account. There is plenty of liquidity in the policy along the way if needs change and there's a death benefit in place if things really change. At the end of the 10th year, the CRAT reaches the end of its run and we're ready for Step 3, when the pure power created by your philanthropic legacy is revealed.

The Sixth Action

This action is all about the distribution of the charitable remainder to your selected charities. This action completes the cycle that defeated accidental philanthropy and starts a new one of multigenerational charitable giving. You are raising the bar for future generations and it feels pretty good. Your charitable remainder can be distributed directly to public charities or used to fund a legacy gift like a Donor Advised Fund (DAF) or Private Family Foundation (PFF). This one simple action has a serious long-term impact and creates the soul of your plan.

Figure 8.3 shows your progress through Step 3.

Option #1: Direct Gifts.   Let's look first at the impact your CRAT distribution has on direct gifts to charity.

- Assets that would have fallen prey to wealth redistribution are now directed by you to go exactly where you want them to go. You can spread the charitable remainder among as many

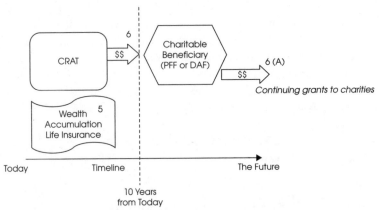

Item #	Action	Impact
6	At the end of the 10-year CRAT term, the remaining balance in the CRAT is distributed to the charitable beneficiaries you select. You could also choose to name a Donor Advised Fund or Private Family Foundation as the charitable beneficiary.	✓ You have used pinpoint accuracy to select where your "accidentally philanthropic" dollars will go by choosing voluntary philanthropy.
6 (A)	A Donor Advised Fund or Private Family Foundatioin will continue to distribute grants to charitable causes in perpetuity.	✓ Your charitable legacy (and family name) will live on through future generations. ✓ Keeps you in the game.

Figure 8.3   Charitable Leverage Creates a Philanthropic Legacy That Could Last for Generations

charitable organizations as you want. Remember, charitable distributions must be noted in the trust before it ends, not at the time of distribution.

- You can further direct each charity as to how they can specifically use your allocated gift. As an accidental philanthropist, your tax dollars are used by congress to do whatever *they want to do*. You win that battle with this step.

- Chances are you'll be alive to see your philanthropy at work. Unlike the traditional lifetime CRTs, your CRAT is only a 10-year deal. There's a good chance you'll be around to participate in the direction of your gift and receive the accolades. In addition, you'll be there to participate in the social and political benefits of being a player. That may not seem important to you, or maybe you're just shy, but there is a lot to be said for the respect and power attributed to the person that writes the checks. It should not be overlooked or minimized. Also, it doesn't hurt to have your kids involved in the process.

- This new level of giving is based on using dollars you were going to lose anyway. It's all about rerouting tax dollars away from government and back toward the causes you care about.

Option #2: A Legacy Gift.   The alternative to leaving a direct gift to charity is to create a legacy gift through a Donor Advised Fund or Private Family Foundation. In my view, this is as good as it gets for the ultimate distribution in a charitable leverage program. The list below explores the impact of that choice.

- Talk about a gift that keeps on giving, the purpose of a legacy gift is to grant money every year to other charitable causes that touch you. The blessings of your actions move from a once and done direct gift to a perpetual legacy. Don't think for a minute that "philanthropy" means you need give a huge gift that will result with your name on a building. You probably know many charitable organizations who struggle every year for any gift. A gift of any size to them is an act of real philanthropy. Your name may not make it onto the front of a building, but it will be written in indelible ink on the hearts of the people you help.

- Things change. Who knows what charitable causes will be important 10 to 20 years from now? Your legacy gift will put you and your family in a position to adapt to changing social needs and respond to emergency requests.

- Building on the preceding bullet points, the perpetual grants of a legacy gift keeps you involved in philanthropy for as long as you want to be. A friend of mine who was a pro athlete in another life, has great way of putting it. He says, "It keeps you in the game." You remain a vital player in the charitable organizations you help each year.

- A perpetual gift can run through multiple generations, recognizing the family name as an ongoing leader in the charitable community. Your children and grandchildren learn from your lessons on philanthropy. You teach them how real wealth transcends what you do for yourself and your family to what you do for others. You give them shoulders to stand on so that after you're gone, they can continue your legacy and establish their own.

Important Planning Note: To Help You Decide How to Direct Your Charitable Remainder, a Little Math Might Help.   There is no right or wrong way to give a gift from the remainder interest of your CRAT. I just want to contrast the type of impact a direct gift has with a legacy gift. Let's say your CRAT will be worth about $500,000 when it ends in 10 years. For the sake of this exercise let's say you'll be 60 at that time and your life expectancy is about 20 more years (age 80). The ages don't really matter, it is the years I'm establishing. If you give the $500,000 all to one charity, or divide it among five at $100,000 each, that's a big gift(s) and a big deal.

Now, let's say you give the same $500,000 to either a Private Family Foundation (PFF) or Donor Advised Fund (DAF). Let's also say that the funds are invested at only 5 percent each year, and you give the same 5 percent away in the form of grants to other charities. Each year your grant would be $25,000. Over the next 20 years, you'll give away $500,000 and your PFF or DAF will still have $500,000 remaining. If you die at that point, your children and or grandchildren will take over and continue the legacy gift in the family name. Or the $500,000 could be distributed outright.

Both gifts work and each style accomplishes a different objective. I should also point out that the legacy gift could be discontinued at any time and distributed directly to your charities. Either way it's nice to be in a position to distribute a gift of this size. No one needs to know that you did it with dollars you potentially would have lost to taxes. We'll just keep that among us girls.

Whether you choose a direct gift to charity or a legacy gift as the remainder beneficiary of your CRAT, it is your call and yours alone. The best part of your new-found philanthropic side is that you fund it with "house money." The tax dollars that would be taken *from* you are now controlled *by* you. If you don't mind that your tax dollars are used to fund research on olive fruit flies in France, or used to produce dog biscuits in the shape of a lobster by the Lobster Institute, then you don't need this strategy. But if you think you could direct your dollars better than congress, then you need to be in control of your tax destiny. Control over your money is the ultimate victory in your battle against redistribution.

Step 4: Charitable Leverage Creates a Financial Legacy for You and Your Family

The payoff, just like a hammer drives the nail with the power of physical leverage, so does the CRAT provide powerful funding for the wealth accumulation insurance policy through the power of charitable leverage. Now, in Step 4, it's time to reap the personal benefits. Figure 8.4 is a review of the final step in this powerful plan.

As you know, the CRAT funding of the insurance policy stops after the 10th year. Step 3 showed you what happens to the CRAT at that time, but what happens to the insurance policy? The answer is pretty simple, though in the form of another question. What do you want to do with it? That's the beauty of super-funding the policy through the CRAT cash flow. There are no further premium payments required to keep it in force. In fact, you do not need to do anything to the policy; it just continues to (hopefully) accumulate earnings until you're ready to start drawing on it. The date you start taking income, somewhere off in the future, is completely controlled by you. Unlike a qualified retirement plan, there arc no age rules for distribution or penalties for early withdrawals. You are the King of your contract. It's good to be the King.

Before you even get to that magic date when you start to take your deferred income, the policy provides a couple of key benefits. There are only two things that can happen to you along the road to

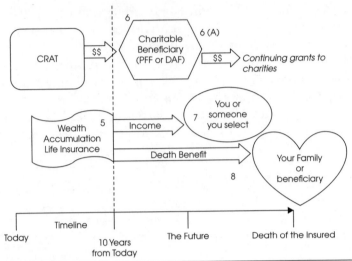

Item #	Action	Impact
7	At the end of the CRAT term, the insurance policy is fully funded and continues to build a tax-sheltered cash value account until you tap it for tax-free income.	✓ The donor has successfully transferred a taxable asset to an account that will generate substantial tax-free income. ✓ The cash value account is liquid and accessible. There are no government penalties or taxes.
8	The tax-free insurance proceeds are paid to your family or other beneficiary.	✓ Provides a source of tax-free financial security for the family of the insured.

Figure 8.4   Charitable Leverage Creates a Financial Legacy

retirement, either you're gonna live or you're gonna die. The policy provides solutions for both.

The Seventh Action

If you need cash along the way toward your "retirement" date, you can always tap your policy. You can loan the money to yourself and never bother to pay it back. If you don't pay it back, it negatively impacts your future income stream. The value of having a heavily funded insurance contract with a lot of cash accumulation is that it gives you options for access to cash quickly if the need arises. I know I'm repeating myself, but it bears repeating, *you can take your money at any time for any reason without incurring a government penalty or income tax.* You don't need to prove anything to anybody, there's no hardship rules or limitations. There doesn't need to be a disaster pending for you to reach into your policy. I have had clients of mine tap their contracts for college education (wait, that was me), vacations, even weddings. Living with money available is a pretty handy thing.

The Eighth Action

The death benefit is in place from minute one. If you die before you get to personally benefit from the cash accumulations, your beneficiaries will receive the tax-free insurance proceeds. If the policy is designed properly, the insurance benefit will include a flat insurance amount (called the "face amount") plus all of the accumulated earnings in your cash value account. The face amount will more than cover the original transfer to your CRAT and the accumulated earnings will insure (pardon the pun) that your family gets the rest—immediately.

Not to back the hearse up to your door, but if you die during the first 10 years, your family (or beneficiaries) would receive the insurance policy death benefit plus the balance of payments from the CRAT. If you die any time after you start to withdraw your income from the policy, your beneficiaries would get the remaining insurance death benefit.

Let's assume you don't die or need cash on the road to drawing your deferred income. Your income may begin at any time and last as long as you want. It's not magic, it's math. The income stream depends on:

1. How much you have accumulated in your policy.
2. What it's earning.
3. How many years you want to take it.

Obviously, using conservative rates of interest and assuming your cash doesn't lose value, the longer you put off drawing your income, and the shorter the period you draw it, will yield the greater income stream.

For most people, their deferred income plan mimics their retirement plan. The typical charitably leveraged program targets income to begin anywhere from age 60 through 70. For planning purposes,

I like to suggest the income run for a period of 20 years if it begins before age 65. Otherwise, I use age 85 as the typical end date and fit the income stream to it. A person age 70, for example, would withdraw income for 15 years (to age 85), a person age 69 would draw income for 16 years (to age 85) and so on. This approach also works well with business owners who are using charitably leveraged plans as a way to provide supplemental retirement income to key employees. We'll cover that and a lot more in Part III.

There are some situations where the income from the insurance policy could start immediately upon the end of funding in the 10th year. This approach works very well for younger folks who are making a boatload of money now, but have no idea how long the gravy train will last. Professional athletes, entertainers, and other young professionals fit this profile. They can use their income stream as a bridge to a traditional retirement plan, or defer it to a normal retirement age with unbelievable results.

The impact of Step 4 is all personal. It is the development of your *personal* wealth accumulation and deferred income plan coupled with the financial security for your family.

- You have transferred a taxable asset out of your estate and then used the cash flow from that asset to build a tax sheltered account with liquidity for your personal enjoyment. When the time is right *for you*, you'll use that tax-sheltered account to generate substantial tax-free income.
- The death benefit of the insurance policy provides a comforting level of family financial security. If you die before your deferred income begins, the death benefit immediately completes your accumulation goals and replaces the original amount you transferred to the CRAT. Since the payment is made in the form of life insurance proceeds, it is distributed to your beneficiaries free of income tax.

Key Planning Note: An Example of What the Policy in Step 4 Could Look Like.   I hate to show illustrations because I can't do it without making some assumptions. It goes without saying—but I'll say so anyway—that assumptions are not guarantees or representative of anything other my own assumptions. I just want you to see what one of these plans looks like. I will do that here for your education only. This is an example of a male age 45 who used his CRAT to fund his wealth accumulation policy to the tune of $95,000 per year for 10 years. We will *assume* that the policy averages a net rate of return of 6 percent throughout the illustration. Take a look at Table 8.2, and then I'll break it down.

Table 8.2 shows the net impact of Step 4 on a friend of ours, Mr. Corleone. God willing, Mr. C. would like to retire at age 65. If he does, his income will be about $165,500 tax-free annually (column 2). Over his 20-year retirement life span, he'll net over $3,300,000 (column 3). But if he can't wait until 65, he can start his income at age 60 at about $133,600 per year tax-free. His total income would be about $2,672,000. It's all math and compound interest.

Mr. C. is in a hazardous line of work and he may not make it to retirement, so his family's financial security is important to him. Column 4 shows that from the very first day of the plan, he is insured for $2,000,000 plus the accumulations in his cash value account. Column 5 shows the remaining death benefit in his policy at age 86, his assumed life expectancy for this model. If he retires at age 65, draws out his $3,310,000 of income and then gets hit, uh, I mean dies, his family will receive another $1,663,000 in insurance proceeds. That's a total benefit package of just under $5,000,000— all tax-free if he does it properly. With all due respect, he would have to crazy not to do this plan. Eh!

Remember, this only shows the results from funding the policy from the CRAT cash flow. It does not take into consideration the first three steps of our plan. But just from this view you can see how profitable the Cash Value Life Insurance Policy (CVLI) can be when it is heavily funded by the CRAT, but then, that's the point behind charitable *leverage*.

Table 8.2 Retirement Projections for a Male Age 45

1 Starting at Age	2 Tax-Free Annual Income	3 Total Income 20 Years	4 Death Benefit in Year 1	5 Remaining Death Benefit at Age 86
60	$133,600/yr.	$2,672,000	$2,000,000 + CV	$1,226,000
65	$165,500/yr.	$3,310,000	$2,000,000 + CV	$1,663,000

This is an illustration of a hypothetical policy on a male age 45, preferred nonsmoker. Assumed IRR of 6% .
This is presented for educational purposes only. This is not a representation of an existing plan.

Summary of How Charitable Leverage Works

I have prepared Figure 8.5 for you to use as a guide to your personal plan. It covers all eight actions in the four-step process. When you break it down step-by-step you see how easy this process is. The best part is that everything flows off of action Item 1. Once you transfer assets to your CRAT, the CRAT takes over. It provides the tax deduction and the tax-sheltered space to sell appreciate securities without tax. It generates the cash flow to superfund your insurance contract, which in turn provides you with tax-free income

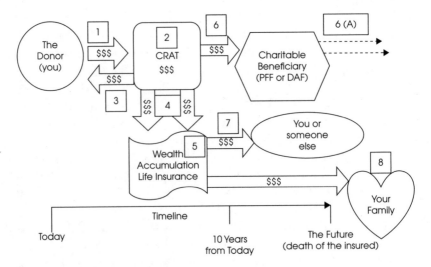

1. The donor transfers cash or appreciated securities into a 10-year term Charitable Remainder Annuity Trust (CRAT) with an annuity rate of 8%–10%.
2. If appreciated assets are used, the CRAT sells the assets and pays no captial gains tax.
3. The transfer to the CRAT creates an income tax deduction, which can be taken against 30% of adjusted gross income and carrried forward for five additional years. Since the CRAT is for a fixed term with a fixed annuity rate, everyone at every age receives the same tax deduction.
4. The CART distributes a fixed dollar annuity payment based on 8%–10% of the original deposit. The fixed payment continues for the full term of years.
5. Each year *all or most* of the CRAT annuity payments is used to pay the premium on a minimum death *wealth accumulation life insurance policy* (VUL or EIUL). The policy is issued on the life of a selected income beneficiary (the donor or someone else—like an adult child).
6. At the end of the 10-year CRAT term, the remaining balance the CRAT is distributed to the selected charitable beneficiaries. 6 (A) If the charity is a Donor Advised Fund or Private Family Foundation, it will continue to make grants annually.
7. At the end of the 10-year CRAT term, the VUL or EIUL is fullly funded and continues to build cash value until the income beneficiary desires to tap it for tax-free income.
8. The insurance proceeds are paid to the beneficaries at the death of the insured providing a source of tax-free financial security for the family members.

Figure 8.5   Personal Plan

and your family with financial security. Ultimately it provides the method to add meaning to your money by creating a philanthropic legacy that will speak volumes about you now and long after you are gone. If you take action Step 1 and become disabled, the plan runs on autopilot. If you die, it completes itself.

The government feels that it can manage your money better than you can. I submit to you that the efficiency shown in Figure 8.5 would say otherwise. When you're in control of your assets, that's the change you can believe in.

CHAPTER 9

Why It Works

*I firmly believe that any man's finest hour, the greatest fulfillment
of all that he holds dear, is that moment when he has worked
his heart out in a good cause and lies exhausted on the field of
battle—victorious.*

—Vince Lombardi

Like freedom fighters using guerilla tactics, we've done the
unexpected, and blown up the existing paradigms. We've made
the transition from mere passive planning using charitable
remainder trusts to the thrilling theater of charitable leverage.
Okay, maybe I am getting a little carried away, but we have created
a new and exciting strategy for fighting back in the war on wealth.

Now that you've seen *how* a charitably leveraged plan works,
we need to answer two more questions. The first is covered in this
section, *why* does it work, or put another way, *what elements make
it a useful strategy?* The second question is *where* does it work? I'm
going to answer that in general terms here and then devote all of
Part III to giving you lots of specific examples.

The keys to why it works lies in the two "E"s, Efficient and
Effective. The application of charitable leverage, like the application
of physical leverage, is an *efficient* mechanism that works simply to

produce a measurable degree of success. The net outcome of applying a charitably leveraged strategy is that it is an *effective* method to avoid accidental philanthropy.

Efficient

When I was a kid and I would ask my Dad what a certain word meant, he'd always respond with, "Look it up." I always knew he would say that, but I'd ask him anyway. If you look up the word "efficient" in the dictionary, you won't find Figure 8.5 from the previous chapter, but you will find a pretty good description of it.

> (adjective) working or producing effectively without wasting effort, energy, or money
>> (*The American Heritage Dictionary of the English Language*, 4th ed., Houghton Mifflin, 2000)

Better still, if you check it out in a thesaurus, you come away with some pretty descriptive synonyms:

> effective, successful, structured, productive, powerful, systematic, streamlined, cost-effective, methodical, well-organized, well-planned, labor-saving
>> (*Collins Essential Thesaurus*, 2nd ed., HarperCollins, 2005, 2006)

At the heart of our *effective, successful, structured, productive, powerful, systematic, streamlined, cost-effective, methodical, well-organized, well-planned, labor-saving* system is its simplicity. Every charitably leveraged strategy and every application is built on the same chassis! There is no mystery. If you know what the chassis looks like, then you'll know how to apply it to your specific situation. Take a look at Figure 9.1 (page 124) and sing along with me.

Item 1 is the CRAT. I bet by now you know this by heart. If you do, then this book is working. If you don't, then read the box in Item 1. The only item that will change in the box is your decision to take an 8 percent, 9 percent, or 10 percent annuity payout. You could take less, all the way down to a

5 percent distribution, but below 8 percent the plan is not as efficient (or effective for that matter).

Item 2 is the annuity distribution or cash flow from the CRAT each year. Again the chassis is always the same, but you can change how much cash flow goes to Box 3 and how much goes into your pocket. Unless I specify otherwise, I put it all (after taxes) into Box 3. That's right; it's the most *efficient* use of the cash-flow.

Item 3 is the Life Insurance Contract designed as a wealth accumulation tool. Your choice inside the box is to pick either a Variable Life policy (VUL), where your cash value is fully invested like your 401(k), but with more costs due to the insurance, or an Equity Indexed policy (EIUL) where the cash value is *not invested* but the interest is targeted to an investment index like the S&P 500.

Item 4 is the ultimate charitable gift in only 10 short years. This drives home the point of charitable intent. You can choose where and how your CRAT is distributed, but you can't choose if—that's built into the chassis. If you don't have charitable intent, you should not do this program. But then again, if you don't do this program, your Uncle Sam will probably do it for you.

Item 5 is the income component of your plan. You can choose how much, when it starts, when it ends, or even if you want it take it at all. You can always leave it in your account to build without tax and tap it as you need it. Your age and objectives will drive your choices. The good news is that you will have choices.

Item 6 relates to the unfortunate realization that none of us will get out of this world alive; it's just a matter of when. How's that for brightening your day? At least when your ticket gets punched the insurance proceeds can be used by your family to avoid a financial hardship.

Logic is about to happen. The chassis never changes, that's the physical element to charitable leverage. But the type of people who *use* the chassis, do change. That's the human element of charitable leverage. I call the human element, the *players* for two reasons. First, they're not all technically humans and second,

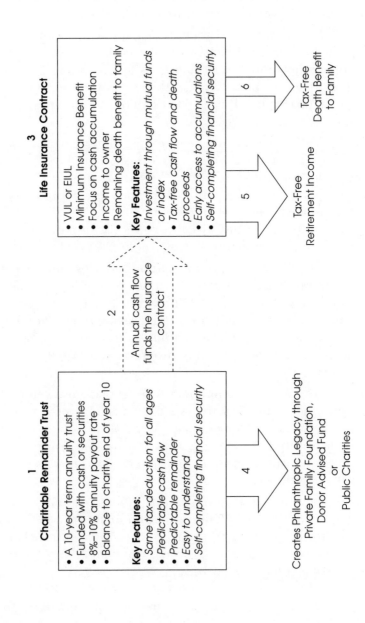

1
Charitable Remainder Trust

- A 10-year term annuity trust
- Funded with cash or securities
- 8%–10% annuity payout rate
- Balance to charity end of year 10

Key Features:
- *Same tax-deduction for all ages*
- *Predictable cash flow*
- *Predictable remainder*
- *Easy to understand*
- *Self-completing financial security*

2

Annual cash flow funds the Insurance contract

3
Life Insurance Contract

- VUL or EIUL
- Minimum Insurance Benefit
- Focus on cash accumulation
- Income to owner
- Remaining death benefit to family

Key Features:
- *Investment through mutual funds or index*
- *Tax-free cash flow and death proceeds*
- *Early access to accumulations*
- *Self-completing financial security*

4

Creates Philanthropic Legacy through Private Family Foundation, Donor Advised Fund
or
Public Charities

5

Tax-Free Retirement Income

6

Tax-Free Death Benefit to Family

Figure 9.1 The Charitable Leverage Chassis

they each "play" a role in how every charitably leveraged plan is utilized. The physical elements in Figure 9.1 are the CRAT and the Insurance Contract (items 1 and 3). The players are the people and institutions affected by the physical elements (items 2, 4, 5, and 6). Missing from the chart is the most important player of all, *the donor.* The chassis never changes but the players do. Get this part, and you're golden.

Remember the flowchart from Figure 5.11? I repeated it in Figure 9.2 without the descriptions so that you will be able to separate the physical element from the players. What you see is the flow chart of how a typical charitably leveraged plan works. The donor contributes the money, the CRAT generates the tax deduction, and on it goes.

I'm going to change the flowchart slightly in Figure 9.3 to identify the players. Since I used numbers to identify the physical elements, I'll use letters here. Let's meet the players.

A. The donor is the person or thing (like a corporation) that funds the Charitable Remainder Annuity Trust. The donor is the only player who can benefit from the tax deduction generated by the CRAT. The donor names the CRAT income recipient (B) and charitable beneficiary (D). In addition,

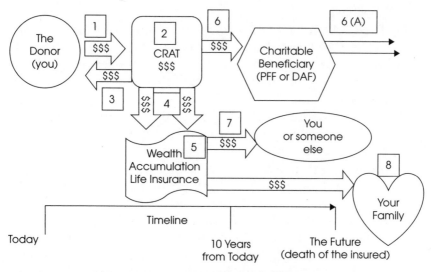

Figure 9.2   A Typical Charitably Leveraged Plan

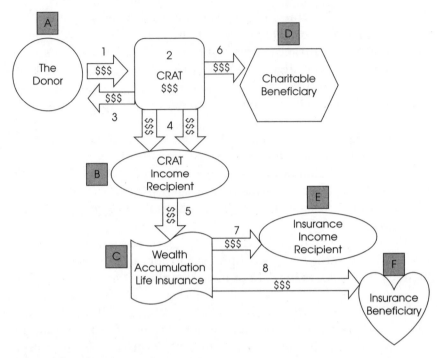

Figure 9.3   Meet the Players

the donor usually calls all the shots with regards to C, E, and possibly F.

B. The CRAT Income Recipient is the noncharitable beneficiary of the CRAT cash flow. Most of the time the income beneficiary is the donor and/or the donor's spouse. In a term of years CRAT, the distribution can continue to a trust on the donor's behalf.

C. The life insurance policy has an owner, insured, and beneficiary. It is important to note that the owner and the insured need not be the same person. The owner is almost always the donor (A) or a trust created by the donor. The important aspect of policy ownership is that the owner controls the policy. The owner determines all uses of the policy cash value. The owner can name the beneficiary of the policy (F) or leave it up to the insured. The 'insured" is the person whose life is covered by the insurance death benefit. In some charitably leveraged applications the insured and the owner are the same person. In other situations the insured cannot be the owner (see the Grandparent Legacy plan). I'm not trying to confuse this issue, trust me, it will become a lot clearer when you see the applications that follow.

D. As if I haven't beaten this into the ground enough, the Charitable Beneficiary is the ultimate beneficiary of the CRAT. It receives whatever is left (remainder) of the CRAT at the end of its term. The charity can be a public charity, Donor Advised Fund, or Private Family Foundation.

E. The insurance income recipients are determined by the owner of the policy. The cash must be withdrawn or borrowed by the owner, but the owner can choose to distribute it to anyone he or she chooses. For example, I as the owner and insured can withdraw cash from my policy and give to my kids, or myself. Or, I as the owner of a company that is owner of the policy insuring one of my key people can withdraw the cash from the policy and give it to any of my employees—or myself.

F. The insurance beneficiaries are the people (or a trust) that receives the tax-free insurance proceeds at the insured's death. Most often it is the family of the donor/income beneficiaries.

Effective

The chassis never changes, but the players do. Now that you know the role of each player, I can show you how to apply a charitably leveraged strategy to provide solutions of lasting value across specific situations.

There are three major categories where a charitably leveraged approach will destroy accidental philanthropy.

1. Personal Supplemental Retirement Plan or Deferred Income Plan
2. A Grandparents Legacy Plan
3. An Employer Sponsored Key Executive Benefit Plan

There is an additional scenario that falls under no specific category but it is so powerful that I had to include it in this book. I call it the IRA Rescue Plan. I will cover that program separately in Part III.

Personal Supplemental Retirement Plan (or Charitably Leveraged Deferred Income Plan)

This is the most straightforward of the charitably leveraged plans and used as the basis for all the others.

General Strategy Characteristics. This strategy recognizes the desire to build a future income stream to supplement any existing retirement plans without the disruption of accidental philanthropy (that'd be taxes). This is the model I used when I illustrated the four-step process showing how a charitably leveraged plan works. The younger age donors will most likely fund the program with cash, while folks nearing the older side of the age spectrum may be more prone to funding it with appreciated stock.

The Players and Their Roles. Almost all the players are the same person. The donor, CRAT income recipient, insurance policy insured and owner, and insurance income recipient are all one and the same. The donor names the charity. A Donor Advised Fund or Private Family Foundation works especially well here because of the number of years remaining in the donor's life after the CRAT ends. (See Figure 9.4 on p.131 for an illustrative overview of the plan.)

Specific Market Applications. Like any other deferred income plan, the younger you start it, the better. The general age range is anywhere from late twenties to fifty-ish. As you move into the fifties, you may need to delay the start of your retirement income to around age 70 to maximize the returns. The optimum age for most people is around 40–45. The first subcategory below pushes the age range lower.

Below is a list of subcategories within this market.

> The Young and the Restless: I define this subcategory as a person with an age range from the twenties to the thirties who currently enjoys a huge and sometimes volatile income with uncertain longevity. The concept of one check–one time is very important to this group. If anything happens to reduce or alter their income after their CRAT is funded, the plan runs on autopilot and all the retirement goals will be met. Examples of this market are:

- Professional Athletes: In a unique twist on traditional retirement planning, this plan works for those who want to start their "retirement" income as measured by when they stop playing professionally. This version of charitably leveraged deferred income assists an athlete in bridging the financial gap that runs from the end of his or her pro career until the start of the league pension (around age 55). In addition, as a group, pro athletes are extremely charitably inclined, especially when the athlete targets his or her philanthropy toward their own Private Family Foundation.
- Entertainers: Ages and retirement dates are all over the ball park, but the security of some downstream tax-free income is a key driving influence. Like the athletes, this group is already inclined toward philanthropy.
- Wall Street: (hedge fund managers, portfolio managers, and the like). Okay, I may need to change this going forward. But I can tell you this, the guys who did a program like this when the going was good, are glad they did.

The Bold and the Beautiful: This subcategory ranges in age from the mid-thirties to mid-forties. They have significant earnings and are, of course, part of the targeted class in the war on wealth. Their earnings are probably more stable than the previous group. The Bold and Beautiful know that traditional retirement plans alone cannot build enough wealth to sustain them in retirement. Though not as philanthropically inclined as the previous group, they like the thought of government control over their assets even less. A charitably leveraged approach may be just what the doctor ordered. Speaking of doctors, examples of this market are:

- Physicians and others in the medical field
- Other professionals (attorneys, accountants, architects—and that's just the As)
- Entrepreneurs

The Old and the Cranky: This group pushes the starting age into the fifties. It's not their fault I didn't write this book earlier. They do need to start their retirement income no earlier than age 70. The insurance contract needs some time to work. This group may be in a position to use appreciated securities to fund the CRAT.

The Dull and the Stupid: I made this subcategory just for me. I was getting silly.

Grandparents Legacy Plan

I said it before and I'll say it again, the grandparents legacy plan is my favorite. Located completely on the other end of the age planning spectrum lives a charitably leveraged plan where the older you are the greater the plan's impact.

General Strategy Characteristics.   The power of this plan is that it provides a strong countermeasure to accidental philanthropy for America's most vulnerable group. The grandparent funds the CRAT. The CRAT funds the insurance policy insuring the life of the adult children (or children) for the benefit of the grandchildren. The insurance contract provides tax-free income to the adult children and a tax-free death benefit for the grandchildren. I cannot wait to show you the case studies in Part III.

The Players and Their Roles.   The Grandparent is the *donor* and names the *charitable beneficiary*. Just think how cool this is when the charitable beneficiary is a Donor Advised Fund or Private Family Foundation in the family name. As the donor, the grandparent gets to use the income tax deduction generated by the CRAT. In addition, donors who are old enough to be grandparents are probably the last remaining people in the United States who still have some appreciated securities in their portfolios. The avoidance of capital gains tax inside the CRAT provides an extra incentive. The grandparent is the primary *income recipient of the CRAT.* The *insured person* is the adult child (or children) of the grandparent. The grandparent can be the owner of the policy or create an Irrevocable Life Insurance Trust (ILIT) to own the policy. If neither one of those two work, the grandparent could name the insured child as the owner. If anyone other than the grandparent is the owner, then the payment to pay the insurance policy premium will be considered a gift. The *income recipient of the insurance* is the adult child. The *beneficiaries of the insurance* are the grandchildren. (See Figure 9.5 on p. 132 for an illustrative overview of the plan.)

Specific Market Applications.   Uh, grandparents. I thought I made that pretty clear. But there are two subcategories.

Charitably Leveraged Deferred Income Plan

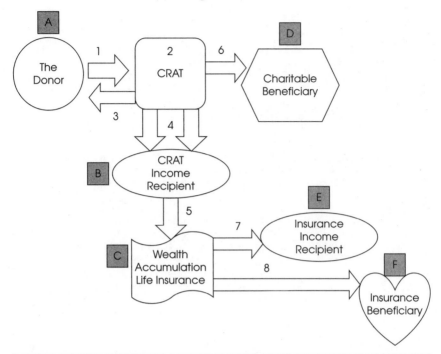

Player	Played by:
A	The individual who chooses to establish the plan for his/her personal benefit
B	B = A. *Note that if A becomes disabled, the program is fully funded and continues as planned*
C	Owner and insured is A
D	A's choice
E	E = A
F	A's choice

Figure 9.4   The Charitably Leveraged Approach to Supplemental Retirement Income

Charitably Leveraged Grandparents Legacy Plan

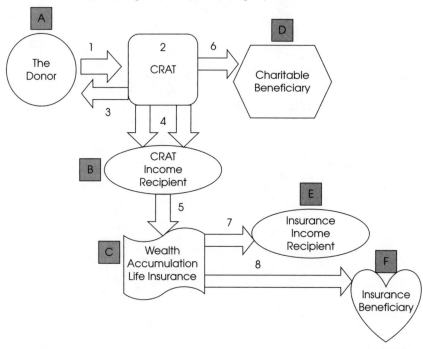

Player	Played by:
A	The grandparent
B	B = A. *Note that if A dies or becomes infirmed the plan continues uninterrupted*
C	Owner is A or Irrevocable Life Insurance Trust (ILIT)
	Insured is adult child of the grandparent
D	A's choice, however, a Donor Advised Fund or Private Family Foundation will perpetuate the family name and the grandparent's legacy
E	If an ILT is used than the trust collects and distributes income to the adult child (Income beneficiary of ILIT)
	If adult child is insured, ownership should transfer to him/her directly for access to cash value
F	Grandchildren of A. Either directly or via the ILIT

Figure 9.5   Grandparent's Legacy Plan

Young and hip, like me. I'm neither, but in my fifties I'm on the young side of grandparenthood. I'll still be my late sixties to early seventies when the grandkids go to college. In my program,

I will control all of the cash flow from the CRAT and own the insurance policies on my kids. That way I can keep my boney fingers on insurance policy cash value to help out with college costs—if the little guys are released from reform school by then.

Old, like "I think I hurt my hip." You can't be too old for this program. In fact, the older the better. The chance to avoid all kinds of accidental philanthropy and perpetuate the family name after you're gone is really powerful. The self-completion feature of a charitably leveraged strategy makes the program that much more appealing. Neither death nor incapacitation will disrupt your noble legacy.

Employer-Sponsored Key Executive Benefit Plans

If you own your own business, or if you are involved in owner-ship of a closely held corporation or LLC, you may well be the next casualty in the war on wealth. Your desire to accumulate savings for future income because you actually earned it will be stifled by the kind of thinking that says, "*I think when you spread the wealth around, it's good for everybody.*" As your company struggles under the burden of taxation, it weighs on your ability to create the extra incentive plan capitalists use to attract and retain the type of talent that can help your company grow. The third application of charitable leverage can be an effective strategy for business owners who want to protect key employees from becoming collateral damage.

General Strategy Characteristics. There are some twists, but largely this program is the personal supplemental retirement plan funded with corporate dollars. The charitable remainder trust element adds a degree of tax deductibility that business owners often miss out on. The result is a partially deductible nonqualified key executive deferred income plan for selected key employees (even if the key employee is you). That's a mouthful for sure, but it is the only plan like it in America, and it's approved by the IRS. The company funds the CRAT. The CRAT funds the insurance policy owned by the corporation on life of the key executive. The key executive receives the income from the insurance policy and names his or her family as the beneficiary.

The Players and Their Roles The company is the donor and names the charity. Some companies already have a foundation in place. Since the company is the donor, it also is allocated the tax deduction. If the company is a regular, or C. Corporation, the deduction can be used against 10 percent of the company's Adjusted Gross Income (AGI). However, most closely held corporations are Subchapter S taxpayers or LLCs with Sub. S status. The benefit of a Sub. S selection is that all the profits and losses flow through to the shareholders. Charitable income tax deductions credited to the S Corporation will flow through as well, and that's a huge benefit to the shareholders. The corporation also controls all of the annual CRAT cash flow. The key executive is the insured person for purposes of the insurance policy.

Depending on the type of benefit plan the corporation creates for the key executive, it can either own and control all of the other player roles, or pass the ownership and control through to the executive.

Charitably Leveraged Nonqualified Deferred Compensation Plan: This is one plan where the corporation controls everything. The key executive receives a promise from the company that upon his or her retirement, he or she will receive some form of extra compensation from the company. It's a nice promise but in reality the executive is nothing more than an unsecured creditor. That's not real popular these days. However, if that's the plan, the corporation would be the owner and beneficiary of the insurance. It would use the cash value to pay the executive.

Charitably Leveraged Executive Bonus Plan: As allowed under IRC§162, the corporation will use the CRAT income to give to the executive the money to purchase the policy in this plan. Therefore, the executive would be the owner of the policy and name his or own beneficiaries.

In either plan the company has control over the cash flow from the CRAT. If the executive leaves early, the company can simply stop the insurance funding and direct the CRAT cash flow elsewhere. (See Figure 9.6 for an illustrative overview of the plan.)

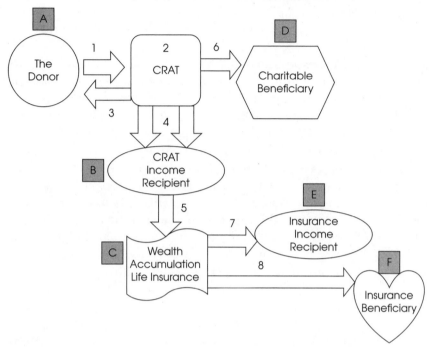

Company Sponsored Executive Benefit Plan

Player	Played by:
A	The company (corporation, LLC, partnership, etc.)
B	B = A. *Note that if CRAT cash-flow is controlled by the company and can be redirected should the executive leave*
C	Owner is A if the plan is a nonqualified deferred compensation plan
	Owner is E if the plan is an Executive Bonus Plan (IRC$162)
D	A's choice, a corporate charitable foundation may be in existence
E	E = A if the plan is a nonqualified deferred compensation plan. Company then distributes income to executive
	E = Executive if the plan is an Executive Bonus Plan
F	F = A if the plan is a nonqualified deferred compensation plan. Company then distributes survivor's benefit to executive's family
	F = Executive's choice if the plan is an Executive Bonus Plan

Figure 9.6   The Capitalist Fights Back through Charitable Leverage

Specific Market Applications.   Any corporate environment where there is a desire to strike a balance between fiscal responsibility and responsible philanthropy is a perfect one for charitable leverage.

> Closely held corporations: Corporations have historically used insurance products as a funding and cost recovery tool for nonqualified key executive deferred compensation plans. But it's the "nonqualified" part of that phrase that hurts the corporation. The government says that if only selected employees are chosen to participate in the plan, then it must be funded with after-tax dollars corporate dollars. That's been tough enough on larger companies, but it can be devastating to smaller companies and closely held corporations.
> The very same companies that create most of the jobs and wealth of this country are targeted for accidental philanthropy through tax. This attack on wealth is not a frontal assault, it comes from out of the darkness. Here's how, just follow the bouncing ball. Most U.S. businesses are not large public corporations, they are small companies and closely held corporations (Sub S corporations and LLCs) run by the people who own them. In these types of companies the net profit passes through to the owners/shareholders. When the top tax brackets increase to 36 percent and 39.6 percent as part of the "change you can believe in," it will impact taxpayers earning $250,000 and up. But, that doesn't mean that everyone below that level stops paying taxes. The bottom line is that profits shared by partners, or Mom and Pop, or owner/shareholders will be taxed more heavily under the new tax increases. We need to earn more to stay even. The increasing tax costs make an after-tax company benefit plan out of reach for most companies. The plan becomes unaffordable and the desire to create a program that attracts and rewards key people falls by the wayside. Talent goes elsewhere, and you know how the rest plays out. The tax deductible charitable contribution to the CRAT and the after-tax CRAT cash flow help put private companies back in the game.
> Family business: In my view, this is the best fit for a charitably leveraged executive bonus plan. All those family businesses out there have one thing in common, a family. Does this ring a bell? How about a plan for the family business where

the major shareholder is the grandparent and the adult child is the key executive. Please tell me you know who the beneficiaries of the insurance policy are. I'll give you a clue, it rhymes with brandchildren.

Professional corporations: Medical, legal, and other professional practices can take advantage of a charitably leveraged strategy as well. In this situation, however, the key person is likely to be the owner.

Partnerships: ditto.

Progress Report

Just like you have to break a couple of eggs to make an omelet, we had to blow up the existing paradigms regarding CRTs, life insurance, and how they work together, in order to create the perfect defense against accidental philanthropy. What we discovered was a new paradigm where the combination of CRT and insurance builds a pile of tax-sheltered cash that will lead to tax-free income. We then walked hand-in-hand through the four-step process behind every charitably leveraged strategy. At that point, Grasshopper, you were ready to learn the secret as to why it works. It's efficient and it's effective, but more importantly, it's simple. The same chassis is used for every strategy, only the players change.

We finished the chapter by applying the "same chassis-different players" principle to three diverse markets: personal plans, grandparent plans, and business plans. I did tease you a little about another plan to rescue your IRA; that's waiting for you in the next section.

The good news is that there is no more new information to stuff into your head (accept for the IRA Rescue Plan). The bad news is that up to this point all you've seen was a bunch of boxes and arrows and circles and more arrows. We're going to fix that in Part III, when I put some numbers in the boxes and then compare this strategy with some alternatives. What lies ahead are case studies, or as I like to call them, war stories of victories in the War on Wealth.

PART

III

WAR STORIES FROM THE BATTLEFIELD

10

How to Use Charitable Leverage to Build a Personal Supplemental Retirement Plan

In a country well-governed, poverty is something to be ashamed of.
In a country badly-governed, wealth is something to be ashamed of.
—Confucius

For a person who fits the *profile shared by the targeted class,* charitable leverage planning will defeat accidentally philanthropic planning every time. I break the profile of the targeted class into five groups. Membership in any one group makes you a target. I'll bet you're a member of more than one.

- The top 10 percent: A great mistake would be made if you considered that only the folks targeted for the tax increase in 2011, the so-called "wealthiest 5 percent," are the targeted class for the war on wealth. The top 10 percent of the taxpayers pay 70 percent of all of the income tax. There are more than 13,500,000 of us! If your income is north of $110,000, you're on the fringe of that group. When your family income grows to $150,000, you are solidly a member, welcome!

- A future retiree: Planning on retiring someday? If you plan on taking more than $150,000 out of your retirement plan, or plan on leaving at least that much of your retirement plan to your kids when you die, you're in the club.
- A business owner: If you own your own business—even if you are the only employee—you're a member. You may not *feel* rich, or *act* rich, but that really is not the point. In this war, you're up against the forces that want to "spread the wealth around." Capitalist equals enemy and you're in the group.
- An investor: There are still people who own appreciated investments—even after the 2008 bloodbath. If you own any investment that will someday be sold for a gain, come on in and join the party! By the way the top 10 percent of the tax-payers pay 94 percent of all the capital gains tax (see group number one). Uncle Sam has his eye on you.
- An asset owner: And if the assets you own exceed $3,500,000 ($7,000,000 joint with your spouse), there's a special room in the club just for you. How dare you grow your wealth! We may not allow water-boarding, but how does a tax enema sound?

This part of the book takes what you've learned about the principles of charitable leverage and applies it to various wealth-building situations. The best way to illustrate the use of our "one chassis–different players" system is to put some math at work in a series of case studies, or what I like to call war stories. I'm going to apply our strategy to three main target areas.

1. Individuals, for their personal deferred income needs.
2. Grandparents, as a way to create multigenerational wealth.
3. Businesses, as a method to create a meaningful benefit plan for selected key employees.

You have already seen how the process works for each market in Chapter 5, so I'm going to go right to the war stories to illustrate the power of charitable leverage. Contained in each war story is a comparison piece that answers the question, "what if I didn't do this?" I think you'll find the results very interesting.

Unless you're a financial advisor reading this, I would not expect that you would have interest in all three target areas, although I invite you to enjoy them all. I mention this because I use a lot of the same language in painting the picture for each situation. After all, I always use same chassis, how many different ways can I explain it? Each war story is intended to stand alone on its own merit. So don't judge me on originality from one war story to the next. My hope is that you'll connect with a story that is close to your own set of circumstances and get a sense of the impact a charitable leverage technique can have in your personal battle against accidental philanthropy. I'm hoping that when you see the potential of changing the paradigm you'll consider a program for yourself. Then all you need to do is find the advisor that's reading the same book you are and you're in business.

We can't do any war stories or comparisons without real numbers. So we need to make some assumptions before we get going.

Assumptions

Where I grew up, in North Jersey, all the Italian families gathered for Sunday dinner. It wasn't anything special to us kids; it was what we did at my grandmother's house every week. Sunday dinner would start around noon and wrap up around six. I thought everybody ate 17 courses and took meatballs home for school the next day. The thing that I remember the most is the way "the men" argued around the table. I'd listen from the kitchen where I ate at the "kids' table" with my cousins. To me, my uncles—Dad included—were the smartest people in the world. You could tell that just by how loud they argued. Each one talking louder than the other, making his point and giving advice to anyone that would listen. One Sunday when I was about nine I remember my grandfather slamming his hand down on the table during one particularly heated conversation, admonishing my uncle Eddie to "Never assume, it makes an ass out of you and me, just spell it." All the men laughed and I laughed, too—mostly because they laughed. I thought I just heard about brightest thing anyone ever said. I didn't know he didn't make it up, I was only nine!

Those days have long past, and all my uncles are gone—Dad included. But I do try to continue the Sunday tradition at my house (with a few less courses). And during the debates around our

Sunday table with me seated at the head, I often quote my grandfather's saying. Well I can't prove that my grandfather *didn't* invent it so I'm going to say that he did. And in that spirit I say to you now that that phrase is never more true than when we start to do financial projections. It opens up all kinds of debate and ultimately takes your eye off the ball. We get so wrapped up with the rates of return used in the projections that we lose focus on the real question, "does the process work?"

Unfortunately, the only way to give you some sense of the power of charitable leverage is to use some assumptions. So, here's the deal. I'm going use conservative, *but realistic* rates in my assumptions and I'll be consistent throughout. I will use the same assumptions for all of the comparisons we do as well. I've made a list below, for you to read and digest. If you disagree with any of my assumptions please call my toll-free debate hotline at 1–800-I'm not interested in your opinion.

Tax Rates

- Income tax rate at 40 percent—reflects the tax rate of increase to 39.6 percent per President Obama's budget. I rounded it up for mathematical purposes.
- Capital gains tax rate at 20 percent—reflects the projected increase in President Obama's budget.
- Qualified dividend tax rate at 20 percent—reflects the projected increase in President Obama's budget.
- Estate tax rate at 45 percent less exemption of $3,500,000—in other words, the first $3.5 million passes free of any tax. The next dollar is taxed at 45 percent. I did not include anything for the state death tax, but If I were you I'd check with a local accountant to find out about your exposure.
- Gift tax rate at 45 percent less $1,000,000—currently the gift tax exemption is frozen at $1,000,000. By the time you read this it might have increased to $3,500,000 to match the estate tax exemption. Again, a quick call to your accountant friend will clear it up.

Investment Rates

- Rate of return for all investments at 6 percent compounded annually—You have to admit this is a fairly conservative projection. Even after the market meltdown of 2008, the Dow averaged about 7.2 percent over the last 20 years (1989 through year end 2008) and the S&P 500 averaged more than 7.4 percent for the same time period. The rate does not include any investment or money management fees.

- Rate of return for the CRAT at 5 percent compounded annually—You would think I'd want to keep all returns on equal footing, and I do for everything else. In the CRAT, however, I want to take advantage of the four-tier accounting rules and to do that I would use a lower projected rate of return to indicate the use of tax-free bonds or bond funds.

- Rate of return for the Donor Advised Fund or Private Family Foundation at 6 percent compounded annually—Assuming the CRAT becomes a DAF or PFF after the 10th year, then the original projected interest rates apply. *However, I will also distribute 5 percent from either legacy gift annually. The net growth then will be 1 percent.*

- Rate of return for the insurance contract at 6 percent compounded annually—Like the investment projections I referenced above, this rate is net of any fees and expenses, but before the cost for mortality (cost of insurance). This is the only fair way to make a comparison because *you are going to pay something for the insurance.* The impact on the insurance policy is that it will drive down the net return by about 1 percent. I think Insurance professionals would agree with this assumption. They may not like it, but they'd accept it as reasonable.

Other Assumptions

- CRAT Applicable Federal Rate (AFR) at 4 percent—The AFR changes from month to month and we get to use the highest rate over the last three months to calculate the tax deduction. Over the last 20 years the monthly rate has ranged from as high as 11.6 percent in May of 1989, all the way to the historic low of 2.0 percent recorded in February 2009 (that figures). Both rates are aberrations. If we average the rates over the last five-year period (including guesstimating an average rate of 2.4 percent for the balance of 2009) we come up with 4.3 percent. I think we'll trend higher, but 4 percent is a good rate to use for this exercise.

- Hypothetical insurance policy—The insurance contract is a hypothetical one based on what is available on the retail market from a number of A+ rated companies, as rated by A.M. Best, the watchdog rating agency of the insurance industry. *They did such a marvelous job watching A.I.G.*
- Insured's health—Assumes a nonsmoker in good health.
- Life expectancy—We need to end the illustrations somewhere. I assume death of the insured at age 85. However, in calculating the withdrawal amounts from the insurance policy, I made sure that the policy stays in force beyond age 100.
- Lapse protection—All the policy calculations assume the use of a lapse protection rider. This will prevent a phantom 1099 upon a policy lapse.
- Insurance Tax Authority—Throughout the descriptions of the life insurance policy, I use phases like: "tax-free death benefit," or "tax-free cash accumulation" and "tax-free income." I make these statements based on the assumption that the death benefit qualifies as tax-free under the scope of IRC§101(a). The cash value of the insurance policy qualifies under one of the tests under the guidance of IRC§7702(a). Further, I assume that loans from the insurance policy are not includable as income under IRC§72 and IRC§72(e)(5).
- CRAT Tax Authority—All CRAT examples I use comply with the regulations under IRC§1.664–1and Reg. 1.664–2(a)(1)(i). For Term of Years guidance I complied with Reg. 1.664–3(a)(5)(i). All my calculations pass the 5 percent or greater probability of exhaustion test under Rev. Rule 77–374. Finally, CRAT distributions rules are set forth in Reg. 1.664–1(d)(1).
- Annual costs are not included—I assume that the annual *fees to* maintain your CRAT will be minimal. The power *of charitable* leverage *is not* reserved for the wealthiest among us. Since we *are not* creating a complex trust arrangement, the annual cost to maintain a CRAT is no big deal. You or your accountant can do the work in a couple of hours. CRAT set up requires the drafting of a legal document, which is already prepared and approved by the IRS, and an application for a Tax ID number, which you can get over the phone. My educated guess is that the legal fees ought not to be a roadblock. However, you do need to be financially healthy to participate.

After all, the CRAT is an irrevocable trust. You receive the annuity payment each year, but you can't reach back into the CRAT and pull money out to spend on something else. For this reason, the absolute minimum amount I would ever commit to a charitably leveraged arrangement would start at $100,000. Typically, the plans I work on don't go below $250,000. I like to use a CRAT funding amount of $1,000,000 for my examples because it's easily divisible and multiplied so that you can fit it into your situation and be reasonably close in your math. Besides, $1,000,000 is fun to work with.

And Now, the Disclaimers

Assumptions are just that. Earnings assumptions that I use throughout this book are for illustrative purposes only. They are not guarantees or warrantees of future returns. Read the material in this chapter for educational purposes only.

I am not engaged in rendering legal, accounting, or other professional service. If you need legal advice or other expertise you should seek out the services of a competent professional.

In order to comply with requirements imposed by the IRS, I need to tell you that any tax advice contained in this book is not intended or written to be used, and cannot be used, for the purpose of avoiding tax-related penalties under the Internal Revenue Code or promoting, marketing, or recommending to another party any transaction or tax-related matter(s) addressed herein. Can you tell I didn't write this last paragraph?

Now, On with the Show

We've seen that the war on wealth takes place on many fronts, assaulting us with numerous weapons of mass redistribution. The attack on your retirement assets is particularly nefarious. Your qualified retirement plan (pension, profit sharing, SIMPLE, SEP, 401[k], IRA, TSA, etc.) builds tax deferred until you start to take your withdrawals. Then the fun begins. At that point you'll get slammed with taxes assessed at what could be a much higher tax bracket then where you are now. In the first chapter, I illustrated how the potential confiscation of your qualified retirement plan at your death may actually leave as much to government as you do to your family.

With these factors in mind, many of us look for alternative methods of accumulating funds that we can later turn into retirement income. Others look for a way to supplement their retirement income with additional dollars that will not be savaged by taxes. That's where the charitable leverage strategy comes in. The supplemental retirement income approach funded by charitable leverage was what I used as the example throughout Chapter 7 when we blew up the paradigms. *Basically, it is an alternative method to accumulate wealth for retirement while avoiding accidental philanthropy.* It is designed for the person who would rather build his or her charitable legacy than feed the coffers of a wasteful government. It allows you to add meaning to your money.

In Chapter 9 I suggested that the supplemental income approach could be applied to three types of preretirement age candidates:

- The Young and the Restless
- The Bold and the Beautiful
- The Old and Cranky

I'm going to give you a war story and comparison for each, but I'm going to do it out of sequence. I'm going to start with the Bold and Beautiful because it is the most typical use of charitable leverage and becomes the basis for the grandparent and business programs in later chapters. Then I'll go back and do the Young and Restless and the Old and Cranky. In a way I guess you can think of me as your Guiding Light.

Charitably Leveraged Supplemental Retirement Plan for the Bold and Beautiful

The hardest years in life are those between ten and seventy.
—Helen Hayes

The individual who fits the profile of the bold and the beautiful ranges in age from the early thirties to mid-forties with at least 20 years to "retirement." They have the kind of earnings that pushes them into the targeted class in the war on wealth. They may not be as philanthropically inclined as the other groups we look at, but they must have some degree of chartable intent to accept this approach. Perhaps the thought of accidental philanthropy helps to motivate them. This target group is populated by young entrepreneurs, professionals, and physicians, among others. Please don't be insulted if I left out your group, I have limited mental capacity—just ask my wife.

To best illustrate the Supplemental Retirement Plan approach. Let's revisit our old friend, Mr. Schmooley. You may remember that Mr. Schmooley is a married business owner somewhere in his mid-sixties. This story isn't about him, however, it is about his son. You see, 45 years ago, when the Schmoolster was just newly married to the lovely Mrs. Schmooley they became the proud parents of a baby boy. The timing was a little questionable, if you get my drift. Anyway, young master Schmooley grew up nicely and fulfilled his mother's dream by becoming a doctor. This story is about his quest for the ultimate supplemental income plan.

Dr. Schmooley Heals His Retirement Plan

Dr. Schmooley is a 45-year-old orthopedic surgeon. He is married to Jennifer, age 42. They have three children. He has a pension plan with his practice, but he knows that it will not provide him with the all of the income he will need in retirement to remain in his current lifestyle. He also wants to be absolutely certain that his family financial situation is secure before, during, and after he retires. His dad always taught him that family comes first.

After meeting with his financial advisors, they project that he will need to generate an additional $10,000 per month after taxes when he retires to meet his income needs. For those of you without a calculator, that's $120,000 per year. In a 40 percent tax bracket, he would need about $200,000 more income per year to net the needed $120,000 after taxes. After all, Uncle Sam needs to get his share, right?

Meanwhile, the development folks from the hospital where he practices have approached him to support a new sports medicine facility devoted to working with injuries arising from youth, high school, and college sports. Initially, the idea appeals to him, especially since that's where he makes his living, but he is uncomfortable committing that type of money directly to the hospital. Dr. S. is cautious and pretty damn smart. He knows that hospital administrations can change. Politics being what they are, he'd like to be in a position of power if in fact he chooses to donate any money.

That may well be a moot point anyway, after the meeting with his advisors. The money he'd need to commit to reach his retirement goals would put a serious kibosh on any philanthropic thoughts he had in mind.

At this point most people like Dr. Schmooley would resign themselves to the old adage of *you can't have everything.* But here's

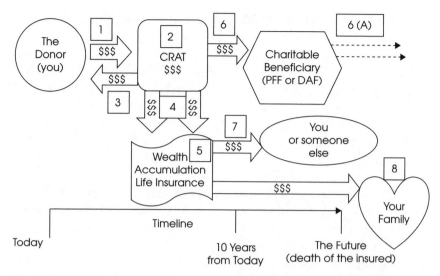

Figure 11.1   The Flowchart of a Typical Charitably Leveraged Plan

the good news. Through the power of charitable leverage you can come pretty damn close.

You may remember Figure 11.1. I used it earlier to summarize the typical charitably leveraged plan. Dr. Schmooley is going to use that design to solve his retirement-planning dilemma and avoid accidental philanthropy.

Action and Impact

Let's go through the action steps and address the impact each has on the good doctor and his family.

1. **Action:** Doctor Schmooley funds his CRAT with $1,000,000 (combination of CDs, treasuries, and money market funds—all current income stuff). Look, I never said the guy was broke; he's an orthopedic surgeon for God's sake.
   - **Impact:** The money in the CRAT is creditor proof. That's a pretty big deal to physicians—especially surgeons.
   - **Impact:** Charitable leverage is in place and operational. If Dr. S. becomes disabled or dies, the plans he made are self-completing.
2. **Action:** After reviewing his income needs, he creates a 10-year term CRAT with a *9 percent* distribution rate. He names himself as

the income recipient with Jennifer as the successor. His annual trust distribution will be $90,000 per year. He's charitable—but Dad also taught him that charity begins at home.

- Impact: The CRAT will distribute the fixed payment of $90,000 regardless of the account earnings. His income is assured.
- Impact: Since he is funding the CRAT with current assets, he losses out on the ability to shelter capital gains. On the other hand he can take advantage of four-tier accounting to generate tax-free income from the CRAT. Using a combination of tax-free bonds and/or bond funds his CRAT will generate a return of 5 percent annually. Because it is required to distribute a fixed payment of $90,000 each year, the trust principal will decrease, but 95 percent of the distributed income will be tax-free.

3. Action: Dr. S. will receive a tax deduction for his contribution to the CRAT. Based on a 10-year term with a 9 percent annuity rate, and a 4 percent Applicable Federal Rate (AFR), the tax deduction will be $270,000.
   - Impact: In the doctor's 40 percent tax bracket, a tax deduction of $270,000 is the equivalent of putting $108,000 in his pocket.

4. Action: Dr. Schmooley uses the after-tax income from the CRAT to fund a wealth accumulation style Cash Value Life Insurance policy (CVLI) funded at the minimum death benefit relative to the premium payment.
   - Impact: Since Dr. Schmooley controls the CRAT cash flow, he can change the amount of money he directs to his policy if circumstances change.

5. Action: Dr. S. is the owner and insured of the policy. A trust for Jennifer and the children is the beneficiary.
   - Impact: The annual premium of $85,000 is generated by the after-tax CRAT cash flow.
   - Impact: The death benefit starts out at $1,800,000 and will increase by the value of the cash value accumulations each year.
   - Impact: The cash value of the policy is assumed to grow by 6 percent net of fees and expenses but not including the cost of insurance.
   - Impact: The cash value is accessible to Dr. S. at any time without tax or government penalty.

6. Action: The CRAT ends in the 10th year, and *controlled* philanthropy begins. The projected value of the CRAT will be just under $500,000. Dr. Schmooley can direct this gift

directly to the hospital, but because he is so smart, he names a Supporting Organization under the hospital's banner as the beneficiary. The Supporting Organization will be known as the Schmooley Family Charitable Fund.

- Impact: Each year the fund will distribute 5 percent of its investment value as directed by the doctor and his family. Assuming the fund investment return is 6 percent, the net growth each year is 1 percent.
- Impact: The fund will distribute about $25,000 each year, increasing as the trust principal grows. Over the course of his life (death assumed at age 85), Dr. Schmooley's family fund will have contributed just over $864,000 to the hospital and *directed its use.* Do I really need to tell you the type of political power that brings to Dr. S?
- Impact: The total projected philanthropy by age 85 generated including the balance in the family fund is more than $1,500,000.

7. Action: At the retirement age of 65, Dr. Schmooley begins to draw on the cash value of the insurance policy and continues for the next 20 year.
   - Impact: Based upon the projected rate of 6 percent (before insurance cost), Dr. S. will receive $125,000 per year from the policy, tax-free. His total projected income will be $2,500,000. If he dies during the retirement years his wife or children would receive the remaining death benefit.

8. Action: For illustrative purposes we assume that Dr. Schmooley dies at the end of age 85, after receiving the full $2,500,000 of distributions from his cash value. At that point the policy will provide another $1,117,000 to his family, tax-free.
   - Impact: Charitable leverage is completed by providing tax-free cash to the doctor's children, fulfilling the last remaining goal of his retirement plan.

The overall Impact of the Dr. Schmooley's charitable leverage strategy looks pretty darn good. His $1,000,000 investment created $3,725,000 of benefits to himself and his family, and another $1,500,000 to charity—on his terms. It breaks down as follows:

- A tax deduction of $270,000, projected tax savings of $108,000.
- Tax-free retirement income of $125,000 annually, $2,500,000 total.

The Power of Charitable Leverage for Dr. Schmooley, age 45

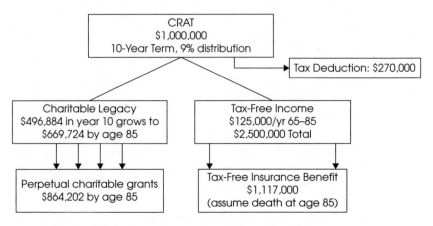

Total Projected Benefits to Family and Charity $5,258,926

Figure 11.2 The Impact on Dr. Schmooley, His Family, and His Charities

Presented for educational purposes only. Based on the projections as stated throughout this chapter

- Another $1,117,000 to his family, also tax-free.
- A charitable legacy of more than $1,500,000 consisting of gifts of $864,000 with another $670,000 remaining in the family fund.

(For a graphical representation of this impact, see Figure 11.2.)

But, Is This the Best Plan for Dr. S.?

I may be convinced, but like I said, Dr. Schmooley is cautious and smart. So he asks a reasonable question, "If I didn't commit $1,000,000 to this plan and put it into a tax-deferred account instead. How would that compare?" Let's take a look.

A Couple More Ground Rules

You already know how I feel about assumptions, but whenever we do a comparison we need to use them. To keep the playing field as level as possible; let's establish some basic, but very important, ground rules.

1. What's good for the goose is good for the gander. In other words, whatever rules we apply to one investment technique, we must also apply to the other. For example, an investment return of 6.0 percent net of fees and costs will be used for *all* of the other investment projections except as noted. I hate the word "retirement" but it does serve a purpose. It defines a period of time that is some day in the future. Therefore "retirement income" is really "income that is deferred for some day in the future." Let's agree that it's just a lot easier to say retirement but know that no one is obligated to start their retirement income until they are ready to do so.

2. Charitable intent is a key factor. A charitable remainder trust, like the one modeled in this comparison, is used as a planned giving instrument and not a tax shelter device. Dr. Schmooley must possess a desire to benefit his hospital or some other charity in order to fully appreciate the power of charitable leverage.

3. Reasonable people use reasonable assumptions. The assumptions I stated at the beginning of Part III are the ones we will use for this exercise. The insurance policy I use is a hypothetical indexed product that resembles what's available on the open market from major life insurance companies. The numbers are accurate for the projections used. It does bear repeating that I deduct the cost of insurance after I credit the interest rate. This has the effect of driving the return on the policy down by about 1 percent or more, but I feel it is a more accurate representation of the insurance contract.

The Lifecycle of a Retirement Investment Plan

Dr. Schmooley's retirement plan investment strategy is one where the objective is to build or grow the account with no income distributions until age 65. When he starts his retirement, the program shifts focus from growth to income. At the end of Dr. Schmooley's life (assume age 85) the balance of the retirement plan is transferred to his family. Our comparison then is divided into four phases:

1. The investment: The total dollars transferred to the retirement investment plan strategy. Dr. Schmooley is age 45 at the funding phase.

2. The accumulation phase: The 20-year period of time that the retirement account will grow until the retirement age. During this phase no income will be distributed to allow for maximum growth. More importantly, taxes are deferred until the income phase. The best example of this type of investment would be a tax-deferred variable annuity. In any event, we're going to assume that the retirement account grows at 6 percent tax-deferred.

3. The income phase: The time when the growth earned from phase two is converted to income. In a perfect world, this phase would last until Dr. Schmooley dies, but for comparative purposes we need to control the environment. Therefore, I use a period of 20 years (i.e., from age 65 to 85). For further insight, I break the income phase into two measurements
   • Annual income: shows the yearly cash flow.
   • Cumulative income: calculates the cash flow over the 20-year retirement period.

4. Transfer: This is a nice way of saying that when Dr. S. dies, whatever remains in the retirement plan will be transferred to Jennifer and his children. As you already know, I use age 85 as the age of mortality.

Dr. Schmooley Funds his Retirement Account and the Growth Begins.   Dr. S. transfers the same $1,000,000 that he would have used to fund his CRAT into a tax-deferred retirement account earning 6 percent tax deferred. By the time he reaches age 55, the account is valued at $1,790,850. At age 65, the account is valued at just over $3,200,000. (See Figure 11.3.)

Retirement!   When Dr. S. reaches age 65; he begins to withdraw money from his account. His goal is to use the account to generate $125,000 per year after taxes for 20 years ($2,500,000 total). Since the account is tax-deferred on a last-in, first-out (LIFO) basis, he will need to withdraw enough money each year to pay the income tax due in a 40 percent tax bracket. In other words, he will need to withdraw $208,333 to net $125,000 after tax. Thus, he will pay $83,333 of his earnings to tax each year. I think we call that accidental philanthropy. (See Figure 11.4.)

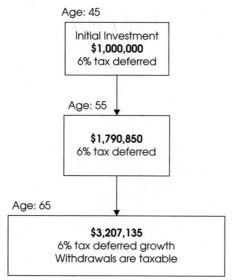

Figure 11.3   Funding and Growth

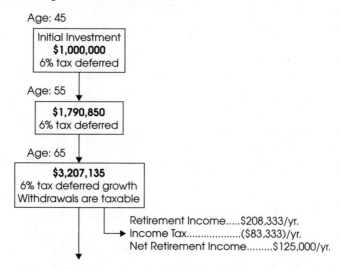

Figure 11.4   Income and Taxes

Dr. Schmooley's Retirement Investment Life Cycle
(Assumes 6% growth; 40% tax bracket)

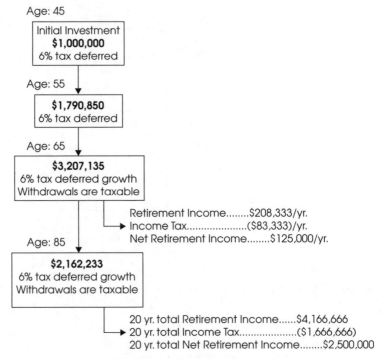

Age: 45

Initial Investment
$1,000,000
6% tax deferred

Age: 55

$1,790,850
6% tax deferred

Age: 65

$3,207,135
6% tax deferred growth
Withdrawals are taxable

Retirement Income........$208,333/yr.
Income Tax....................($83,333)/yr.
Net Retirement Income........$125,000/yr.

Age: 85

$2,162,233
6% tax deferred growth
Withdrawals are taxable

20 yr. total Retirement Income......$4,166,666
20 yr. total Income Tax....................($1,666,666)
20 yr. total Net Retirement Income........$2,500,000

Figure 11.5   A Lot of Income and Whole Lot of Taxes

Cumulative Retirement Income By the time the doctor reaches
age 85, his retirement account has generated $2,500,000 total net
retirement income, and he still has $2,162,233 remaining in the
retirement account. Unfortunately, he had to withdraw $4,166,666
to achieve that net income. He paid an extra $1,666,666 in taxes
just to get the income he needed. That's a lot of waste. I wonder
if he knows he could have used that money for his hospital? (See
Figure 11.5.)

Account Transfer to Dr. Schmooley's Family The retirement
account is transferred to Jennifer and/or the Schmooley children
at the good doctor's demise. In addition to the taxes already paid,
the retirement account balance of $2,162,233 (less the original
basis of $1,000,000) is subject to more income tax. The Income

Dr. Schmooley's Retirement Investment Life Cycle
(Assumes 6% growth; 40% tax bracket)

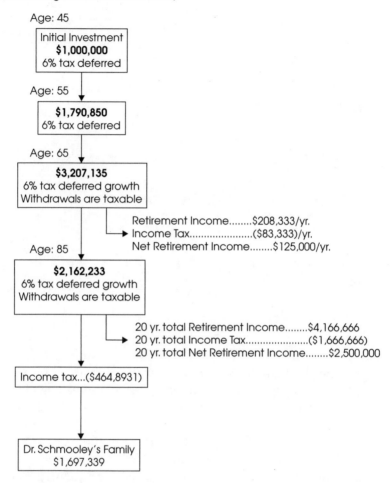

Age: 45

Initial Investment
$1,000,000
6% tax deferred

Age: 55

$1,790,850
6% tax deferred

Age: 65

$3,207,135
6% tax deferred growth
Withdrawals are taxable

Retirement Income........$208,333/yr.
Income Tax......................($83,333)/yr.
Net Retirement Income........$125,000/yr.

Age: 85

$2,162,233
6% tax deferred growth
Withdrawals are taxable

20 yr. total Retirement Income........$4,166,666
20 yr. total Income Tax......................($1,666,666)
20 yr. total Net Retirement Income........$2,500,000

Income tax...($464,8931)

Dr. Schmooley's Family
$1,697,339

Figure 11.6   Estate Transfer, and More Tax

tax bill at death is an additional $464,893. The net transfer to Dr. Schmooley's family is $1,697,339. (See Figure 11.6.)

Measuring the Impact Let's look at Table 11.1 to measure the impact. Dr. Schmooley started out with $1,000,000 that he wanted to invest to supplement his retirement income. His goal was to generate $120,000 per year after taxes after age 65. Whatever he didn't use in retirement he wanted to pass along to his children. The war on his wealth raged

Table 11.1   The First Part of the Comparison

	Dr. Schmooley's Retirement	
	Traditional Planning	Charitable Leverage
(1) Starting Amount	$1,000,000	
(2) Capital Gains Tax	0	
(3) Net to Fund the Retirement Account	$1,000,000	
(4) Tax Deduction	$0	
(5) Tax Savings	$0	
(6) Total Retirement Income (20 yrs)	$2,500,000	
(7) Net to Family at death	$1,697,339	
(8) Total Combined Family Wealth	$4,197,339	
(9) Total to Charity	$0	
(10) Total to Taxes	$2,131,559	
(11) Combined Wealth to Family and Charity	$4,197,339	

along two fronts, the battle for income taxes during the retirement years, and the battle for more taxes at the transfer of his plan to the children. When the fighting ended Dr. S. thought he made out okay. But you and I know better. The IRS won and charity lost big.

1. He generated $2,500,000 for his retirement.
2. His family inherited another $1,697,339 at his death.
3. The total financial benefit to his family was $4,197,339.
4. He didn't leave a penny to the hospital from this plan. Any gifting would have had to come from other funds.
5. But he did pay $2,131,559 in taxes.

Dr. Schmooley says, "I invested $1,000,000 and created over $4,000,000 of wealth for me and my family over my lifetime. 4 to 1 that's a damn fine job." But Doc Schmool, what about your charitable desire toward the hospital? And what about paying more than $2,000,000 in taxes? Two to one in taxes, that's not so good. "Well my boy," the doctor says, "you can't have everything."

Yes you can Doc, yes you can.

The Lifecycle of Dr. Schmooley's Charitably Leveraged Retirement Investment Strategy

The first thing that strikes you when you view the figures is that there are a couple of extra parts in a charitable leverage strategy. Where the previous example used one retirement account, the charitably lever-aged strategy uses three. God forbid that you should have to open two extra statements every month. Believe me; it'll be worth the extra effort.

Dr. Schmooley (Age 45) Funds His CRAT

Dr. S. transfers the $1,000,000 of current income assets to his 10-year CRAT with a 9 percent annuity rate. The doctor agrees to create the Schmooley Family Fund under the hospital's public foundation to act as the charitable beneficiary. The funding of the CRAT triggers two events (see Figure 11.7):

1. Generates a current income tax deduction for the present value of the future gift to charity: The tax deduction based on the AFR of 4 percent and 9 percent annuity rate, will be approximately $270,000. In Dr. Schmooley's tax bracket of 40 percent, the tax savings from the deduction is $108,000.
2. Provides a stream of annuity income each year for the next 10 years: The annual fixed-dollar annuity payment from the CRAT will be $90,000 each year for the next 10 years. The cash flow from the CRAT is taxed under the "four-tier accounting" rules. Since the CRAT was funded with investments that had no gains, the CRAT account could invest in tax-free bonds and bond funds. The combination of the investments should gen-erate no more than 5 percent taxable income. The tax due on the annuity each year would be about $4,500. The net cash flow to invest in the retirement plan is $85,500.

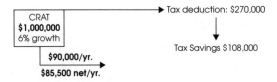

Figure 11.7   Dr. S. Funds His CRAT

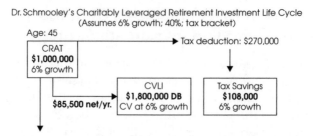

Figure 11.8   The CRAT Creates the Leverage That Funds the Plan

The CRAT creates the charitable leverage that funds every facet of the retirement plan. If Dr. S. were to become disabled at any time, the retirement plan funding could continue automatically. If he were to die prematurely, the plan would complete itself for the benefit of his wife and children. The funding of the CRAT puts the doctor is position to use both the *saving* from the tax deduction and the *cash flow* to achieve his retirement goals (see Figure 11.8.)

- Tax savings: The tax deduction must be recognized for the important role it plays in our comparison. Tax savings represent real dollars that can be invested. Following the ground rules we established for this comparison, *Dr. Schmooley will invest the tax savings into the exact same investment as the retirement account used in the traditional plan (i.e., a tax-deferred variable annuity earning 6 percent net after expenses).*
- Cash flow: The CRAT cash flow will fund the wealth accumulation style Cash Value Life Insurance policy (CVLI) I've referenced throughout this book. Again, keeping everything on a level playing field, I have used the same 6 percent net return on the policy before deductions for the mortality costs. I would guess that after the mortality costs are deducted the indexed-type policy of variable life contract would generate an internal rate of return of about 4.5 percent to 5 percent. I used $85,000 of the $85,500 for the premium payment. He can take Jennifer out for the weekend with the balance.

The Accumulation Phase—Age 45 to 65

Ten years into the plan (age 55), the CRAT has done its thing acting as the charitable lever and will be distributed to charity at the end of the 10th year. In this example, *the charity is the Schmooley*

Family Charitable Fund, which will be directed by Dr. Schmooley and anyone else he adds to the advisory board. As far as clout goes Dr. Schmooley has it. Assuming a 5 percent net return during the first 10 years, the value remaining in the CRAT *after the annuity distributions* stands at $496,884. (See Figure 11.9.) It is now in place for perpetual philanthropy. But even before the CRAT term ended, Dr. S. had a seat at the table by maintaining the right to change the charitable beneficiary during the CRAT term. At any time, he could have directed the remainder elsewhere. How much attention do you think the hospital paid to him?

Second, the CVLI funding is now complete. The cash value is about $988,000 and will continue to grow toward the retirement date without tax. The tax-free insurance benefit is up to $2,757,150 providing Jennifer and the kids with a comfortable level of financial security. Also, if Dr. S needs cash prior to age 59½, he can withdraw it from the CVLI without tax or 10 percent penalty that accompanies other tax-deferred accounts.

Third, the tax savings that was deposited into the tax-deferred account continues to build at an invested rate of 6 percent. By the 10th year the account is up to $193,425.

By the doctor's age 65 the accumulation phase is complete. His CVLI policy cash value is worth more than $1.68 million with a death benefit of more than $3.1 million. The tax savings that were invested at the beginning have grown to $346,396. He will not need

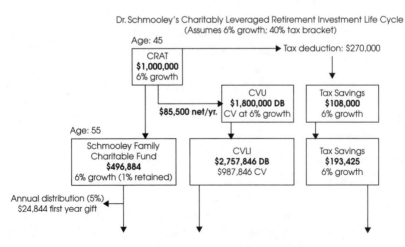

Figure 11.9   The Accumulation Phase After 10 Years

this account to provide his income goal, so it will continue to grow (or it could be used for other cash needs).

The CRAT was replaced by the *Schmooley Family Charitable Fund* 10 years earlier. It has become an ongoing means of addressing the Schmooleys' charitable intentions. Though not obligated to do so, the fund distributes 5 percent of its net investment assets each year to support the hospital's sports medicine facility. Continuing with the 6 percent net investment return, the *Family Charitable Fund* will distribute about $27,000 in the first year and retain about 1 percent. Each year thereafter, as the fund grows, so will its annual distributions to charity. By the time he reaches retirement age, the doctor's charitable fund has grown to $548,000. In addition, it has already distributed $260,000 in gifts and grants. (See Figure 11.10.)

Retirement, Charitably Leveraged Style

The CVLI is in place to provide Dr. Schmooley with his income goal of $125,000 per year, after taxes, starting at age 65 and continuing for 20 years ($2,500,000 total). The major difference between this approach and the traditional one is that the cash flow from the CVLI is considered an insurance policy loan and not subject to income tax. Insurance loans do not require repayment. If it remains unpaid, the loan amount is deducted from the death benefit. *The death benefit throughout this study assumes that the loan is outstanding at the time of death and repaid by the insurance proceeds.* The CVLI used in this example is one that employs a lapse-prevention feature, ensuring that the tax-free cash flow remains that way. If Dr. S. dies during the income phase, his wife and children would receive the remaining balance of the cash value account plus the insurance benefit, income tax-free. Since he needs only the CVLI to provide the income for his retirement needs, the Tax Savings Retirement Account can remain invested for growth. (See Figure 11.11.)

Cumulative Retirement Income

As the retirement years come to a close, Dr. Schmooley is now age 85. His insurance policy has provided $2,500,000 of income without tax. The balance of the cash value account is down to $463,000 but the death benefit for the family is holding at $1,117,000. In addition, the tax savings account, proving the power of compound interest is now up $1,110,289.

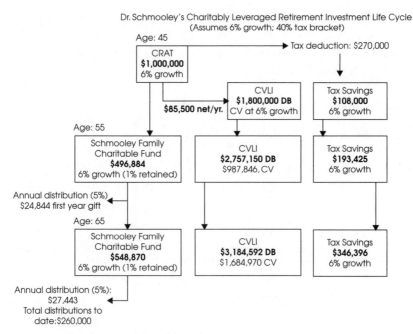

Figure 11.10   The Accumulation Phase at Age 65

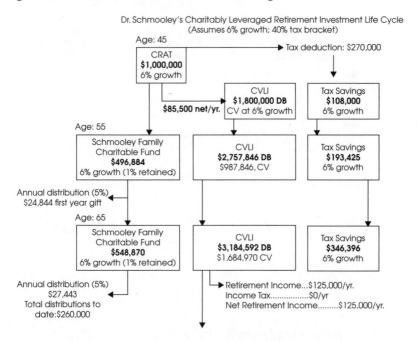

Figure 11.11   A Charitably Leveraged Retirement

The Schmooley Family Charitable Fund, with the fully grown Schmooley children on the advisory board, has grown to $669,724. Since its inception the fund has granted $864,000 of charitable support. (See Figure 11.12.)

Account Transfer at Dr. Schmooley's Death

Unfortunately all good things eventually come to an end, and so it is for our hero, as Dr. Schmooley complies with our comparison by getting hit by a meteor just before his 86th birthday. Though he may have been motivated by his personal retirement

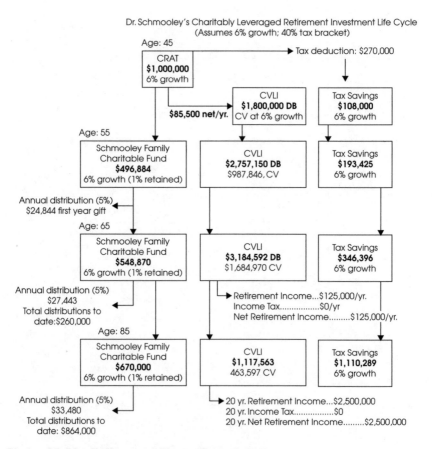

Figure 11.12   Retirement Phase Completed

needs, the remaining value in the Schmooley Family Charitable Fund ($670,000) coupled with gifts of more than $864,000 generated by the fund, has created a philanthropic legacy of more than $1,500,000. The Schmooley family name lives on as his children and grandchildren oversee his charitable mission.

Looking next to the Tax Savings Account, its value by age 85 is $1,110,289. Though it pains me greatly, we must treat the transfer of that account in the same way as the traditional tax-deferred retirement account. Therefore, the tax savings account less the basis of $108,000 is subject to ordinary income tax upon estate distribution. Assuming a 40 percent tax bracket, the tax due would be $400,915. The net amount from the tax savings deferred account that will be transferred to the family would be $709,373.

The insurance pays the remaining death benefit of $1,117,000 to Dr. Schmooley's heirs free of income tax. Combined with the after-tax proceeds of the Tax Savings Account, the total wealth transferred to his family would be $1,826,936. (See Figure 11.13.)

Measuring the Impact

When Dr. Schmooley chooses to avoid accidental philanthropy, he unlocks the power of charitable leverage. He started with the same $1,000,000 investment as the traditional approach but added far more meaning to his money.

- He generated $2,500,000 of personal retirement income. That's the same as the traditional plan.
- His family received $1,826,936 at his death, compared to $1,697 339 in the traditional plan.
- The total financial benefit to his family was $4,326,936 as compared to $4,197,339. That's an increase of about $129,000, but I view it as a wash. While the family does come out a few bucks ahead, what wins the day is yet to come.
- He created a philanthropic legacy of more than $1,500,000 under this approach *as opposed to leaving nothing for his legacy in the traditional plan.*
- He reduced his taxes to $400,915 as compared to the $2,100,000 he paid under the alternative method. He may

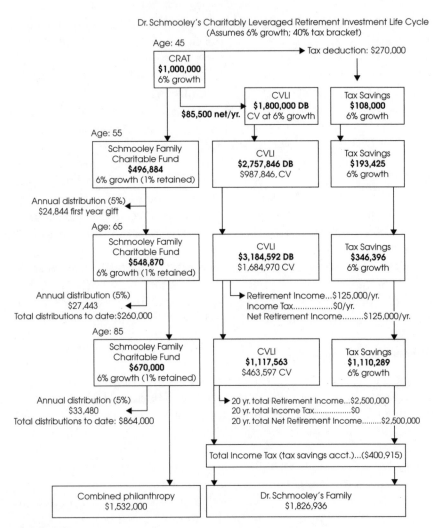

Figure 11.13   The Full Impact of Charitable Leverage at Estate Settlement

not have chosen to become a philanthropist in the traditional plan, so the IRS chose it for him, to the tune of $2,131,559.

• The combined impact of charitable leverage to family and charity is $5,860,936.

Table 11.2 compares the results of the two paths.

Dr. Schmooley started with the same $1,000,000 seed and produced essentially the same personal results. But did he? If he

Table 11.2 Which Path Would You Choose?

	Dr. Schmooley's Retirement Comparison	
	Traditional Planning	Charitable Leverage
(1) Starting Amount	$1,000,000	$1,000,000
(2) Capital Gains Tax	0	0
(3) Net to Fund the Retirement Account	$1,000,000	$1,000,000
(4) Tax Deduction	$0	$270,000
(5) Tax Savings	$0	$108,000
(6) Total Retirement Income (20 yrs)	$2,500,000	$2,500,000
(7) Net to Family at death	$1,697,339	$1,826,936
(8) Total Combined Family Wealth	$4,197,339	$4,326,936
(9) Total to Charity	$0	$1,534,000
(10) Total to Taxes	$2,131,559	$400,915
(11) Combined Wealth to Family and Charity	$4,197,339	$5,860,936

selects the traditional approach, he will have nothing to show for the taxes he paid. His $2,131,559 worth of accidental philanthropy will never give him the right to say how his *gift to the government* should be used. No one will ever know how much he gave toward such valuable projects as "Olive fruit fly research." There is no list of donors in the war on wealth, only casualties—and nobody even knows their names.

12

Charitably Leveraged Supplemental Retirement Plan for the Young and Restless

Blessed are the young, for they will inherit the national debt.
—Herbert Hoover

By now you get what I've been saying about how we can beat accidental philanthropy by using charitable leverage. The war story discussed in Chapter 11 showed you what most of us would think of as a typical retirement-planning scenario. But what about the man or woman who falls outside of the norm? How would this plan work for someone who is young, has the means, and wants to draw his or her income early? Would a charitably leveraged plan stand up?

Who are these people? They are professional athletes, entertainers, investment bankers, entrepreneurs; they are people who earn a whole lot of money in a short period of time with a very uncertain future. The problem lies in trying to convince the invincible that there is such a thing as a rainy day.

The Pro Choice War Story

No, it's not about that choice, it's the other Pro choice. Nowhere is this problem of too much–too soon more evident than in professional sports. The March 23, 2009, issue of *Sports Illustrated* ran a stunning article by Pablo S. Torre called "How (and Why) Athletes Go Broke." In it he reveals the brutal reality of life after sports. He says that, "By the time they have been retired for two years, 78 percent of former NFL players have gone bankrupt or under financial stress because of joblessness or divorce. Within five years of retirement 60 percent of former NBA players are broke." He goes on to paint similar disheartening stories across professional athletics.

The professional leagues do have pension plans. Most kick in at age 55 with reduced payouts available at younger ages. The hard part for many athletes is getting there. The money is here today but may not be there tomorrow. The article in *SI* seems to bear this out. After reviewing a charitable leverage plan for himself, a former NBA player challenged me with the unique financial dilemma of professional athletes to see if I could adapt the strategy to act as a bridge to get to the professional from the end of his playing days to the start of the league pension. It sounded like something worth looking at and I'm glad I did.

I used as my model a 25 year old with a nice new contract complete with bonus. The structure of the plan is the same as everything you've seen so far except that instead of using a retirement date of age 65, I targeted age 35 as the date. Like the other plans, I ran the retirement income for 20 years. That's a good match for the athlete because that's when the full league pension kicks in.

The other significant change in this model is that I wanted to see how much the Pro had left of his investment by age 55. The other models end with the subject dying at age 85. I want to be prepared for the worst if the Pro dies, but I think we all know that by age 55 the odds are pretty good he's going to be alive and kicking.

The role the CRAT plays in this program is meaningful and important. It is meaningful because athletes are unbelievably charitably inclined, you'd be hard-pressed to find one that isn't giving something back. A number of Pros have their own Private Family Foundations. That actually sounds better than it is since many of the foundations go out of business after the player retires and the funding stops. The CRAT will drop into the Pro's foundation at the end of the 10th year, keeping his philanthropic endeavors funded, without any additional contributions from him. It's important because if the player is not charitably motivated, this is not the plan for him.

Action and Impact

So, here's how we did.

1. Action: The Pro (age 25) transfers $1,000,000 to a 10-year CRAT with a 9 percent annuity rate. (See Figure 12.1.) It is the same CRAT we used for Dr. Schmooley. Even though the Pro is 20 years younger, his CRAT benefits are exactly the same.
   - Impact: He gets the same $270,000 income tax deduction, same $108,000 tax savings, and the same CRAT fixed distribution of $90,000 per year.
   - Impact: Since we're using the same assumptions throughout, the Pro will net $85,500 from the CRAT each year. He takes the net CRAT income and funds his Cash Value Life Insurance policy (CVLI). The policy initial value based on his age is $3,500,000 plus his cash accumulation.
   - Impact: Of increased importance in this scenario is the self-completing aspect of charitable leverage. If the Pro's career ended suddenly due to injury, the CRAT would continue to fund all aspects of this retirement strategy. That's a pretty big deal and should not be overlooked.

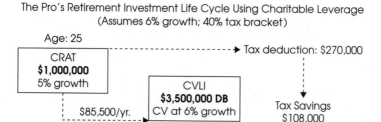

The Pro's Retirement Investment Life Cycle Using Charitable Leverage
(Assumes 6% growth; 40% tax bracket)

Age: 25

CRAT
$1,000,000
5% growth

$85,500/yr.

CVLI
$3,500,000 DB
CV at 6% growth

Tax deduction: $270,000

Tax Savings
$108,000

Figure 12.1   The Pro Funds the CRAT

2. Action: When the Pro reaches age 35, the CRAT is transferred to his Private Family Foundation and the CVLI is fully funded. (See Figure 12.2.) Now the fun begins.

   - Impact: The foundation must spin off 5 percent of its net portfolio each year. Without the Pro ever contributing additional money, his foundation will create the cash flow to keep him involved and vital in the charitable causes that are important to him.
   - Impact: Working backward with the CVLI, I calculated the maximum funds that the policy could distribute each year for the 20-year period from age 35 to 55 without putting the policy in jeopardy of lapsing. I stuck with our 6 percent net return before insurance costs. That magic number was $84,327 tax-free.

3. Action: By the time the Pro completes the retirement cycle at age 55, his foundation is worth $606,000, and his cumulative grants total $547,000. His total philanthropy to that point is $1,153,000. What's really cool is that all of that charitable giving was generated by the same lever that created the CVLI.

   - Impact: The total tax-free income from the CVLI was $1,684,740.
   - Impact: Even better is that the Pro still has $160,000 remaining in the cash value of the policy and a death benefit for his

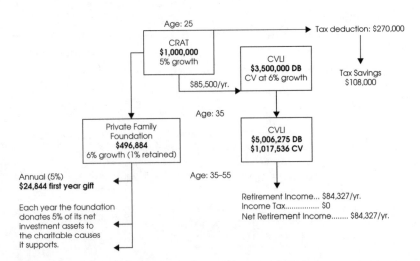

Figure 12.2 "Retirement" Income Starts at Age 35

family of $2,488,000. He's only 55 years old, both cash value and the death benefit will grow for the rest of his life! (For a graphical representation of this impact, see Figure 12.3.)

By choosing charitable leverage, the Pro successfully built a bridge from the end of his career to the start of his league pension. His $1,000,000 transfer generated more than $1,684,000 of tax-free income and more than $1,000,000 for charity. In addition, he created a substantial philanthropic program that allowed him to stay in the game after his playing days were long over. *And he did it all without paying one penny in taxes.* Imagine how much good his foundation will do in the 30 years that still lay ahead of him? You don't have to; I'll do it for you. Under the current projections, by the time he's 85, his foundation will have given away $1,600,000 and they'll still have $817,000 in the till, for a total of $2,400,000. All done with dollars that were destined for accidental philanthropy.

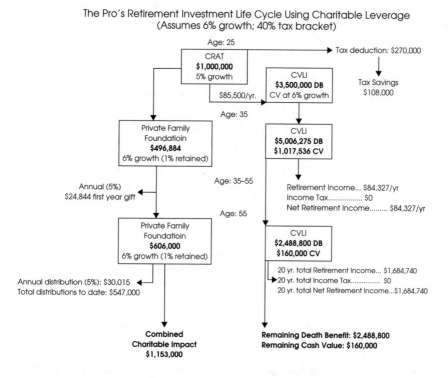

Figure 12.3 The Cumulative Impact of Charitable Leverage

But, Is This the Best Approach?

I think that no other comparison shows the need for the subject to have charitable intent more than this one. The results come out just about dead even, the question is, is the Pro willing to accept accidental philanthropy in exchange for a greater degree of liquidly over the first 10 years? The answer lies in his charitable motivation.

A typical retirement plan develops over three phases: the investment and growth phase, the withdrawal/retirement income phase, and the transfer phase. In a typical retirement plan, the subject is usually in his or her seventies or eighties when the income phase ends. So naturally the transfer of the remaining account coincides with his or her death. Obviously this scenario is a little different in that the Pro will only be age 55, but we still want to run this comparison over all three phases.

The Investment and Growth Phase

We start the lifecycle when the Pro invests $1,000,000 into a tax-deferred retirement account earning 6 percent net of fees and expenses. Ten years later, at age 35, the account has grown to $1,790,850. (See Figure 12.4.) This is where I believe a point can be made about liquidly. In a traditional tax-deferred plan, the retirement account is accessible, but with a steep price. All of the earnings are taxable and the withdrawal is subject to an additional 10 percent penalty imposed by the government for distributions

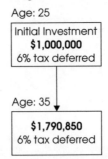

The Pro's Retirement Investment Life Cycle
(Assumes 6% growth; 40% tax bracket)

Age: 25

Initial Investment
$1,000,000
6% tax deferred

Age: 35

$1,790,850
6% tax deferred

Figure 12.4 Funding Phase—The Investment Is Accessible, But Very Expensive

prior to age 59½. That is a heavy price to pay and is supposed to act as a deterrent. The charitably leveraged approach, on the other hand, uses the CRAT as the funding tool. As you know, the CRAT is an irrevocable trust, and no one—not even the Pro—can take the money out. The only liquidity over the first 10 years will be found in the CVLI. The good news is that early withdrawals are not subject to tax or penalty.

The Withdrawal/Retirement Income Phase

When the Pro reaches age 35, he begins to withdraw money from his account. For the purposes of this comparison, we're going to match the income he will be getting from the CVLI in the charitably leveraged approach; $84,237 after tax ($1,684,740 total). Since the account is tax-deferred on a last-in, first-out (LIFO) basis, he will need to withdraw enough money each year to pay the income tax due in a 40 percent tax bracket. When his withdrawals exhaust all of the earnings, he'll start taking distributions against the original basis, and the taxes will stop. That event will occur in the 13th year. While paying taxes on the withdrawals, he will need to take $140,495 out of his account to net $84,237 after tax. Thus, he will pay $56,158 of his earnings to tax each year. In addition, he will be subject to that 10 percent government penalty for withdrawals prior to age 59½. *It should be noted here that I did not take the 10 percent penalty into account in these calculations.* (See Figure 12.5.)

On taxes alone, over the 20 year retirement phase the Pro will be forced to withdraw $2,407,762 to match the $1,684,740 generated by the charitably leveraged plan. That amounts to $723,022 in wasted tax dollars. That is an awful lot of accidental philanthropy in exchange for some early access to an account that was earmarked for retirement in the first place.

The Transfer Phase

When the Pro reaches age 55, he can stop taking money from his retirement account because his league pension will kick in. He made it, paid a lot of taxes, but he made it. As I stated earlier, in a typical retirement plan, the client is usually in his or her seventies or eighties when the income phase ends. So naturally the transfer of the remaining account coincides with his or her death or possible gift for estate-planning purposes. In this scenario, the Pro is

The Pro's Retirement Investment Life Cycle
(Assumes 6% growth; 40% tax bracket)

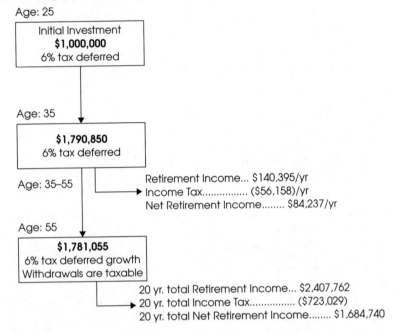

Figure 12.5   The Pro Draws against the Retirement Account Subject to Taxes and Penalties

only 55 when his income phase ends, so we're probably not talking transfer at all. If he is still is living, the remaining $781,055 could be used any number of ways ranging from spending it all, to leaving it in the account for the future. (See Figure 12.6.)

A transfer upon death should not be dismissed out of hand, however. It is important to note that if the Pro does die prematurely, the same account balance of $781,055 is what will be transferred to his beneficiaries. While this seems fairly obvious here, it becomes an important issue when we do the comparison to the charitable leveraged strategy.

Not So Fast, Goldberg.   Before I complete this comparison, I'd like to tell you a story.

It seems there was this drill sergeant in the Army who was particularly coarse and abusive. He possessed no known people skills. He was called on

The Pro's Retirement Investment Life Cycle
(Assumes 6% growth, 40% tax bracket)

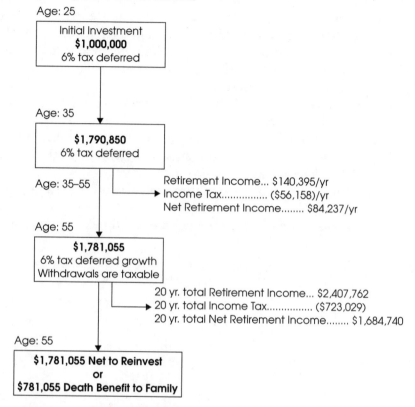

Figure 12.6   The Cumulative Impact

the carpet a few times for his actions, and on this day was getting reamed yet again by his commanding officer. "Sarge," the Captain screamed, "I've had it up to here with the complaints about you. This is a modern Army, you need to adapt to change, you must be sensitive to the troops' feelings. This is your final warning. Now I'm going to give you one last chance to prove to me that you can change. Private Goldberg's mother died yesterday and you're going to tell him. Use tact, use diplomacy, be sensitive. Or you are out. Do I make myself clear?"

With a quick, "yes sir," and a salute, the sergeant was off to do his task. He thought for a minute and called the troops to assemble. When they were standing at attention, the sergeant stood back and barked, "All those men whose mothers are still living, take two steps forward . . . not so fast, Goldberg!"

Given a quick look at the results, you might say that the traditional plan comes out on top. There is only $160,000 of cash value remaining in the CVLI policy as compared to more than $780,000 in the traditional approach. Sure the death benefit of the CVLI blows away the competition but we agree that death at age 55 is not that likely. Is this it? Is this the war story where accidental philanthropy wins? Not so fast, Goldberg.

One of the key features of the charitably leveraged plan is that it generates an income tax deduction of $270,000. In the Pro's 40 percent tax bracket that amount equates to 108,000 real dollars in his pocket. In order to keep this comparison on a level playing field, (no pun intended) we need to invest those savings in exactly the same manner as the tax-deferred retirement account (i.e., a variable annuity earning 6 percent net). Figure 12.7 illustrates the impact on the Pro's plan when we take the tax savings into consideration.

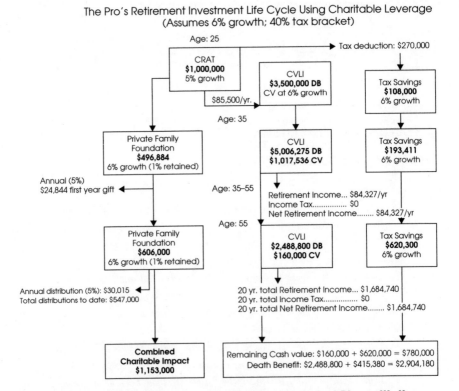

The Pro's Retirement Investment Life Cycle Using Charitable Leverage
(Assumes 6% growth; 40% tax bracket)

Figure 12.7   The Impact of the Charitably Leveraged Plan with the Tax Savings Considered

Now that changes things a little, doesn't it? When we consider the use of the tax savings in the fairest way possible, the cash available at age 55 is almost dead even. Table 12.1 has the stats and they're worth taking at look at. The combined personal wealth generated by the same $1,000,000 in the traditional approach is

Table 12.1   The Comparative Impact of Accidental Philanthropy Versus Voluntary

	The Pro's Retirement Investment Lifecycle	
	Traditional Approach	Charitable Leverage
(1) Starting Amount	$1,000,000	$1,000,000
(2) Total Personal Income (ages 35–55)	1,684,740	1,684,740
(3) Net cash remaining to invest at age 55	$781,055	$780,000
(4) Tax combined wealth	$2,465,795	$2,464,740
(5) Death benifit to family at age 35	$781,055	$2,904,180
(6) Total to charity	$0	$1,153,000
(7) Total to taxes	$723,029	$45,000
(8) Combined wealth to family + charity	$2,465,795	3,617,740

Row Descriptions:
1. Starting Amount: the total dollar amount contributed to the investment plan or CRAT.
2. Total Personal Income (ages 35–55): the total net income of $84,267/yr for 20 years.
3. Net cash remaining to invest at age 55: remaining cash in the investment vs. CVLI + accumulated tax savings after Column 2.
4. Total combined wealth: Column 2 + Column 3.
5. Death benefit to family at age 55: Cash payment to family if the owner dies at age 55. Charitable leverage includes (a) CVLI pays the insurance benefit tax free + (b) tax savings a accumulation account less taxes.
6. Total to charity: total gifts made to charity by age 55 (Foundation balance + gifts from the Foundation).
7. Total to taxes: projected income taxes due assuming a 40% tax bracket.
8. Combined wealth to family + charity: Column 4 + Column 6.

$2,465,795 as compared to the charitably leveraged plan, which produced $2,464,740. At a $1,058 difference I'd call it a dead heat. But is it? The price tag of the traditional plan is $723,029 in income tax payments. I think you know what we call that. Whereas if I factor in the taxes due on the original CRAT distributions, the total tax bill will be $45,000.

Obviously, the charitably leveraged program kills the traditional plan in the case of the Pro's premature death due to the tax-free death benefit associated with the CVLI policy. Unfortunately from time to time we are reminded that young people do die. In that case the death benefit provides the Pro's family with a substantial degree of financial security from the very beginning. I'm not going to belabor this point because if a 25 year old was that concerned about dying he could buy term insurance pretty cheaply. Of course, the cost would swing the combined personal wealth column back in favor of the charitably leveraged plan.

The real difference in the program is in the impact on Pro's social philanthropy. Under the traditional plan, dollars lost to taxes go unaccounted and undirected. The Pro has no control over the distribution of his wealth. The charitably leveraged approach reduces the tax exposure and instead creates more than $1,000,000 for the charitable and social programs that are uniquely important to him and his family.

In summary, it is the total package that makes a charitably leveraged strategy so attractive. It is not right for everybody, but for the Pro athlete with a desire to give something back is an effective method of bridging the gap to retirement while staying in game socially.

The Choice to Confound Congress Through Compound Interest

What about the rest of the young business leaders, physicians, professionals, entertainers, and entrepreneurs whose income is substantial but subject to huge swings (or not). As a group they may live large but they also have a pretty good grasp on building a secure retirement. The year 2008 fired a shot across their bow and they may now be ready for some reasonable expectations. Similar to the Pro athlete the member of this group may view the word "retirement" as simply a point in time to start receiving deferred income.

They may not have as an immediate view of retirement as the Pro, but they view age 65 as the outer marker. Unfortunately, they are not as charitably inclined as their professional athlete brethren. Perhaps if they felt the target they wear on their back, they'd think differently. Perhaps not, I can only do so much.

What I can do is provide some insight into how we can work a little charitable leverage magic into their otherwise pretty cool lives. Let's see how this strategy will perform at various retirement ages. Here's the plan: We'll take a quick look at the plan structure and then run a couple of tables, one for a 30-year-old targeting "retirement income" ages of 50, 55, 60, and 65 and the same deal for a 35 year old.

Plan Design

Remember Dr. Schmooley? His charitable leverage strategy looked like the one in Figure 12.8.

The game plan for this current group will be exactly the same as our 45-year-old doctor with the exception that we will begin to distribute the income sooner because the donor is younger. The funding stays the same. The donor will transfer $1,000,000 into a

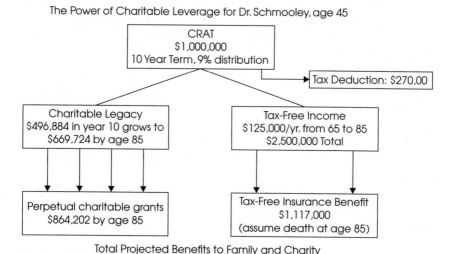

Total Projected Benefits to Family and Charity
$5,258,926

Figure 12.8   A Review of the Good Doctor's Plan

Presented for educational purposes only. Based on the projections as stated throughout this chapter.

10-year CRAT with a 9 percent fixed annuity rate. If you're thinking to yourself, "doesn't this guy ever change his tune?" The answer is sure, you can use an 8 percent CRAT if you want a larger tax deduction and less cash flow, or a 10 percent fixed CRAT if you want a teeny deduction and more cash flow. Other than that, I'm pretty much Johnny One-note.

The 10-year CRAT with the 9 percent fixed annuity rate will provide this gang with the same tax deduction Dr. Schmooley got, and the same one the Pro athlete got. It'll be the same deduction everyone, every age gets when the Applicable Federal Rate (AFR) is at a paltry 4 percent. The cash flow will be exactly the same, too. Bottom line: $270,000 tax deduction, $90,000 per year income—no matter what happens to the trust principal. Don't you love predictability?

Sticking with the assumptions we've used consistently, at the end of the 10th year the CRAT will transfer the remaining balance of $496,884 to the designated charity. Once again I beg you to consider a Donor Advised Fund, Supporting Organization, or Private Family Foundation as the charitable beneficiary. And once again I assume you listen to my sage advice and establish what I call the Family Charitable Fund. The fund will earn 6 percent, distribute 5 percent and retain 1 percent for growth.

No change with the CRAT cash flow either. The net after tax distribution by the CRAT is $85,500. The full boat is used to fund a CVLI insuring the life of the donor/owner. This area is the only place where you'll see some differential between the plans. A younger donor/insured will start with more death benefit than an older one.

Finally, I do want to show the importance of investing the tax savings created by the CRAT tax deduction. You may choose to ignore these results but I think that would be a mistake. You can't just take the tax deduction and toss it aside. It is an important aspect of charitable leverage and the dollars saved are very real and very spendable.

For Jack Bell, Measuring the Impact of Charitable Leverage is Easy as ABC

Jack is a 30-year-old entrepreneur coming off a couple of huge years. Remembering what happened in the economic destruction of 2008, he plans on depositing $1,000,000 of profits into his charitably leveraged supplemental retirement plan. He's not sure when he plans to retire. The earlier the better, but not before age 50.

The strategy, of course, starts with the 10-year CRAT paying a 9 percent annuity rate. The CRAT will fund the CVLI and transfer the remaining balance of $496,884 to the Bell Family Charitable Fund. Now let's look at the menu of outcomes at various "retirement" ages. Jack would like to examine the impact of the (A) retirement cash flow (B) tax savings if invested and (C) the impact on charity.

I prepared the following menu for him.

- Pick the *Income Start Date* from the first column in Table 12.2. That will provide Jack with his tax-free income and insurance benefit projections.
- Pick the *age your retirement ends* (Column 2 on Table 12.2) and match that with the age on the Philanthropy Grid in Table 12.3. Now Jack will know his potential charitable legacy at the end of retirement.

Table 12.2   Retirement Income Projections

Deferred income projections for a 30 year old who funds a 10-year CRAT (9% fixed annuity) with $1,000,000

1 Income Starts at Age	2 20 years Income Ends at Age	3 Annual Income	4 Total Income	5 Death Benefit at Funding Age	6 Remaining Death Benefit after Retirement
50	70	$133,460	$2,669,800	$3,000,000	$2,249,000
55	75	$175,350	$3,507,000	$3,000,000	$2,620,000
60	80	$228,600	$4,572,200	$3,000,000	$2,904,000
65	85	$293,900	$5,878,000	$3,000,000	$3,217,000

Table 12.3   Charitable Legacy Projections

CRAT value at end of year 10 = $496,884. CRAT then transfers to Charitable Family Fund

Retirement End Age	Grants to Date	Fund Balance	Total Philanthropy
70	$864,000	$670,000	$1,534,000
75	$1,035,000	$704,000	$1,739,000
80	$1,215,000	$740,000	$1,955,000
85	$1,400,000	$778,000	$2,178,000

- Pick any age on Table 12.4. That will show Jack what his tax savings have grown to at that point in time.

It's not that difficult. Let's look at tables 12.2–12.4 and then I'll give you a couple of examples.

Jack decides to start his retirement income at age 55; his annual projected cash flow from the CVLI policy will be $175,350. His cumulative tax-free income to age 75 will be $3,507,000. His family's financial security is supported by the additional $2.6 million insurance benefit. He's feeling pretty good.

He'll feel even better when he checks the way his charitable family fund is projected to perform. Knowing that his retirement income will end at age 75, he chooses to use that as the measure on his charitable legacy. He goes to Table 12.3, checks across the row that shows age 75 and sees a charitable legacy of more than $1,700,000, which includes grants and fund value.

He then looks at age 75 on Table 12.4 and finds that his tax savings will have grown to $1,486,577 by that age. His charitably leveraged package that he started with $1,000,000 has the potential to yield $3,507,000 in personal income, another $3,555,000 after tax for his family (which *includes* paying 40 percent tax on the tax

Table 12.4   Tax Savings Growth Projections

$108,000 tax savings invested in a tax deferred account at 6%

Age	Tax Savings Account Compounded at 6%
30	$114,480
35	$144,528
40	$193,411
45	$258,828
50	$346,370
55	$463,522
60	$620,297
65	$830,097
70	$1,110,857
75	$1,486,577
80	$1,989,376
85	$2,662,234

savings account), and more than $1,700,000 for his charities. Total personal and charitable wealth of $8,762,000 created with a single transfer of $1,000,000. It's not for nothing I call it the power of charitable leverage!

With this menu, Jack (and you) can mix and match various projected results with different ages. Invite your friends over and let them join in on the fun.

And Now, a Word from Ms. Hanks

Ms. A.J. Hanks a 35 year old from Los Angeles writes, "What about a well-heeled working girl like me? What would happen if I tossed a cool million into the charitably leveraged ring? Would I do as well as Mr. Bell?" Well, A.J. from L.A., tables 12.5–12.7 are for you.

Table 12.5   Retirement Income Projections

Deferred income projections for a 35 year old who funds a 10 year CRAT (9% fixed annuity) with $1,000,000

1 Income Starts at Age	2 20 years Income Ends at Age	3 Annual Income	4 Total Income	5 Death Benefit at Funding Age	6 Remaining Death Benefit after Retirement
50	70	$100,665	$2,013,300	$2,520,000	$1,446,000
55	75	$132,370	$2,645,400	$2,520,000	$1,700,000
60	80	$172,530	$3,450,600	$2,520,000	$1,947,000
65	85	$222,185	$4,443,700	$2,520,000	$2,236,000

Table 12.6   Charitable Legacy Projections

CRAT value at end of year 10 = $496,884. CRAT then transfers to Charitable Family Fund

Retirement End Age	Grants to Date	Fund Balance	Total Philanthropy
70	$701,000	$637,000	$1,338,000
75	$864,000	$670,000	$1,534,000
80	$1,035,000	$704,000	$1,739,000
85	$1,215,000	$740,000	$1,955,000

Table 12.7 Tax Savings Growth Projections

$108,000 tax savings invested in a tax deferred account at 6%

Age	Tax Savings Account Compounded at 6%
35	$114,480
40	$144,528
45	$193,411
50	$258,828
55	$346,370
60	$463,522
65	$620,297
70	$830,097
75	$1,110,857
80	$1,486,577
85	$1,989,376

The first thing you may notice is that there is not much difference in the Charitable Legacy and Tax Savings tables. That's because they're based on compound interest and distribution assumptions so everything appears to be five years later. The tax savings at age 60 on Mr. Bell's (age 30) Table 12.7 equates to the 65 year old on A.J.'s Table 12.4.

Still, mostly because of her age and the power of compound interest, A.J.'s projections produce remarkable results for herself and her charities. If she chooses to retire at the "normal" retirement age of 65, she can look to more than $222,185 of annual tax-free income. Her total retirement income to age 85 will be $4,443,700. Her children will be the beneficiaries of another $2,236,000 of tax-free insurance proceeds. In addition, her tax savings account will have grown to more than $1,989,000,

Ms. Hanks is an active advocate for the child literacy programs throughout her state of California. The foundation that she creates will be funded by the termination of her CRAT at her age 45. It will generate $1.2 million in education grants by the time she reaches age 85. She plans that her children will become active participants in the foundation. They will have a fund balance of $740,000 to continue Mom's legacy.

A.J.'s charitably leveraged deferred income plan will provide $4,443,700 of income for her retirement, another $3,472,600 for her children (which includes paying 40 percent tax on the tax savings account), and $1,955,000 to the charitable causes she loves. Her $1,000,000 seed grew to $9,870,700 of real wealth for family and philanthropy!

Controlling Their Assets

The young and restless will benefit from the power of compound interest combined with the power of charitable leverage. It is that tandem that can deal a death blow in the battle over control of their assets.

13

Charitably Leveraged Supplemental Retirement Plan for the Old and Cranky

If I knew I was going to live this long, I'd have taken better care of myself.

—Mickey Mantle

At the far end of this target group are people from all professions who are in their fifties and may still want to pad their retirement income. They are not really old, but compared to the other folks in this category, they're (we're) relics. They *are* cranky because this is the application where charitable leverage must be tweaked to produce competitive results. There just isn't enough time to allow the CRAT to do its work and produce a meaningful retirement income. Do the math, if you are 58 and you'd like to retire at age 65 you only have seven years to work—I need 10. I can hear Scotty now calling up from the engine room on the Starship Enterprise, "Captain, she's not going to make it—we need more power!" It's hard to write with a Scottish brogue, but you get my point. To be fair, any investment that only has seven years to perform is not going to look so great.

So Now What Do We Do?

To have any shot of generating a competitive alternative to traditional planning and provide a decent future income, I have prepared the list below of the factors needed for a successful charitably leveraged plan for the 55 and older set.

- You must be willing to push the "retirement income" date or "deferred income" date back to age 70. Logically, we'll still carry the income stream to age 85 as life expectancy. By putting off the start date to age 70 and shortening the payout period to 15 years, we have a fighting chance in the War on Wealth.
- An appreciated asset changes everything. Remember those? That's the stuff that was valued lower when you bought it compared to where it is now. You know that capital gains tax is one of the harshest weapons in the government arsenal and it will get worse in 2011 when it increases to 20 percent. Funding your CRAT with appreciated assets will allow you to deflect that bomb and use the savings for your benefit and for the benefit of your charity.
- You may need to think outside the box. I've been saying that a charitably leveraged strategy should be funded with publicly traded securities, but it can be funded with appreciated real estate or closely held stock. In fact, some of the largest plans I've done were based on appreciated closely held stock. There are a lot of rules that surround this application, and it's a little far afield of this book. If you think you may be in a position to use charitable leverage to shelter the gains on real estate or closely held stock, talk first to your accountant. He or she can crunch the numbers and do the research to support your plan. You may also want to work directly with a charity that has a support staff to help you.
- *Most importantly* charitable intent must be a top priority. With just about all of the other age groups and techniques we can sort of *back into* charitable intent because the numbers are just so damn compelling. However, the

O&C crowd will see that on a straight up, cash versus cash comparison with a traditional short-term retirement investment, the charitable leverage approach will probably provide a little less cash to the remaining beneficiaries at death. You *will* pay less tax and you *will* avoid accidental philanthropy but the savings will favor your charity more than your children. But, that was kind of the original intention, wasn't it?

How We Produced for the Guy Who Sold Produce

Joe the Grocer is a 58 year old from Florida who owns a pretty substantial chain of grocery stores (what did you expect he'd own?). After 30 years of watching the stock market bounce around, and after losing 30 percent of his investment wealth in 2008, Joe says the only market he can control is his own. Joe's not exactly stupid and he's growing wary of the antibusiness attitude of a left-leaning Washington. He has started negotiations with a public chain to buy his stores.

Joe is a patron of the arts and serves on the board of the nonprofit Performing Arts Center in his community. They are always up against fund-raising issues. When he sells his business he intends to create a charitable fund that would support the center.

He's still sitting on about $3,000,000 of stock that has only $100,000 in basis he accumulated over the years (it used to be a lot more). He'd like to lock in his gains and get out of the stock market, but if he does he will need to write a check in the amount of $580,000 payable to the U.S. Treasury for the capital gains tax. As much as he hates the thought of taxes, he can't stomach any more losses. His financial advisor tells him he could lock in a tax-deferred annuity at 6 percent for the next 12 years (there is no such thing but I'm trying to make this interesting—read between the lines—I'm using the 6 percent tax deferred comparison rate, get it?). Joe likes the sound of that.

He and his advisor calculate that Joe needs about $190,000 after taxes to supplement his retirement income. He could use current assets to get him from now to age 70 and then use the annuity to start kicking in money from 70 to 85. Let's follow on his mathematical journey:

- Current value of the stock $ 3,000,000.
- Value after the sale: $2,420,000 (loses $580,000—Joe not happy)
- Invested tax deferred at 6 percent, the account would be worth $4,870,000 by the time he needs it to spin off income at age 70.
- In a 40 percent tax bracket he will need to withdraw $320,000 to net $192,000 after taxes. He becomes a little nauseous at the thought of paying $128,000 of income tax each year.

Joe starts to sprint for the bathroom, when he realizes that over the 15 period from age 70 to 85, in order to reach his income goal of $2,880,000, he'll need to withdraw $4,800,000 from his annuity. "That's $1,920,000 of my money!" he shouts as he slams the bathroom door.

When he emerges from the potty, his advisor hands him a towel. Joe says that he's okay and then asks how much his wife and children will receive of the account when he dies. The advisor happily exclaims that the account will be worth $3,771,000 at age 85. Then he mumbles something under his breath that Joe cannot make out so he asks him to repeat it. The advisor says, "$3,771,000 is the total account balance, $2,420,000 is your basis, so the ordinary income tax is $540,400. The net to your family is $3,230,600." Joe spins around and heads back to the throne room.

Figure 13.1 shows you what Joe's chart looks like.

Lucky for Joe, he had the smarts to compare the retirement income strategy to a charitably leveraged plan. He found it able to meet all of his needs and was far easier on his stomach.

- Current value of the stock, $3,000,000 is deposited into a 10-year CRAT with an 8 percent fixed annuity rate (4 percent Applicable Federal Rate [AFR]).
- Value after the CRAT sells the stock: $3,000,000 (loses nothing to capital gains tax—Joe is starting to smile).
- Transfer to the CRAT creates a tax deduction of $1,053,385, which will come in handy if Joe sells the grocery biz this year. In any event the tax savings in a 40 percent bracket is $421,350. Joe trots down to his financial advisor and buys that 6 percent annuity with the tax savings.
- The CRAT distributes $240,000 each year subject to 20 percent capital gains tax. The net income distributed to Joe is $192,000 per year for 10 years.

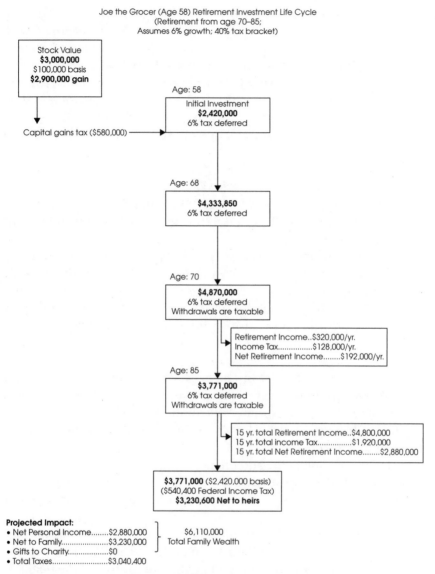

Figure 13.1   Joe the Grocer's Retirement Projection

Joe takes all of the CRAT distribution and buys a CVLI policy designed in the wealth accumulation strategy used for a charitably leveraged plan. The death benefit of the policy is $2,933,000 plus cash accumulations.

At the end of the 10th year the CRAT will fund Joe's philanthropic legacy for the Performing Arts Center. He will use the CRAT remainder of $1,868,000 to establish a trust for the center, which will spin off 5 percent of its net investment assets each year.

Joe will start withdrawing his retirement income goal of $192,000 at age 70 and continue to age 85. His total retirement income will be $2,880,000. He will not pay tax. (Joe likey.)

When Joe goes to that great grocery store in the sky, age 85, the results will look like this:

- Total income to Joe: $2,880,000.
- Total cash to family: $4,066,840 resulting from the remaining insurance proceeds added to the tax savings annuity (after paying income tax).
- Total Charitable Legacy: $3,933,660, which is a combination of the Charitable Fund of $2,212,270 and the total of grants given to the Performing Arts Center of $1,721,390. Joe the Grocer's name and legacy will live on in the performing arts community, and others will follow thanks to the example he set.

He did pay $1,124,000 in taxes; $480,000 of that was the tax on the CRAT distributions in the first 10 years. The other $644,000 was the income tax on the annuity distribution, which could have been avoided if Joe had transferred the annuity to his children when he first purchased it.

The bottom line to Joe and the people and causes he loves amounts to $10,880,520 as compared to $6,110,000 in the original plan.

Figure 13.2 shows you what Joe's charitably leveraged chart looks like.

Table 13.1 shows a side-by-side comparison of the two approaches. The combination of $1.9million *less* in taxes and $4.7 million *more* for his family and charity was enough to convince Joe to seal the deal.

The strength of this war story lies in the fact that Joe had appreciated property that he could use to fund the CRAT. A cash versus cash comparison would have been much closer. In either case the desire to avoid accidental philanthropy makes a strong case to at least look at an "apples to apples" comparison. That was a little produce humor in honor of Joe, who may still be old, but he's no longer cranky.

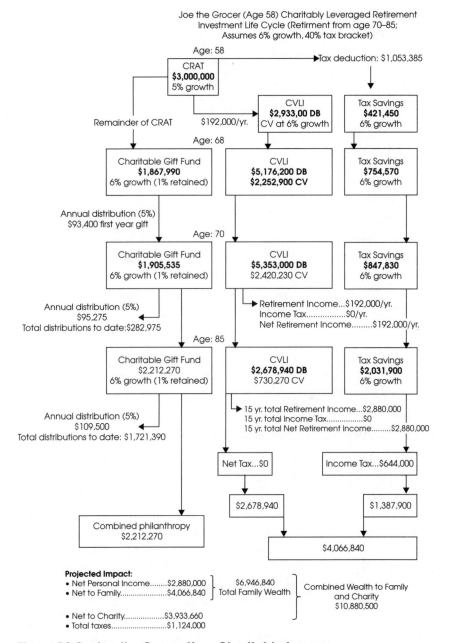

Figure 13.2   Joe the Grocer Uses Charitable Leverage

Table 13.1   A comparison for Joe

	Joe the Grocer (Age 58) Retirement Investment Life Cycle (Retirement from age 70–85)	
	Traditional Planning	Charitable Leverage
(1) Starting Amount	$3,000,000	$3,000,000
(2) Capital Gains Tax	$580,000	0
(3) Net to Fund the Retirement Account	$2,420,000	$3,000,000
(4) Tax Deduction	$0	$1,053,385
(5) Tax Savings	$0	$421,350
(6) Total Retirement Income (15 yrs)	$2,880,000	$2,880,000
(7) Net to Family at Death	$3,230,000	$4,066,840
(8) Total Combined Family Wealth	$6,110,000	6,946,840
(9) Total to Charity	$0	$3,933,660
(10) Total to Taxes	$3,040,400	$1,124,400
(11) Combined Wealth to Family and Charity	$6,110,000	$10,880,500

Final Thoughts on the War Stories

As we walk the battlefields where the War on Wealth is fought, the skirmishes over control of the accumulation and distribution retirement assets are among the fiercest. Traditional retirement strategies fall prey to the covert attacks that transform earnings into taxes, and taxes into entitlements, bailouts, and pork. The victims are our families and the charities we support. The simple math that the government forces cannot seem to do is that the more they take, the less we can give. Worse yet is that the war on wealth focuses on selective targets. They are America's best and brightest who produce the most, employ the most and earn the most. They used to be revered as capitalists, now they are reviled as "the wealthiest Americans." Like the accumulation of wealth through education, hard work, and long hours is a bad thing.

The war stories in this chapter showed some examples of how people like you and me can take back control of our money. They also show how we can build what we want and give it to who we want, when we want. I shared with you the stories of folks who took the time, did the math, and then made the decision to become active philanthropists instead of accidental ones. It is your money, your family, your philanthropy, fight for it!

14

How to Use Charitable Leverage to Fund the Grandparents' Legacy

Nobody can do for little children what grandparents do.
Grandparents sort of sprinkle stardust over the lives of little
children.

—Alex Haley

And then it happens. With a little more than a few months warning, your son or daughter makes you a grandparent. You aren't ready for it, nobody is. *"How did I get here? Where did the time go?"* As your friends offer you their congratulations, you flashback to those early years of parenting and then on to the teen years. There's a lot of "could've" and "should've" in those memories. "I should've said this . . . ," or "I could've done that . . . " But this is real life and *there are no do-overs.*

And then it happens. You hold the baby for the first time. In those deep blue eyes you see your own children; you see yourself and the next generation all at once. It all kind of blurs together. Some of us cry, some of us lock it up inside, all of us taste the bitter with the sweet. You think ahead to a new child growing up. You smile when you envision the coming years of more t-ball games, more dance recitals, more challenges, more opportunities. That's when it hits you; you realize that what lies in your arms is *your* future. It is a future full of possibilities. *You do get a do-over.* In fact, you get a lifetime of them. Suddenly, the past fades and the time ahead is exciting and full of promise. Then the best part happens. The baby starts to cry, and you hand him back to his mom. This is going to be great!

What will your legacy be? What will you leave your grandchildren? Will it be memories, mementoes, money? All of that stuff is important for sure, but is that it? How about leaving some footprints that will not wash away? How about setting the bar a little higher for your children and grandchildren—and maybe even their children? That's the driving force behind the strategy on the following pages, what I call *The Grandparents' Legacy.*

A Life Well Lived, a Legacy Well Planned

My career as a financial planner has taken me on some wild rides with some very tough clients. Not tough like, "I'm going to kick the crap out of you" tough. But tough, like, "you do what you have to do to be a great business leader" tough. I've been doing this kind of work for a very long time. I have worked with some of the crustiest, crudest, crunchiest characters you'd ever want to meet. I've seen them boss, yell, scream, and bully their way to the top of their business world. Most are great guys, some you probably would not want to hang out with. But they all have one thing in common. When you ask them about their grandchildren, they turn into a babbling pile of goo. They may be crunchy on the outside, but they're chewy on the inside.

They may not carry that same sentiment about their children. You know the drill. "I fed them, clothed them, paid for their school, gave them whatever they wanted—certainly more than my parents ever gave me, and they still forget my Birthday, or Mother's Day." Sound familiar? But the grandchildren, now that's a whole new ball game. I have come to agree with the author and humorist, Sam Levenson, who said, "I believe that the reason grandparents get along so well with their grandchildren is that have a common enemy, their parents!"

Of course, we've learned that there is another enemy lurking in the shadows. That enemy threatens to attack the so-called "wealth" that we've spent a lifetime *working* for, and redistribute it to fulfill their political agendas and obligations. You may think like many of my grandparent-clients who say, "I may think my kids are ingrates, but they're *my kids*. And I sure as hell would rather see them and my beloved grandchildren get the fruits of my labor than some government entitlement program." For publication purposes, I removed the curses—it shortened the sentence considerably.

Assuming that a grandparent has the desire to create a charitable legacy instead of becoming an accidental philanthropist, a charitably leveraged strategy will enable him or her build and shelter wealth for the next two generations with a large degree of control. In the bargain, the grandparent will receive a substantial income tax deduction while creating a philanthropic legacy that will tell his or her story for years to come.

To illustrate this strategy, here's what we're going to do. First, I'll put some real numbers in the figures I used earlier. As we review each step of the four-step process you get a better feel for the action-impact dynamic. Then you're in position to enjoy the process in the context of a war story and comparative alternative.

The Grandparents' Legacy example that follows uses the assumptions I stated at the beginning of Part III. In addition, I've added the following information:

- The Grandparents (GP) are both age 70.
- The Adult Child (AC) is age 40.
- The Grandchildren (GC) are the children of AC. They are ages 14 and 12.
- The public stock to be transferred to the CRAT is valued at $1,000,000 with a $250,000 cost basis.

Step 1: The Grandparents Start the Conversion from *Accidental* Philanthropy to *Active* Philanthropy

The grandparents (GP) start the process by transferring the $1,000,000 stock position with a $250,000 basis into their 10-year term CRAT. They select an 8 percent annuity rate. The stock is sold inside the CRAT and reinvested in conservative growth and income securities. Upon the sale of stock, not one single dollar is lost to capital gains tax.

- Scoreboard: GP $150,000 (capital gains tax savings)
- Accidental philanthropy: 0

The transfer to the CRAT generates an income tax deduction for the present value of the gift. There's not a whole lot to calculate. If *you* did a 10-year CRAT with an 8 percent distribution rate and the Applicable Federal Rate (AFR) was 4 percent, *you* and everybody else would receive the same tax deduction of $351,000. Think about what GP can do with that deduction. They can use it to take additional money out of their IRA, or it can be used to offset the gain of some of their stock that was sold outside the trust. They could even use it against the taxable portion of the CRAT income in the next step. If the AFR was 3 percent, the tax deduction would be $317,000. If it were 5 percent, the deduction would be $382,000. The bottom line is that in their 40 percent income tax bracket, a $351,000 income tax deduction is like putting an extra $140,500 of honest-to-God spendable money in their pocket.

- Scoreboard for this round: GP $140,500 (income tax savings)
- Accidental philanthropy: 0

The other feature of this step is that the transfer of the $1,000,000 asset to the CRAT removes it from GP's taxable estate. If it's not in the estate, then there's no federal or state estate tax. I'd say ol' GP did pretty well for themselves with this little maneuver. (For a graphical representation of these action items, refer to Figure 14.1, which shows your progress through action 3.)

Step 2: The Grandparents Control All of the Cash Flow

As we move through the next three steps, keep in mind that once the CRAT is funded by the stock transfer, the entire charitable leverage process is locked in. The unfortunate truth about those of us who are old enough to be grandparents is that the potential for all kinds of health issues comes into play. It is a comforting benefit of

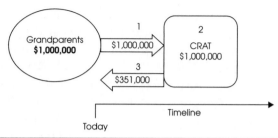

Item #	Action	Impact
1	GP transfers $1,000,000 of stock (with a cost basis of $250,000) to a 10-year term (CRAT) with an 8% annuity rate.	✓ Removes the $1,000,000 of stock from GP's taxable estate. ✓ Protects the assets from the claims of creditors.
2	The CRAT trustee sells the appreciated stock. The CRAT pays no capital gains tax.	✓ $150,000 that would have been lost to capital gains remains in the CRAT to be reinvested.
3	The transfer of $1,000,000 to the CRAT creates an immediate income tax deductiion of $351,000.	✓ Potential tax savings of $140,500. ✓ The tax deduction can be taken against 30% of adjusted gross income and carried forward for five years.

Figure 14.1   GP Starts the Conversion from Accidental Philanthropist to Active Philanthropist

a charitable leverage strategy that provides grandparents with the assurance that their legacy plan will go on even if they don't.

The 8 percent fixed annuity rate is determined on the day GP creates the CRAT. The amount of $80,000 will be distributed to whomever GP selects for the next 10 years. There is no guessing, no measuring, and no messy cleanup. Ready for this? You just set it, and forget it. *Even I can't believe I just said that.* When GP creates the CRAT they select how often they want the income distributed. Most of the CRATs that I've designed distribute the annuity payment quarterly, starting in the fourth month following the funding. While the GP would receive $20,000 per quarter, in our example all calculations are based on annual payments to avoid any confusion.

The GP select themselves as the income recipients of the CRAT payments with a trust as a back-up should some awful fate befall them. Naming themselves as income recipients provides maximum control over the rest of their charitable leverage strategy. As the annuity income is distributed, it becomes subject to tax under the four-tier accounting rules. Since the GP avoided capital gains tax on $800,000 of appreciation when they sold the stock, the best they could hope for would be capital gains tax treatment on the trust income. Therefore, it is in their best interest to keep the CRAT balance invested in growth securities and mutual funds. They could also invest in stocks that pay qualified dividends, taxed at the 20 percent rate. They want to stay away from any investment that generates ordinary income. The $80,000 annuity payment under this investment model will avoid ordinary income tax at the 40 percent rate and fall to the next tier, which would be capital gains tax treatment taxed at the 20 percent rate. The GP net income from the CRAT then, is $64,000 ($80,000 less 20 percent).

GP uses the $64,000 net CRAT payment to purchase a wealth accumulation–style life insurance policy (like the ones I've described ad-nauseam throughout this book) on AC. Based upon AC's age and health status, the minimum insurance face amount relative to the premiums was just under $2,000,000. So what the hell, we rounded it up to $2,000,000 plus the cash value account. As the years go by and the cash grows so will the policy insurance benefit.

AC is the insured but *GP is the owner.* This structure gives GP complete control over all of the cash disbursements. GP already controls where the $64,000 annuity payment goes each year. Now they can control access to the cash value of the insurance policy as well. This is a very important design feature for the grandparent who loves his or her kids, but really-really loves the grandkids. They may not want their kids to have access to the cash value early because they may spend it—you know how kids are. With GP in control, they can tap the policy on AC's behalf and help out with education or other needs. This is an extremely popular planning technique. At some point GP will transfer the policy ownership to AC. When that event occurs, the cash value in the policy will be considered a gift for gift tax purposes. That's not a big deal but you need to know about it.

The Grandchildren (GC) are the beneficiaries of the policy on AC's life. GP would be best served to name a trust for the benefit of GC. Another planning technique is to have an Irrevocable Life Insurance Trust (ILIT) own the insurance policy. The trustee could withdraw cash from the policy for the income needs of AC, or the cash needs, including college education of GC. If this is the method chosen by GP then the annual payments to the

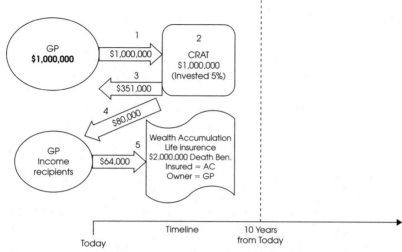

Item #	Action	Impact
4	Each year the CRAT distributes a fixed dollar annuity payment of $80,000 back to the GP. The annuity income is taxed under the favourable four-tier accounting rules. In this case only 20% is subject to tax. GPs' net income each year is $64,000.	✓ The investment performance of the CRAT impacts the *charity not GP. GP always receive the full $80,000.* ✓ The $80,000 annual payment continues for the full 10-year term even if it exceeds the GPs' joint lives.
5	GP uses the $64,000 annuity to purchase an Equity Index UL insurance policy, GP is the owner of the policy, AC is the insured. A trust for GC is the beneficiary. The face amount of the policy is $2,000,000 plus cash value.	✓ Cash builds in the policy free from tax. ✓ Cash is available to GP to use for any need of AC or GC. ✓ GP can transfer ownership to AC whenever they choose. The transfer is a gift.

Figure 14.2   CRAT Cash Flow Funds the Insurance Contract

insurance policy will be treated as gifts. Either way it is a sweet package funded by dollars that GP was going to lose to tax. (For a graphical representation of these action items, refer to Figure 14.2, which shows your progress through action 5.)

Step 3: The Grandparents' Defining Moment— A Charitable Legacy

I try to have fun when dealing with the subject of charitable leverage, I mean c'mon some of this stuff can get pretty slow. But when it comes to this part of the Grandparents' Legacy I have to be serious.

Remember those crusty guys I was talking about at the open? I've seen tears form in their eyes when we get to this point. The idea of using what would have been wasted tax dollars to create a charitable legacy in the family name is compelling. But when I show what the impact the legacy can have on future generations, it moves to whole new level.

The CRAT moves on to the designated charity at the end of the 10th year. I encourage my grandparent-clients to name a Donor Advised Fund (DAF) in the family name or create a Private Family Foundation as the charitable beneficiary. In this example the CRAT has been earning at the rate of 5 percent per year while distributing a fixed rate of $80,000. One does not need a calculator to figure out that the value of CRAT will decrease over the 10 years. As I said earlier, a declining CRAT account is part of the charitably leveraged design. Simply put if the money is not in the CRAT, it's in your hands. It's okay with the IRS, too. Before the CRAT is approved it must pass what's called the 5 percent probability test. That test was created by a revenue ruling that specifically referenced fixed payout annuity trusts like the one used here. In short, the ruling uses an investment return on the original transfer ($1,000,000) indexed to the AFR at the time of the CRAT creation (4 percent in this case). Based on that rate and the payout of $80,000 per year, if the trust has a greater than 5 percent chance of exhausting the principal (i.e., there would be nothing left for the charity), then the trust is denied.

The point of avoiding accidental philanthropy is to utilize the potentially wasted tax dollars to create a meaningful gift. In this case the CRAT value will be about $622,660 by the time it is transferred. If the gift ends there with a direct payment to charity I believe that the grandparents miss out on a valuable opportunity to speak to their grandchildren long after they are gone. If instead the gift is given to the GP Donor Advised Fund or Private Family Foundation, gifts and grants from the funds may be given in perpetuity.

For example, let's say that the $622,660 from the GP CRAT is transferred to the GP Family DAF. The fund will voluntarily distribute 5 percent of its net investment value each year as grants to other charitable causes (family foundations are mandated to do the same). Let's also assume that the DAF invests the $622,660 at 6 percent per year. In the first year of the DAF (the 11th year of the overall plan) it grants $31,000 to other charities ($622,660 × 5 percent). By the time the 21st year roles around the DAF will be worth $759,763 and it would have given more than $685,000 in grants. By the 35th year, long after GP are gone (AC age 85), the DAF will be worth $882,000 and will have made grants for more than $1,297,000. The total philanthropy to that date is more than $2,100,000!

All along the way AC serves on the DAF advisory board with GC standing in the wings ready to serve when they are of age. They are part of every decision, every meeting, and every gift. AC and GC will live the legacy created by GP for the rest of their lives. Who knows it may inspire them to do their own philanthropy. (For a graphical representation of these action items, refer to Figure 14.3, which shows your progress through action 6.)

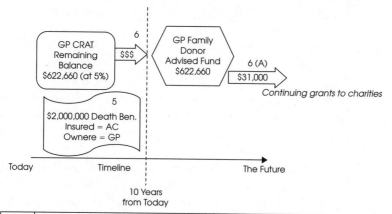

Item #	Action	Impact
6	At the end of the 10-year CRAT term, the remaining balance will be distributed to the GP Family Charitable Fund (A Donor Advised Fund). At an assumed investment return of 5%, the remaining balance in the CRAT will be $622,660.	✓ You have used pinpoint accuracy to select where their "accidentally philanthropic" dollars will go by choosing voluntary philanthropy.
6 (A)	The GP Family Charitable Fund will continue to distribute grants to charitable causes that are selected by the GP's family well into the future. In addition to GP, AC, and GC may sit on the board.	✓ If the Fund earns 6% and distributes 5%, it will grant more than $31,000/year to selected charitable causes. ✓ The GP Legacy (and family name) will live on through the AC and GC, and possible beyond.

Figure 14.3   The Grandparents Add Meaning to Their Money

Step 4: The Grandparents Create a Financial Legacy for the Next Two Generations

With the CRAT now gone and the DAF in its place, the grandparents are ready to watch the cash-flow benefits of charitable leverage unfold for their children and grandchildren. I'm going to show you the power of this arrangement over the lifetimes of GP and AC, with the ultimate beneficiaries being the GC. AC is age 40 when the plan starts and as I've said earlier, I use age 85 as AC's life expectancy. At that point, the remaining insurance policy death benefit is paid to the GC who will be in their fifties. The insurance benefit provides a pretty nice kickoff to the GCs' retirement plans, thanks GP. Anyway, the whole scenario plays out over a 45-year timeline. Any projections I could make for a period this long are subject to question as I stated in the section on "assumptions," but that's not going to stop me from making them. I've used a pretty conservative return of 6 percent net after expenses for all investments. In this case that would be the *net* return on the DAF and the *gross* return on the insurance policy *before the cost of insurance is deducted* (this is the only fair way to do it). With the cost of insurance included, the internal rate of return of the insurance policy will average about 5 percent. In other words, these are pretty reasonable assumptions. One last thing about the DAF, I assume it will grant 5 percent of its net asset value to other charities every year. Therefore, the projected growth of the fund is only 1 percent net.

GP continues to control the insurance policy until they die or decide to transfer it to AC. When AC reaches the magic retirement age for this exercise (age 65), the withdrawals (and policy loans) are used to generate tax-free income for the next 20 years. Based upon our assumptions, the policy will generate a little more than $120,000 annually. The projected income over the 20-year period is more than $2,400,000. If AC dies at age 85 after just having cashed the last $120,000 check, the GC will inherit the tax-free insurance proceeds of another $1,700,000. The total tax-free multigenerational benefit is more than $4,100,000! How's that for a financial legacy?

On the charitable side, the DAF value at AC's age 85 is projected to be about $882,000, but the DAF had already given away $1,297,000 of gifts. The total charitable legacy in the family name is more than $2,000,000. Here's the best part, *the DAF is still operational*

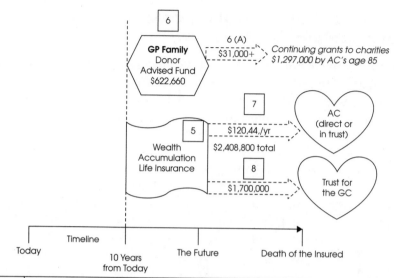

Figure 14.4 The Grandparents Create a Multigenerational Financial Legacy

Item #	Action	Impact
7	With the insurance policy *fully funded* by the CRAT, It continues under GP control unit ownership is transferred to AC. The chart shows AC's retirement withdrawals from age 65 to 85 (20 years).	✓ If the Insurance earns 6% net return, it would provide AC with over $120,000 per year tax-free income from age 65 to 85 ($2,408,880 total).
		✓ If AC dies during the "retirement years" the remaining death benefit will be paid to a trust for GC.
8	The tax-free insurance proceeds are paid to a trust for the grandchildren. The chart above assumes death of AC at age 85.	✓ If the insurance earns 6% net return, there would be another $1,700,000 of death benefit for GC at AC's age 85.
		✓ Under the assumptions used here, the $1,000,000 formely taxable asset in the GP's estate will generate over $4,100,000 *tax-free* to AC and GC while providing over $2,000,000 to charity.

with $882,000 in it and the grandchildren in charge! I wonder who they'll think about every year when they make their grants?

The combined benefits to family and charity generated from the original GP transfer of $1,000,000 is more than $6,000,000. (For a graphical representation of these action items, refer to Figure 14.4, which shows your progress through action 8.)

Is that enough of a legacy for you?

Summary: The Power of Charitable Leverage on the Grandparents' Legacy

Based on the assumptions used in this example, the $1,000,000 seed planted by the grandparents, *which was targeted for accidental philanthropy*, has grown into more than $6,400,000 of real financial benefits for themselves, their children, their grandchildren, and charity. (See Figure 14.5.)

What Figure 14.5 doesn't show is the impact that charitable leverage has on your soul. It doesn't show the impact it has on America's soul. Very simply, we as grandparents and Americans can draw a line in the sand and choose how at least some of our tax dollars are spent. That's good for us, it's good for our families, it's good for the charities that are important to us, and it's good for the country we live in. Your money, your charities, your choice, isn't that how capitalism and free markets are supposed to work?

For all of the worrying you've ever done about your finances and for all of the complex estate planning you've done, I need to

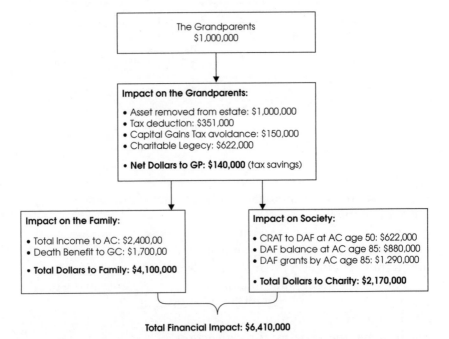

Figure 14.5   **The Seed from the Grandparents Grows into Meaningful Benefits for Family and Charity**

tell you something. Your grandchildren will not talk to their children about how effective your estate planning was. *You will never be remembered for the taxes that you saved—even though your family may have benefited from it.*

But I can tell you this with certainty, because I live it personally and I see it with the families of my clients every year. Long after you are gone, when your grandchildren sit with their children to discuss who will receive that year's grants from the charitable legacy you created in your family name, they'll know who you were, they'll know what you stood for.

They will remember you.

CHAPTER

15

A Grandparents' Legacy War Story and Comparison

Grandchildren: the only people who can get more out of you than the IRS.

—Gene Perret

The best way to feel the impact of a charitably leveraged grandparents' legacy strategy is to view an actual war story with real people and real numbers. You find that the story that follows mirrors the four-step process you read about in the previous chapter. Enjoy the story of the Italian kid with a high school education who made good—maybe too good.

The Battle Over the Dry Cleaner's Legacy

Back story:

Peter Curto is 72 years old. He and his wife, Mary, had just sold their dry cleaning business in Paterson, New Jersey about four years ago and were preparing to move to Florida, when Mary was diagnosed with cancer. She passed away a year later. Pete put off the move to Florida temporarily to stay close to family while he regrouped.

Pete and Mary worked long and hard over the years and built a nice estate primarily through real estate investment in strip malls like the one where their business was located. They also amassed a substantial stock portfolio. Following the settlement of Mary's estate, Pete was left with a current taxable estate of $5,000,000. As he says, "Not bad for Italian kid with a high school education!"

Part of the $5,000,000 estate is one particular stock (ABC Corp), which Pete inherited 20 years ago when his uncle Vito died. At that time the stock was valued at $200,000. It is now worth just north of $1,000,000. Vito was a pretty savvy guy, and everyone agreed, a very good dresser. He was handsome and a lifelong bachelor. Nobody asked why, and if anybody knew anything, nobody talked about it. Anyway, Pete inherited the stock and thought that one day he'd pass it along to his daughter. ABC Corp pays a 1 percent dividend so the income it spins off each year has no impact on Pete's lifestyle.

It's been three years now since Mary passed, and Pete, being of good Italian stock (and according to my wife is like most men—he can't live alone—except of course for Uncle Vito) has met someone. So, the plan is that the move to Florida is back on with a new Mrs. Curto. Before Pete makes the move south, he wants to wrap up any loose ends of his estate plan. In a nutshell, he wants to make sure that his entire estate is transferred to his (and Mary's) only child, their daughter, Gracie (age 40), and his grandchildren Steven (age 13) and Sophia (age 11).

Gracie has been divorced for five years and was working in the family business until it was sold. Now, with college diploma in hand and a Master's in Social Work, Gracie intends to pursue her passion. She has landed a low-paying, but fulfilling, job with Catholic Charities in Paterson. She'll tell you that for the first time in a long time, she's really happy. Her dad, on the other hand, worries about her future and wants to make sure that she and her children are financially protected.

The last piece of information in this story is that Pete had always been a benefactor of many charitable causes for all the years he was in business. He intends to continue to do so in retirement. He would like to do something more meaningful in his estate plan—he just doesn't know what. He wants to find a way to honor Mary and is thinking of tying it into the hospice program that took such good care of her, him, and Gracie during her last days. In addition, he is proud of the fact that he grew up with nothing and built a great business and reputation in Paterson. He would like to see the family name continue to grow in prominence in the community. It was never just about money with him, it was what he could do with it. He wants his grandchildren to grow up knowing the responsibility they have to their family and their community.

Pete wants to get on with living his life and needs to wrap up his plans in Jersey before he moves on. He has noble thoughts about charity, but for him it's family first. All he wants to do is keep the assets he and Mary worked so hard to build, in the family. His estate plan does leave everything to Gracie and the grandkids, but he thought he could do something clever with the ABC stock. He didn't know that the government had other plans.

The Stats on the Curto Family

Grandparent	Peter Curto (age 72)
Adult Child	Gracie Curto (divorced) (age 40)
Grandchildren	Steven (age 13); Sophia (age 11)
Pete's Gross Estate	$5,000,000
Target Asset	$1,000,000 of ABC Corp. Stock ($200,000 basis)
Pete's Tax Bracket	40 percent
Capital Gain Tax Rate	20 percent
Estate Tax Rate	45 percent after $3,500,000 exclusion per person based on 2009 unified credits

Other Assumptions Used in this Example

- Investment return at 6 percent net after expenses
- Insurance return at 6 percent net after expenses *but* before cost of insurance
- CRAT investment return at 5 percent
- AFR used for CRAT at 4 percent
- DAF return at 6 percent
- DAF grants at 5 percent

- Growth in DAF at 1 percent
- Life expectancy to age 85

A Pain in the . . .

Pete looks at a couple of options focusing on the transfer of Vito's stock to Gracie. Both give him a stomach ache.

- If he dies with the stock: Pete's estate is $5,000,000. Using his full $3,500,000 free pass on the federal estate tax, his estate tax bracket at death would be 45 percent. If Pete transfers the stock at death, it would lose $450,000 (45 percent). Gracie would only receive $550,000.
- If he sells the stock: He would have to pay tax on the gain of $800,000. The sale would cost Pete $160,000. The remaining amount to invest would be $840,000. If Pete dies from the shock of the capital gains tax, the $840,000 balance would be included in his estate and subject to another 45 percent tax. He'd lose another $378,000! The government would take more ($538,000) than his daughter would receive ($462,000).
- If Pete gifts the stock to Gracie: The gift of $1,000,000 reduces Pete's estate tax exclusion from $3,500,000 to $2,500,000 exposing another million dollars of Pete's estate to the 45 percent tax. Therefore, when Pete dies, the estate taxes cost will be $450,000. In addition, the stocks carry Pete's basis of $200,000 when gifted. When Gracie sells the stock for income, she'll be the one to pay the capital gains tax of $160,000.

Any of three options above make Peter Curto a victim of the War on Wealth and the people he loves most, Gracie, Steven, and Sophia, collateral damage. Death and taxes, or taxes, death, and more taxes. It's not much of a choice. (See Figure 15.1.)

Actions and Impact

Sometimes it takes a wakeup call like the one in Figure 15.1 or the one the United States of America is getting right now, for us to get in touch with our charitable side. Pete got in touch with his and here's what he did.

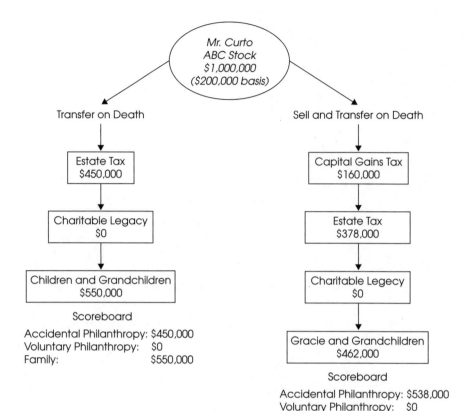

Figure 15.1   Death and Taxes, Taxes, Death, and More Taxes

1. Action: He transferred the ABC stock to his 10-year term CRAT with an 8 percent annuity rate. Pete selected a Donor Advised Fund under a public foundation to act as the charitable beneficiary.
   - Impact: He removed the asset from his estate (no more estate tax).
   - Impact: He protected the asset from the claims of creditors.
   - Impact: He locked in a self-completing element of his plan should he die or become disabled.
2. Action: Pete's transfer of $1,000,000 of appreciated stock to the CRAT generated a $351,000 income tax deduction.
   - Impact: The tax savings from a $351,000 income tax deduction in Pete's 40 percent income tax bracket is $140,400.

3. Action: Acting as his own trustee, Pete sold the ABC stock inside the CRAT.
   - Impact: The sale avoids the tax on the capital gain of $800,000.
   - Impact: Saving $160,000 of potential loss to accidental philanthropy.
   - After the sale, the CRAT has the full $1,000,000 to invest as opposed to $840,000 he would have if he sold it outside the trust.
4. Action: The CRAT distributed $80,000 per year to Pete for the next 10 years. If he dies during that time he names Gracie and the next income recipient.
   - Impact: Under four-tier tax accounting, Pete will pay tax on the distribution at the capital gains tax rate of 20 percent. His net income each year is $64,000.
5. Action: Pete uses the annual cash flow from the CRAT to fund Gracie's retirement plan. He knows that she's following her passion but unfortunately her passion doesn't pay very well. This gives Pete the ability to re-route an asset that was going to get destroyed by taxes and use it to give his daughter a stable income in retirement.
   - Impact: Pete purchases a wealth accumulation–style insurance policy exactly like the one in the grandparents' legacy example (in fact, it is the same one).
   - Impact: Gracie is the insured. The initial death benefit of the policy is $2,000,000 plus any accumulations of cash.
   - Impact: Pete is the owner and premium payer. He uses the after-tax cash flow of $64,000 for the payment. The grandchildren are the beneficiaries (in trust).
   - Impact: As the owner, Pete has control over the policy until he transfers it to Gracie. Gracie is the contingent owner. He likes this arrangement for a number of reasons:
     - If Gracie should remarry—a distinct possibility, Pete can keep this property outside of Gracie's control. "You never know if she's going to make another mistake," says Pete. Who am I to argue?
     - If things go really bad, he doesn't have to give Gracie anything. Not likely, but like the man said, "you never know . . ."
     - If Pete wants to use some of the cash for Steve and Sophia's college, he can do it.

- The most likely of all scenarios is that he will transfer the ownership to Gracie in a few years, and she will use it to supplement her retirement income.

6. Action: At the end of the 10th year, Pete will be 82, Gracie turns 50 and the CRAT turns into The Curto Family Donor Advised Fund, honoring the memory of Mary Curto. The value of the fund on the date of transfer, based upon our assumptions is $622,660.

   - Impact: The Advisory Board of the Curto Family Fund is Pete, Gracie, Steve, and Sophia. The primary mission of the fund is the support of hospice care and cancer research in Mary Curto's name. But the board has the latitude to support any other deserving organization.
   - Impact: The Curto Family Fund will distribute 5 percent of its net asset value each year. For example, it will distribute $31,133 in the first year. By the time Gracie is the age her dad was when he set up the plan, the value of the fund will be $767,000 and they would have given grants totaling another $761,000.
   - Impact: At some point Steven and Sophia may wish to add their children to advisory board. And even though they never met their great-grandfather or great-grandmother, they'll know who they were and what they stood for.

7. Action: Probably long after Peter is gone, Gracie will begin to draw from the insurance policy that she now owns to provide herself with tax-free retirement income.

   - Impact: She starts her income at age 65 to the tune of $120,446 tax-free annually.
   - Impact: Her income runs for a period of 20 years—to age 85. Her total income is $2,408,920.

8. Action: Upon Gracie's death at the end of age 85, the remaining insurance proceeds are paid to Steven and Sophia, now age 58 and 56 respectively.

   - Impact: They will share $1,742,000 or $871,000 each—tax-free.
   - Impact: They will also oversee the Curto Family Fund, which is now valued $882,000 and generated an additional $1,297,000 in grants in their grandmother's and grandfather's name.

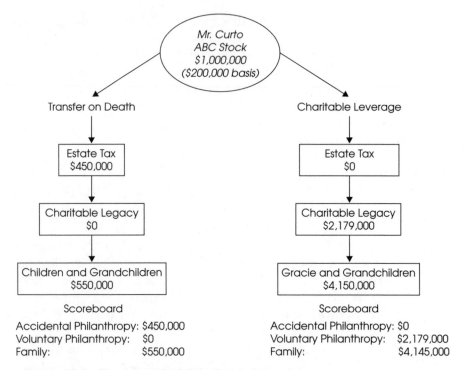

Figure 15.2   The Impact of Charitable Leverage

What did Peter Curto accomplish through charitable leverage? He took an asset of $1,000,000 that was going to lose about half its value or more to the war on wealth, and he chose instead to give it to charity—on his terms. Charitable leverage generated a tax savings to him of $140,400, tax-free family financial benefits of $4,150,000 (income to his daughter of $2,408,000, another $1,742,000 cash to his grandchildren), and more than $2,179,000 to charity. You know what Mr. C., that's *not bad for Italian kid with a high school education!*

For a graphical representation of the impact, see Figure 15.2.

"But What if I Don't Put My Money in a Charitably Leveraged Plan?"

That's a good question that invites a comparison. What would happen if Pete did sell the $1,000,000 of ABC stock, bit the bullet on the capital gains, and invested the proceeds for Gracie's retirement? What if we ran an "apples to apples" comparison of the charitably leveraged strategy with the best arrangement we could make for Gracie and her children over the same 45-year timeline? That's a long time to make up the $160,000 capital gains tax loss. Coupled with the fact that an alternative method would not include any money going to charity, it would have beat charitable leverage, right? Accidental philanthropists unite; it may not be such a bad deal after all. You tell me.

More Ground Rules and More Assumptions

The only ground rule for this comparison is this, what's good for the goose is good for the gander. In other words, whatever rules we apply to one investment technique, we must also apply to the others. For example, an investment return of 6 percent net of fees and costs will be used for *all* of the investment projections except as I already noted (CRAT at 5 percent and insurance policy at 6 percent before the cost of insurance). I know this skews the numbers in favor of the alternative investment, but honestly, do you think I'd do this if I didn't know how it would come out?

I will refer to the new investment for Gracie as the "Retirement Account." I'll assume that an investment like that will be tax-deferred until the money is withdrawn at her retirement. That way I can justify using a 6 percent overall net investment return. A variable annuity would be a good example of an investment for the retirement account. Further, I will assume her tax bracket will be at the 40 percent rate (39.6 percent rounded up for the calculations). I can justify that rate because that's the bracket the retirement income distribution will push her into. Lastly, to make the comparison easier to follow, I'll break it into the same time periods as the charitably leveraged plan.

Gracie at Age 40. Pete Funds the Investment

Easy enough, Pete is going to sell the stock, pay the capital gains tax and buy a tax deferred variable annuity with the proceeds. Enjoy the flow chart in Figure 15.3, this is about as easy as they get.

The Investment Grows on the Road to Retirement

At 6 percent compounding annually, the tax-deferred investment grows nicely on the way to Gracie's retirement. In 10 years (age 50) the investment is worth more than $1,504, 000. By age 65 the account is worth more than $3,605,000! (See Figure 15.4.) That's the power of compound interest.

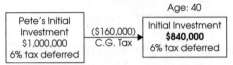

Figure 15.3   **Pete Funds the Investment for His Daughter**

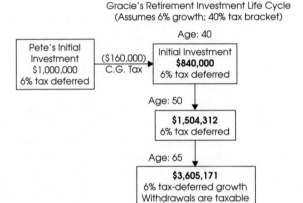

Figure 15.4   **Growth on the Way to Retirement**

I know this comparison is about numbers, but you need to know that if Steven or Sophia needed any money for college, a withdrawal from the retirement account would cost Gracie ordinary income tax plus a 10 percent government penalty for early withdrawal prior to age 59½. Just thought I'd throw that in.

Retirement!

When Gracie reaches age 65, she begins to withdraw money from her account. Her goal is to use the account to generate $120,446 per year after taxes for 20 years ($2,408,920 total). Since the account is tax-deferred on a LIFO basis, she will need to withdraw enough money each year to pay the income tax due in a 40 percent tax bracket. Until she starts hitting her original basis of $840,000, she will need to withdraw $200,743 to net $120,446 after tax. Gracie will lose $80,297 of her earnings to tax each year. Once that money leaves her account, Uncle Sam takes over

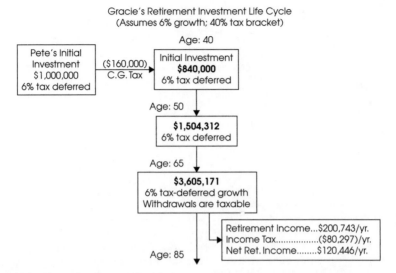

Figure 15.5   Annual Retirement Income with a Little Accidental Philanthropy on the Side

and she loses all control over how it is spent, but I guess you already knew that. (See Figure 15.5.)

Cumulative Retirement Income

By the time Gracie reaches age 85, her retirement account has generated $2,408,920 total net retirement income, and she still has about $3,734 743 remaining in her account. Unfortunately, she had to withdraw $4,014,866 to achieve that net income. She had to pay an extra $1,605,946 in taxes. That's a lot of accidental philanthropy, but that's just my opinion. (See Figure 15.6.)

Account Transfer to Gracie's Children

The retirement account is transferred to Steven and Sophia at Gracie's death. As if the tax payments of more than $1,600,000 weren't enough, the WMD used in the War on Wealth are deployed once again. The retirement plan balance of $3,734,743 is subject to both income tax and federal estate tax. If we assume that the retirement account is the only asset in Gracie's estate then her estate tax would be $105,634 (using up her $3,500,000 transfer exemption). This, of course, is a ridiculous assumption since we already know

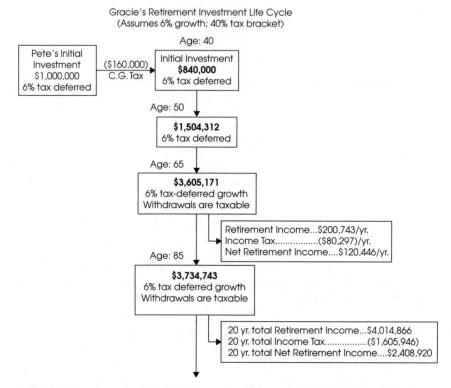

Gracie's Retirement Investment Life Cycle
(Assumes 6% growth; 40% tax bracket)

Age: 40

| Pete's Initial Investment $1,000,000 6% tax deferred | ($160,000) C.G. Tax | Initial Investment **$840,000** 6% tax deferred |

Age: 50

$1,504,312
6% tax deferred

Age: 65

$3,605,171
6% tax-deferred growth
Withdrawals are taxable

Retirement Income...$200,743/yr.
Income Tax.................($80,297)/yr.
Net Retirement Income....$120,446/yr.

Age: 85

$3,734,743
6% tax deferred growth
Withdrawals are taxable

20 yr. total Retirement Income...$4,014,866
20 yr. total Income Tax.................($1,605,946)
20 yr. total Net Retirement Income....$2,408,920

Figure 15.6   Cumulative Retirement Income with a lot of Accidental Philanthropy on the Side

that her father's estate was $5,000,000 and she was the sole heir. But, what the hell, let's go with it.

The income tax is far worse. Except for her original basis of $840,000, the entire tax-deferred retirement account is subject to income tax in Gracie's 40 percent bracket. The bill is a whopping $1,157,897 of fresh new taxes. The total tax bill at estate settlement is $1,263,531. The net transfer to Pete's grandchildren is $2,471,212 ($3,734,743 less $1,263,531). (See Figure 15.7.)

Measuring the Impact

In order to measure the impact, let's look at Table 15.1. Peter Curto started out with $1,000,000 that he wanted to invest for his daughter's retirement and his grandchildren's future inheritance.

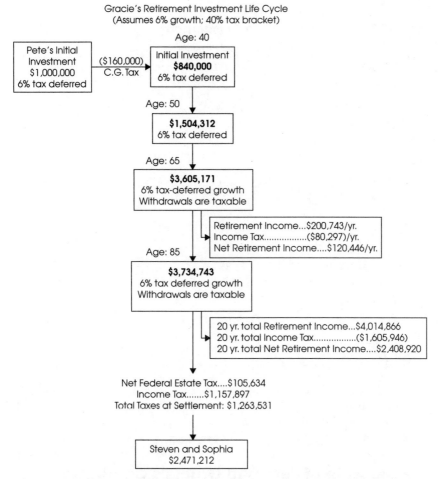

Gracie's Retirement Investment Life Cycle
(Assumes 6% growth; 40% tax bracket)

Age: 40

Pete's Initial Investment
$1,000,000
6% tax deferred

($160,000)
C.G. Tax

Initial Investment
$840,000
6% tax deferred

Age: 50

$1,504,312
6% tax deferred

Age: 65

$3,605,171
6% tax-deferred growth
Withdrawals are taxable

Retirement Income...$200,743/yr.
Income Tax.................($80,297)/yr.
Net Retirement Income....$120,446/yr.

Age: 85

$3,734,743
6% tax deferred growth
Withdrawals are taxable

20 yr. total Retirement Income...$4,014,866
20 yr. total Income Tax................($1,605,946)
20 yr. total Net Retirement Income....$2,408,920

Net Federal Estate Tax....$105,634
Income Tax.......$1,157,897
Total Taxes at Settlement: $1,263,531

Steven and Sophia
$2,471,212

Figure 15.7   The Distribution to the Grandchildren and More Taxes

This former dry cleaner from Paterson, New Jersey, was then subjected to a vicious battle for control over the distribution of his wealth. When smoke cleared from the battlefield here's what happened:

- He generated $2,408,920 to his daughter.
- His grandchildren inherited another $2,471,212 at her death.
- The total financial benefit to his family was $4,880,132.

Table 15.1   The First Part of the Comparison

	Traditional Planning	Charitable Leverage
(1) Starting Amount	$1,000,000	
(2) Capital Gains Tax	($160,000)	
(3) Net to Daughter's Retirement Acct	$840,000	
(4) Tax Deduction	$0	
(5) Tax Savings	$0	
(6) Total Retirement Income to Daughter	$2,408,920	
(7) Net to Grandchildren at Daughter's death	$2,471,212	
(8) Total Combined Family Wealth	$4,880,132	
(9) Total to Charity	$0	
(10) Total to Taxes	($3,029,477)	
(11) Combined Wealth to Family and Charity	$4,880,132	

- He didn't leave a penny to charity, hence there was no legacy.
- But he did manage to pay $3,029,477 in taxes.

The Lifecycle of Pete and Gracie's Charitably Leveraged Plan

Even after paying more the $3,000,000 in taxes over the lifecycle of this investment, Pete still did pretty well by his daughter and grandchildren. He never did get to that charitable gift *he intended* to create to honor Mary though. I guess that dream was just another casualty in the War on Wealth. And that's the rub isn't it? In effect, congress has said, "That's okay Pete, we can better direct your money than you could anyway. We'll see to it that *right* people and organizations that we choose, will get it." I guess the government feels that while Pete was smart enough to build a nice business and amass a large estate, he came up a little short in the distribution department. But then again, Pete was willing to become an accidental philanthropist to achieve the goals he had in mind for his daughter and grandchildren.

Hey Pete, it's your money and you can give when you want to. Let's see how the charitably leveraged approach compares. First, we know that there are more pieces to this approach then there are with the traditional plan. Where the previous example used one Retirement Account, the charitably leveraged strategy uses three. That shouldn't be much of a roadblock, since the three accounts may be coordinated and managed under one roof. More importantly, the impact on the Pete, Gracie, Steven, and Sophia *and his charities* may just be worth it.

Gracie at Age 40. Pete Funds the CRAT

I don't know, have you seen this process enough? I never get tired of it. Pete transfers the $1,000,000 of ABC stock (with the $200,000 basis) to his 10-year CRAT with an 8 percent annuity rate. Pete selects a Donor Advised Fund under a public foundation to act as the charitable beneficiary. The funding of the CRAT triggers two events: (a) it generates a current income tax deduction for the present value of the future gift to charity, and (b) it provides a stream of annuity income each year for the next 10 years. Right off the bat the trust has use of the full $1,000,000 instead of the $840,000 shown in the traditional approach. The tax deduction (based upon the average AFR of 4 percent) will be approximately $351,000. In Pete's tax bracket of 40 percent, the tax savings from the deduction is $140,450. In addition, the fixed dollar annuity payment from the CRAT will be $80,000 each year for the next 10 years. The cash flow from the CRAT is taxed under the favorable "four-tier accounting" rules. The tax due on the annuity each year would be $16,000 (20 percent capital gains rate). The net cash flow to invest in Gracie's retirement plan is $64,000. (See Figure 15.8.)

- Tax savings: The tax deduction is a big deal and it plays an important role in our comparison. We can't ignore the fact that the tax savings represents real money that can be invested, so following my "what's good for goose..." doctrine, *Pete will invest the tax savings into the exact same investment as the retirement account used in the traditional plan (i.e., a variable tax-deferred annuity earning 6 percent net after expenses).*

Figure 15.8   Pete Funds the CRAT

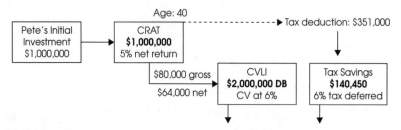

Figure 15.9   The CRAT Creates the Leverage That Funds Everything Else

- Cash flow: The CRAT cash flow will fund a wealth accumulation–style Cash Value Life Insurance policy (CVLI) exactly like the one we've been talking about for what seems like forever. Again, keeping everything on a level playing field, I have used the same 6 percent net return on the policy before deductions for the mortality costs. (See Figure 15.9.)

The CRAT Does Its Thing on the Way to Gracie's Retirement

Ten years into the plan (Gracie age 50), the CRAT has completed its role as charitable lever and will be distributed to the Curto Family Donor Advised Fund. Pete (for the remainder of his life), Gracie, and the grandchildren will serve on the advisory board. Assuming a 5 percent net return, the value remaining in the CRAT stands at $622,660. As the CRAT passes to the DAF, it sets the stage for a lifetime of philanthropy and the defeat of accidental philanthropy.

Second, the CVLI funding is now complete. The cash value is about $755,848 and will continue to grow toward the retirement date without tax. The tax-free insurance benefit is up to $2,755,848 (face amount of $2,000,000 plus accumulated cash) providing

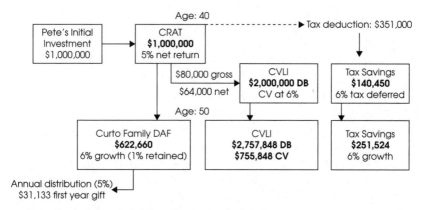

Figure 15.10   The CRAT Acts as the Charitable Lever

a serious amount of financial security for Pete's grandchildren. Unlike the traditional plan, if cash is needed for college or any other expense prior to Gracie's age 59½, she (or Pete if he still owns it) can withdraw it from the CVLI without the tax or 10 percent government penalty.

Third, the tax savings continue to motor along at an invested rate of 6 percent. By the 10th year the account is up to $251,524. (See Figure 15.10.)

Retirement!

By the time Gracie reaches age 65 the accumulation phase is complete. Her CVLI policy is worth almost $1,700,000 with a death benefit of $3,695,436. The tax savings that were placed in a tax-deferred investment account have grown to $602,793. She will not need this account to achieve her income goal, so it will continue to grow (or it could be used for other cash needs). If she got some good advice, she would be told to transfer the account out of her estate. But we're not going to go there now.

The CRAT was replaced by the DAF 10 years earlier. It has become an impressive method for perpetuating the Curto family charitable legacy. The DAF will distribute 5 percent of its net investment assets each year to the charitable causes it supports. Continuing with the 6 percent net investment return, the DAF will have distributed about $31,000 in the first year and retain about 1 percent. Each year as the DAF fund grows, its annual distributions will increase. As Gracie reaches retirement age, the DAF has grown to $722,888. In addition, the fund will have already distributed more than $500,000.

Now it's time to start the retirement income phase. The CVLI is in place to provide Gracie with her income goal of $120,446 per year, after taxes, starting at age 65 and continuing for 20 years ($2,408,920 total). The major difference between this approach and the traditional one is that the cash flow from the CVLI is considered an insurance policy loan and not subject to income tax. Insurance loans do not require repayment. If it remains unpaid, the loan amount is deducted from the death benefit. *The death benefit throughout this study assumes that the loan is outstanding at the time of death and repaid by the insurance proceeds.* The CVLI used in this example is one that employs a lapse-prevention feature, insuring that the tax-free cash flow remains that way. Each year the scoreboard looks the same: Pete's daughter, $120,446; Uncle Sam, $0. If she dies during the income phase, her children would receive the remaining balance of the cash value account plus the insurance benefit, income tax-free. Since the CVLI is all that is needed to provide income to Gracie, the Tax Savings Account can remain invested for growth. (See Figure 15.11.)

Cumulative Retirement Income

As the retirement years come to a close, Gracie is now age 85 (she doesn't know that I'm going to kill her off at the end of this year). Her insurance policy has provided $2,408,920 of income without incurring any taxes. The balance of the cash value account is now about $670,000. However, the tax savings account, which has been compounding nicely at the 6 percent illustrative rate for the last 45 years, is now worth a tidy sum of $2,049,234!

The Curto Donor Advised Fund, with the grandchildren at the helm, has grown to $882,061. In the names of Peter and Mary, the DAF has distributed $1,297,009 in gifts, scholarships, and grants to the exact causes they cherished. (See Figure 15.12.)

Account Transfer to Gracie's Children

Gracie's dead. Frankly, I was getting tired of this whole crew. Kidding, I'm kidding. As I stated earlier, the transfer phase assumes

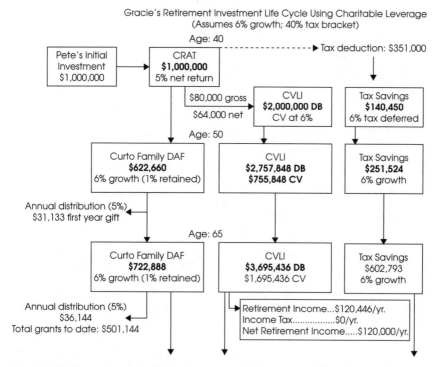

Gracie's Retirement Investment Life Cycle Using Charitable Leverage
(Assumes 6% growth; 40% tax bracket)

Figure 15.11 **Gracie Enjoys a Tax-Free Retirement while Continuing Her Family's Charitable Legacy**

that Gracie dies at the end of age 85. The combined charitable legacy started by her father is now $2,179,070. The Curto family's philanthropic mission continues with Pete's grandchildren, Steven, and Sophia, and possibly *their children* advising the DAF.

Looking next to the Tax Savings Account, its value by age 85 is $2,049,234. This is important: In reality Pete would have created a trust for the grandchildren and funded it with the tax savings of $140,450 way back when. There would have been no gift tax, no generation-skipping tax, and Gracie could have been the income beneficiary of the trust. If he had done that, the entire $2,049,234 would not be transferred at Gracie's death incurring any tax at all. Unfortunately for all of us, and in keeping with the goose-gander thing, we will treat the transfer of that account the same as the traditional tax-deferred account. As much as it sickens me to say it, the tax savings account less its basis would be subject to ordinary income tax upon estate distribution. Assuming a

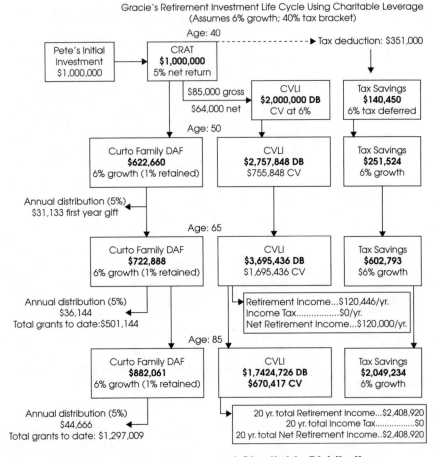

Figure 15.12   Cumulative Income and Charitable Distributions

40 percent bracket and only a $140,450 basis, the tax due would be $763,513. The net amount transferred to the grandchildren would be $1,285,720. I know every war has its casualties, but this one could have been avoided.

The insurance pays the remaining death benefit of $1,724,664, to the Steve and Sophia free of income tax. Combined with the after-tax proceeds of the Tax Savings Account, the total wealth transferred to Pete's grandchildren would be $3,010,384. The transferred amount falls below the $3,500,000 threshold for estate tax. Avoidable income tax notwithstanding, I think the Curto clan came out pretty good. (See Figure 15.13.)

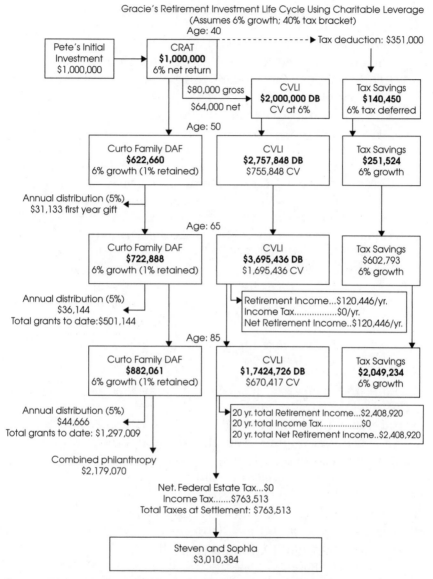

Figure 15.13 The Full Impact of Charitable Leverage at Estate Settlement

Measuring the Impact

I love the smell of charitable leverage in the morning, it smells like victory. Was the choice to avoid accidental philanthropy a good one for Pete? You tell me.

- He generated $2,408,920 to his daughter. That's the same as the traditional plan.
- His grandchildren inherited another $3,010,384 at her death, compared to $2,471, 212 in the traditional plan.
- The total financial benefit to his family was $5,419,304 as compared to $4,880,132. That's an increase of $539,172. We could stop there because charitable leverage provided more to Pete's family. But that would leave some men on the battlefield.
- He created a philanthropic legacy of $2,179,070 fulfilling his charitable intentions. He didn't leave a penny to charity in the traditional plan, and there was no legacy.
- He reduced his taxes to $923,513, which includes all of the taxes he paid on the CRAT distributions ($160,000) and a needless additional $763,513 at estate settlement, just to play fair. That's still more than $2,100,000 less than the $3,029,477 in taxes he paid in the traditional plan. In reality he would have dropped his tax cost to $160,000.
- The combined impact of charitable leverage to family and charity is $7,598,374 as opposed to $3,029,477 they would have received in the traditional plan.

Table 15.2 compares the results of the two paths.

In this comparative analysis, the choice of charitable leverage over accidental philanthropy is compelling. I don't know if it will work for you, but wouldn't you like to know? Everyone's situation is different and your assumptions may be more aggressive. But the unmistakable truth is that you cannot control something you do not possess. Once the taxes are paid, they're gone and out of your control. If you let the government tax your success, they will. If you let them redistribute your hard work to causes you don't care about or entitlement programs you do not respect, they will.

The war on wealth is real, and it is here. If you are in the class of Americans who have been targeted by this administration (and it is a hell of a lot larger than the top 5 percent of taxpayers) you *will* lose money and the *power* of what it can do. That charitable nature of Americans like you, me, and Pete is part of this country's soul. But as the government gets bigger and grabs more power convincing more people that they need big brother to survive, your power will be diminished. The impact of the War on Wealth

Table 15.2 Which Path Would you Choose?

	Traditional Planning	Charitable Leverage
(1) Starting Amount	$1,000,000	$1,000,000
(2) Capital Gains Tax	($160,000)	$0
(3) Net to Daughter's Retirement Acct	$840,000	$1,000,000
(4) Tax Deduction	$0	$351,128
(5) Tax Savings	$0	$140,450
(6) Total Retirement Income to Daughter	$2,408,920	$2,408,920
(7) Net to Grandchildren at Daughter's death	$2,471,212	$3,010,384
(8) Total Combined Family Wealth	$4,880,132	$5,419,304
(9) Total to Charity	$0	$2,179,070
(10) Total to Taxes	($3,029,477)	($923,513)
(11) Combined Wealth to Family and Charity	$4,880,132	$7,598,374

will be felt more acutely by grandparents than any other group. We're the ones who have the bulk of the assets, we're the ones who aren't awash in debt, we're the ones with the most wealth in retirement plans, and we're the ones who still have gains left in our portfolios. We are easy pickings for a government in desperate need of cash. When you accept accidental philanthropy you lose the chance to direct your wealth, and tell your story to the next generation and the ones that follow. Your life has been well lived, shouldn't your legacy be well planned?

16

How Businesses Can Use Charitable Leverage to Attract and Retain Key Employees

We make a living by what we get, but we make a life by what we give.

—Winston Churchill

Businesses of all kinds can play in the charitable leverage game. Mom and Pops, partnerships, LLCs, Regular or C Corporations, Subchapter S Corporations, closely held family corporations, Professional Corporations and Associations, and even public companies (though we're not going to discuss them here) can participate as warriors in the War against Wealth. And why not, is there any group more disparaged than business owners?

- Personal tax rates are scheduled to climb to 36 percent and 39.6 percent, which affects the sole proprietor, partnership, Subchapter S Corporation, and LLC choosing an S or partnership tax status.

- Our corporate tax rates are the highest in the world. If a C corporation retains more than $75,000 of earnings, it is in a 34 percent tax bracket. More than $100,000 and it slides into a 39 percent bracket.
- Professional corporations like physician practices are in a flat 35 percent bracket.

If this does not represent a tax on success, I don't know what does. For the record, unfair business taxation did not start with the Obama Administration; it has been around through Democratic and Republican presidencies and congressional control by both parties. So we either complain about it or do something about it. I just did all that I'm going to do about the first, and I'm going to spend the balance of this chapter focusing on the second.

Relief from the Tax on Success

There have been volumes written about the tools and techniques available to business owners for providing benefits to key employees. They range from the creative to the very creative—and sometimes suspect. The problem stems from a simple rule from our friends at the IRS, which I will paraphrase: "My dear corporation, if you would like to deduct the cost of providing a retirement benefit to your employees, you better make damn well sure that you include *all* full-time employees." You can bundle them in groups, but you must include them all.

The challenge that faces business owners of all sizes is that sometimes the routine retirement plan is just not enough for the best and brightest stars of the company. Sometimes those best and brightest are our own children. As business owners we constantly struggle to find ways to attract and retain talent. If possible, we'd like to attach strings. We want to put a plan in place that will reward a key person for staying with the company, but we also want that plan, or at least a part of it, forfeited if that key person leaves. We want the key employee to think twice about the benefit left on table should he or she walk.

When you combine the challenge of the last paragraph with the love note from the IRS, as a business owner, you are screwed. The only choice you have to create a special supplemental retirement benefit or deferred income benefit to *selected key employees* is to fund that benefit with after-tax dollars.

In some cases the company may choose to make the *promise* to the key employee to pay a special supplemental retirement benefit and *not fund it at all.* That's known as nonqualified deferred compensation. The key executive becomes nothing more than an unsecured creditor of the corporation. In the wake of the collapse of the economy that took a bunch of businesses with it, let's just say these plans don't carry the weight that they used to.

So, let's go back to the after-tax funding challenges of the business owner.

- If a C corporation funds the plan, it is subject to a 34 percent to 39 percent tax.
- If a sole proprietor, partnership, Subchapter S Corporation, or LLC funds the plan, the shareholders pay tax on someone else's benefit at the rate of 35 percent to 39.6 percent.
- If a professional corporation funds the plan, the tax is a flat 35 percent.

You know where I'm heading with this, but before you get there ahead of me, I want to add a strong word of caution. Obviously, I am about to make a case for charitable leverage, I'll bet the chapter heading gave you a hint, but please pay attention. Charitable leverage brings with it certain tax benefits, which we are about to discuss. *A charitably leveraged plan, however, should not be used simply for its tax benefits.* There are so many twists and turns in the tax code, that if a business owner or shareholder is solely motivated by tax incentives, their tax advisors might better serve them by looking elsewhere for relief. The philanthropic rewards of the charitably leveraged plan outweigh the tax benefits. Having said that, if the package including the tax benefits inspires your company to considerer philanthropy, I don't think anyone would complain.

What's in a Name?

First, let's agree on what we call this benefit. It is a deferred income benefit. It's been called deferred compensation, or supplemental retirement income, or supplemental deferred income. I'm calling it "Deferred Income," because I'm the one writing about it and I get to name it. When you write your book, you can call it whatever you want.

Second, the deferred income plan is offered to selected people who are viewed as key players in your organization. They have been called Key Employees, Key Executives, and Key Persons (for the more politically correct). I think "employee" is too cold and I will never be accused of being politically correct, so I'm going with "Key Executive." The Key Executive can be any type of key person, no jacket, tie, or skirt is required. Any winning coach at a university is a Key Executive.

Finally, the Key Executive's Deferred Income Plan must be offered by some employer. The employer runs the gamut of business ownership. I, being of simple mind, will just stick with "Employer." As I go through the examples I break down the tax benefits to the different business forms. There you have it, Employer Sponsored Key Executive Deferred Income Plan. Wait, I forgot the best part. It will be called a *Charitably Leveraged* Employer Sponsored Key Executive Deferred Income Plan. Man, that's a long name. How about we agree that from this point forward I just refer to it as "The Plan" and you'll know what I mean.

A Charitably Leveraged Employer Sponsored Key Employee Deferred Income Plan (The Plan) is the meshing of fiscal responsibility and responsible philanthropy. It is fiscally responsible because it offers businesses of all sizes a way of providing this important benefit to the best and brightest with less overall costs. It exercises responsible philanthropy through direct gifts or a private foundation created by the company. The part I like the best is that we get to use the same one-chassis system that you've come to know and love. Once again the only thing that changes is the players.

Two Types of Employer-Sponsored Plans

The Plan can be used in one of two traditional key executive benefit models:

1. A nonqualified deferred compensation plan
2. An executive bonus plan

I just want to cover the basic differences between the two models; otherwise we get bogged down in minutia.

Nonqualified Deferred Compensation Plan

A deferred compensation plan is a promise by the employer to pay a deferred income benefit to the executive at some future point in time—usually at retirement. The executive receives no current taxable compensation because he hasn't gotten anything. All he or she has is an unsecured promise by the company. If the company goes belly-up, the executive is on the outside looking in, and that ain't looking good. When the executive retires, the company pays the deferred payments. At that point, the income is taxable to the executive and tax deductible as compensation by the company. Usually companies "informally fund" deferred compensation agreements by purchasing life insurance on the executive. The company is the owner and beneficiary of the policy. The death benefit is used to recover the costs of the payments at the executive's death. Cases where the executive elects to defer his or her own compensation for future payment falls under the scope of IRC§409A and way way way outside the bounds of this book. In short, deferred compensations plans are very sophisticated and require specialized attention.

Executive Bonus Plan

The executive bonus plan, also called a Section 162 plan, allows for the purchase of life insurance on the life of a select employee with premiums paid by the employer. The employer includes the premium payment in the taxable wages of the employee. The employee is the owner of the policy, names the beneficiary, and has all the rights to the policy cash values. The employer has no rights in the policy's cash values or death benefit. With the executive bonus plan, the employer will take an income tax deduction under IRC§162 for the amount of the bonus, which is usually equal to the premium. The employer can pay the premium directly to an insurance company, to the employee, or to the employee's trust. In some cases the company can "gross up" the bonus to cover the executive's tax obligation.

Same Chassis—Different Players

With the elementary descriptions of the two types of executive benefit plans out of the way, let's look at how we can add charitable leverage. In a nutshell, the funding of either plan is exactly the same, as are benefits the company receives from using a CRAT. The differences occur over how the cash flow from the CRAT is used. Let's bring back an old favorite, "the players guide," to differentiate between the two models. The letters

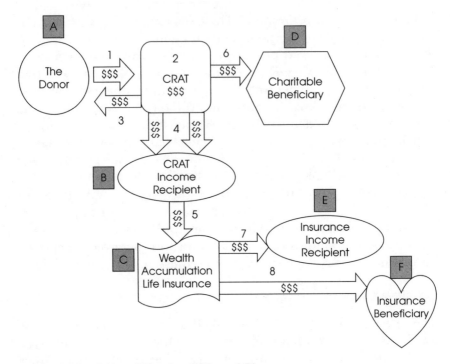

Figure 16.1   Same Chassis—Different Players

A through F in Figure 16.1 align with the letters on the breakdown that follows.

A. The Donor

The donor of the charitable leverage plan is always the employer. This would seem fairly obvious since this is an employer sponsored plan. The employer can be any of the forms of business ownership; there no restrictions. Look at what happens when we get the employer involved.

- The Employer/Donor funds the CRAT.
- The CRAT is the good ole 10-year term, 8 percent annuity model. The tax code specifically allows a company to fund a charitable remainder trust as long as it is a "term of years" variety. We have that base covered with the 10-year CRAT.
- The income tax deduction goes back to the donor. This is a very important feature because the tax deduction is not

attributed to the funding of the benefit plan; it is qualified as a *charitable income tax deduction* for the present value of the future gift to charity.

- A C Corporation would apply the tax deduction against 10 percent of the corporate AGI.
- A Subchapter S Corporation passes the tax deduction through to its shareholders. That is a humongous benefit that can defeat accidental philanthropy at its strength, the attack on the business owner. Most closely held corporations elect S status because it provides the asset protection of a C corporation without the double taxation of the corporate and personal brackets. An S corp. allows the flow-through of income and deductions to the shareholders. The exposure to accidental philanthropy is the strongest against the business owner at that point because as profits flow through to the shareholder/taxpayer, income increases subjecting the taxpayer to the income tax increases of 36 percent and 39.6 percent. The shareholder could be subject to taxation on profits that are retained at the corporate level.
- Partnerships and LLCs are treated in the same manner as S corporations.
- Sole proprietors are treated as individual taxpayers.

B. The CRAT Income Recipient

Just as the employer is always the donor of *an employer sponsored* charitable leverage plan; the employer is also the CRAT income recipient. Item 4 in Figure 16.1 shows the annuity distribution each year. The CRAT income over the 10-year period is paid back to the employer for a few good reasons. Control over the CRAT income stream gives the employer the "strings" we were looking for to attach to the Plan. For instance:

- If the Key Executive leaves the company, the employer may simply stop using the cash flow to fund the insurance policy and direct the funds elsewhere, even to another Key Executive.
- If the Key Executive dies during the funding phase, the CRAT annuity payment will be paid directly back to the employer.

- If the Key Executive becomes disabled, the CRAT cash flow will still be available to continue funding the plan or to fund a lesser program.
- Control equals power. The employer controls the CRAT cash flow.

The cash flow from the CRAT (that is paid to the employer first) will be used to fund the insurance policy in the next step.

C. Wealth Accumulation Life Insurance

In the next step, the employer uses the CRAT cash-flow to fund the insurance policy (or policies) Item 5 shows the CRAT income beneficiary (Employer) paying the insurance policy premium on a cash value life insurance policy (CVLI) designed to maximize its living benefits. The executive is the insured. Here's where the deferred compensation plan separates from the executive bonus plan.

Deferred compensation: The employer is the owner *and* beneficiary of the insurance policy on the executive. The policy is purchased as "key-man" insurance. The employer has the rights to the cash value of the policy.

The after-tax cash flow from the CRAT is paid to the CVLI that is owned by the employer.

Executive bonus plan: The executive is the owner of the policy and names the beneficiaries. The executive has all of the rights to the policy cash value.

The after-tax cash flow from the CRAT is paid to the executive (or the insurance company on the executive's behalf). The payment is tax deductible by the employer and considered taxable income to the executive. The executive has access to the tax-free cash value.

D. The Charitable Beneficiary

In the next step, the employer/donor names the charitable beneficiary. The employer would be well advised to create a corporate charitable foundation to receive the remainder interest, if it has not already done so. Imagine the power the charitable foundation brings with it. In addition, the employer can direct the use of the charitable funds back to the communities where their employees live and work. In some rare cases the employer/donor could let the executive choose the charitable beneficiary.

E. The CVLI *Provides the Tax-Free Retirement Income*

As you see throughout the examples I use in this book, the owner of the CVLI withdraws (or borrows) money from the policy at the desired retirement age. Assuming the policy has been funded properly, the cash flow from the policy is tax-free. Once again, the deferred compensation plan separates from the executive bonus plan in this step.

> Deferred compensation: The employer withdraws the cash value from the policy tax-free and uses it to pay the tax deductible compensation to the executive. Under this method, the employer would profit each year by its tax bracket. For example, if ABC Corp. pays Mr. Exec. $50,000 per year in deferred income payments, the $50,000 would be deductible to the corporation. In a 34 percent bracket the cost of the payment would be $33,000 ($50,000 less 34 percent). Since the employer is taking that money from the tax-free cash flow of the CVLI, it will actually earn a 34 percent *profit* on the payment. It used tax-free cash to pay a tax-deductible expense. The tax savings from each payment is $17,000. The employer could increase the compensation paid to the executive to bring the after-tax cost to the employer to zero. The payment to the executive could be increased to $75,000. The cost to the corporation after tax would be $50,000. Hence, the employer breaks even. Really complicated.

> The executive bonus plan: The executive controls the CVLI policy and takes the cash flow whenever he or she feels like it. It works like every other charitably leveraged plan I've shown so far. God, I like this plan so much better.

F. Insurance Beneficiary

When the insured/executive dies, the insurance policy pays the death benefit to a named beneficiary. Again, the two plans require different action steps.

> Deferred compensation: The deferred comp model pays the death benefit back to the employer. The employer then pays the executive's beneficiary the agreed upon survivor's benefit. In many cases the survivor's benefit is just a continuation of the executive's retirement benefit until a specified age.

The executive bonus plan: The executive's named beneficiary receives the tax-free insurance proceeds.

Designing an Employer-Sponsored Executive Bonus Plan

Having reviewed the charitable leverage process discussed above, it appears that the deferred compensation model is far more complicated than the executive bonus one. However, the complexity is due to the nature of the beast and not the charitable lever. Deferred compensation plans do have their place in larger companies where golden handcuffs are a top priority. Care must be taken to comply with the new government regulations regarding non-qualified deferred compensation arrangements. What you need to know is that if plan passes muster within the new IRS rules, funding it through a CRAT will add a tax-deductible and philanthropic dimension to an already popular tool.

For simplicity sake I want to focus on using the executive bonus approach as the Employer Sponsored Plan of choice as we go forward. The good news is that you already know how this plan works for the key executive because you read about it when we were building a personal supplement income plan. In case you forgot, here is a quick review:

- The CRAT is the charitable lever. It provides asset protection while generating a tax deduction, predictable cash flow, and a substantial deferred gift to charity.
- The charitable lever funds the CVLI. The CVLI generates tax-free retirement income with family financial security through the tax-free insurance proceeds.

That's it, it is that simple. One chassis—never changes. All you need to do is substitute the employer as the donor like we did in Figure 16.1 and you have an employer-sponsored plan.

The better news is that since the employer calls the shots, and the Key Executive is the recipient of the bonus, the employer has all kinds of flexibility. Here's what I mean.

- The first rule is that there are no rules. The employer funding the CRAT is a separate operation from the employer funding the CVLI. I am tying them together in the charitably leveraged design.

- The CRAT is funded with cash, not securities. The CRAT is invested in tax-free bonds and bonds funds. Therefore, minimal tax is due on the annuity income. I assume 5 percent.
- The employer can do whatever it wants with the annuity income. For instance:
  - The employer can bonus it all to the executive's CVLI.
  - The employer can bonus some of it to the executive's CVLI and the rest directly to the exec to cover the taxes on the bonus; or,
  - The employer can bonus some of it to the executive's CVLI and keep some of it; or, my personal favorite,
  - The employer can bonus some of it to the executive's CVLI and use the rest of it; to buy key-person insurance on the exec. Pretty clever play I think. The employer uses some of the CRAT cash flow to buy a low-cost permanent death benefit policy on the executive. When the executive dies, the employer receives the tax-free proceeds as a cost-recovery payment.
  - The employer can fund multiple Key Executives from one CRAT.
  - If the Key Executive leaves early, the employer can turn off the funding of the CVLI and direct the CRAT cash flow to another policy.

The best way that I can show you the dynamics behind this approach is by sharing another war story. And this one brings back on old friend.

Schmooley Rides Again

You remember our hero from the first chapter, Mr. Schmooley. I introduced him as a business owner in his mid-sixties. A few chapters later you met his son, the famous Dr. Schmooley, when we designed his personal supplemental income plan. Our thoughts now turn back to good old Schmoolster. It turns out that that sly dog just couldn't get enough of the lovely Mrs. Schmooley, and only three years after the arrival of number one son, out popped young Schmooley number two, known to all as Eddie. Like his brother, Eddie grew up strong and smart, but med school wasn't in the cards for him, he liked the action of entrepreneurship. After college he went to work in Pop's business, Schmoolcorp and now at age 43 is considered the key man.

The problem is that the Schmoolcorp retirement plan stinks for the high-wage earner and Eddie knows it. It is a typical 401(k) plan topping out at $16,500 per year. The contribution comes in the form of a voluntary reduction in pay. In effect, the employees at Schmoolcorp fund their own retirement plans. Eddie can do the math and he knows that he needs a greater volume of savings to meet his retirement needs.

In addition, Eddie is far more community minded than his dad. He believes that if your company derives its income from the community it ought to give something back. It's good for business and good for the soul. I told you he was a smart guy. Anyway, the kid convinces the Old Man to fund a charitably leveraged key executive bonus plan with the profit the company will earn from a large construction project that's coming to fruition. The structure of the plan is depicted in Figure 16.2.

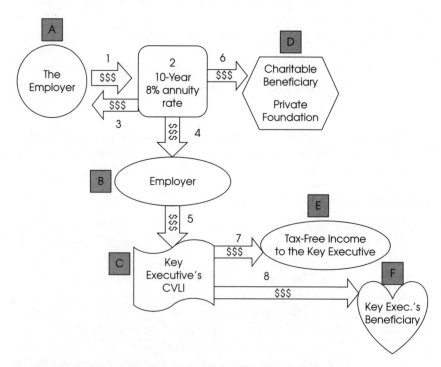

Figure 16.2   Eddie Schmooley's Key Executive Bonus Plan

Figure 16.2 looks eerily similar to Figure 16.1 except that I made some subtle changes that I will expound upon. The letters and numbers I use in the following statement correspond to the chart in Figure 16.2. The Employer, Schmoolcorp (A) will transfer $1,000,000 of the profits (1) to a 10-year CRAT with an 8 percent annuity rate (2). The transfer to the CRAT will generate a $351,000 charitable income tax deduction (3) back to Schmoolcorp. Since Schmoolcorp is a Subchapter S Corporation, the tax deduction will flow through to the shareholders, Mr. and Mrs. Schmooley. Let's pause here for a moment to reflect on what has happened.

- Cash from Schmoolcorp ($1,000,000) has been asset-protected in the CRAT "Lock Box."
- The executive bonus plan is now totally funded with the one transfer.
- The tax deduction of $351,000 flows through to Mr. and Mrs. Schmooley for their personal use. Are you starting to see the power of this? They can use that deduction to attack the tax on withdrawals from their retirement plans, or even against sales of some Schmoolcorp stock to their son.
- In the Schmooley's 40 percent tax bracket, the tax deduction is equivalent to cash in their pocket of $140,400.
- Schmoolco rp has just created the first of two deductions on the executive bonus plan (more to follow).

The CRAT (2) invests the $1,000,000 cash in nontaxable investments. The CRAT annuity cash flow each year (4) will be $80,000. Adjusting for some possible taxable income subject to four-tier accounting, I'm assuming that the net income will be $76,000. The net annuity payment (4) is payable to Schmoolcorp as the income recipient (B).

Mr. Schmooley as the owner of Schmoolcorp is going to use the after-tax annuity payment (4) to fund Eddie's executive bonus plan (C), which will be a cash-building CVLI contract. He has $76,000 "free income" to work with. The payment of the premium (5) will be a tax-deductible expense under IRC§ 162, (the the second deduction I was alluding to earlier). Unfortunately, the payment of the insurance premium creates taxable income to Eddie. That leads us to some simple math. When Mr. S. as the employer, uses tax-free cash to fund a tax-deductible benefit, the cost of the benefit is reduced by his tax bracket. If Schmoolcorp uses the full $76,000 (4) to pay the premium (5), the net cost is $45,600 ($76,000 less 40 percent). Likewise, Mr. S. could pad the bonus to Eddie by 40 percent and the after-tax company cost would be zero. Eddie's IRC §162 bonus would be $126,000 (the company would pay the premium directly and allocate the balance via Eddie's W-2). The after-tax cost to Eddie would be $0. The deduction of the $126,000 bonus would bring the apparent cost to the corporation down to $76,000. But since it receives an after-tax distribution from the CRAT for the same amount, the cost to Schmoolcorp is zero.

With the knowledge of how an executive bonus plan works, and $76,000 of free money to work with, Mr. Schmooley has a couple of pretty snappy options to choose from.

> Option 1: He could bonus the full $76,000 from the CRAT to pay the CVLI policy for Eddie. Schmoolcorp would deduct the payment while Eddie would include it in his income. Schmoolcorp would be ahead of the game by $30,400 with each payment.

> Option 2: He could "gross-up" each payment to $126,000. The net cost to Schmoolcorp would be zero. Eddie would have the full use of the $76,000 since the $126,000 payment would cover his taxes.

> Option 3: He could do a combination based on the CRAT distribution of $76,000 where Eddie receives a $60,000 net bonus (grossed up to $100,000) and Schmoolcorp keeps $16,000 for cost recovery key man insurance. The Schmoolcorp financial statement loves this approach and so do I.

Mr. Schmooley decides that the first option is not so hot because Eddie would need to pay $30,400 each year to taxes either out of his pocket or from the bonus. If he pays the tax from the bonus it will leave just $45,600 for his personal supplemental retirement income plan. While he is not ready to hand over the reins to Eddie yet, Mr. Schmooley does want to him to know how valuable he is to the company. Making the lad pay that much in tax each year will not help him accomplish his goals. After all, Eddie is his son and he wants to do right by him.

Option 2 is doable and it wouldn't cost the company anything on the cash-flow side. The Schmool could be convinced to go this way. After all, Eddie is his son and he wants to do right by him. Then he thinks, it is a lot of money to throw into the kid's retirement though, and he doesn't want to send the wrong message to his bankers, credit being tight and all.

Option 3 has real business appeal to Mr. Schmooley. He thinks that it should appeal to Eddie as well. After all Eddie is his son and someday this will all be his—and he will have to deal with the banks.

What is a Schmooley to do?

I'm going to leave that little cliffhanger for moment so that I can complete the charitable leverage process. Then I'll come back to it. I promise. We're at the point of some key decision making with regard to funding the actual executive bonus. What we do know for sure is that Eddie will be the owner of the CVLI policy (C). He will be income beneficiary of the policy (E) and receive the tax-free cash-flow from the policy (7) at retirement. Further, he will name his wife and children as the policy beneficiaries (F). They will receive the tax-free insurance proceeds at his death (8).

Boss Schmooley and Eddie both agree on how the CRAT remainder will be used. At the end of CRAT term the remaining balance will be transferred to a Charitable Beneficiary (D) named by Schmoolcorp. The beneficiary is the Schmoolcorp Charitable Foundation. The primary focus of the foundation will be on granting merit-based scholarships to deserving youths seeking to further their education in the vocational technical fields. Based on the assumption that the CRAT earns 5 percent and distributes $80,000 per year, the remainder to the Foundation (6) at the end of year 10 will be approximately $622,000. The foundation will then be in a position to award more than $31,000 each year in scholarships. "That," says Eddie, "will leave a lasting impression on our community. In fact some of those scholarship winners may come back to work for us!" Eddie gets it.

Now, let's get back to CRAT cash flow and see if we get this kid some income. Mr. Schmooley decides to split the CRAT income so that $60,000 will go to Eddie's executive bonus Plan and $16,000 will be retained by the company to purchase key man insurance on him. The divided amounts came as a result of calculating the fixed premium payable for 10 years to a maximum death benefit policy insuring Eddie to guarantee a $1,000,000 death benefit. The premium was less than $16,000 per year for 10 years. I rounded it up to make things simple. The $60,000 allocated to Eddie's CVLI policy will be net of the taxes, which will be an additional bonus. The annual net cost to company will be zero.

Figure 16.3 shows what the arrangement will look like for the first 10 years.

By the end of the 10-year CRAT term, Eddie is now 53. Both the key man insurance and his CVLI policy are fully funded with no further payments required. The CRAT remainder funds the charitable foundation. You are familiar with the roles of the CVLI and foundation, but we should spend a minute on the key man contract. Old man Schmooley was right, the key man policy serves a couple of purposes. First, it shows the company's lenders that if the rainmaker dies the company would receive a tax-free benefit of $1,000,000 to be used to keep the place running and hire a potential replacement. If you don't think this is important, talk to a corporate lender in these modern times,. They want no risk of capital loss and certainly no business interruption due to death. Second, the cash surrender value of the insurance policy is carried as *corporate cash asset* on the books. Because the insurance is payable only to the company there is no offsetting future expense—it's all good

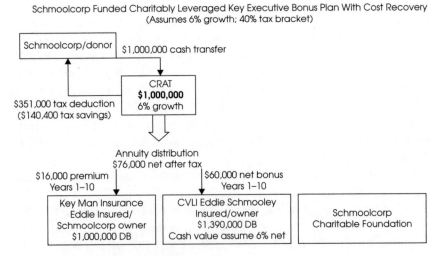

Schmoolcorp Funded Charitably Leveraged Key Executive Bonus Plan With Cost Recovery
(Assumes 6% growth; 40% tax bracket)

Schmoolcorp/donor | $1,000,000 cash transfer

$351,000 tax deduction
($140,400 tax savings)

CRAT
$1,000,000
6% growth

Annuity distribution
$76,000 net after tax

$16,000 premium
Years 1–10

$60,000 net bonus
Years 1–10

Key Man Insurance
Eddie Insured/
Schmoolcorp owner
$1,000,000 DB

CVLI Eddie Schmooley
Insured/owner
$1,390,000 DB
Cash value assume 6% net

Schmoolcorp
Charitable Foundation

Figure 16.3   The First 10 Years

and tax-free. Third, and this may be more important for a larger company with multiple key people, the death benefit provides the company with cost recovery of the original CRAT deposit. Think about the power of that statement. I'll demonstrate just how powerful when we get to the conclusion. Figure 16.4 shows the snapshot 10 years out.

By the time Eddie is ready to "retire" at age 65 his CVLI policy generates $95,500 per year in tax-free supplemental retirement income. The company-owned key man policy is paid up and carried on the books as a $262,000 cash asset. The Schmoolcorp Charitable Foundation has a projected value of $737,000 and has given more than $569,000 in scholarships. All in the Schmooley name. (See Figure 16.5.)

Running the retirement lifecycle to the end shows the overall projected results if Eddie dies at the end of age 85. And what results they are! Eddie receives $1,910,000 in total retirement income; his family receives another $860,000 at his death. The total tax free benefits to the "Key Executive and his Family" amount to $2,770,000, all

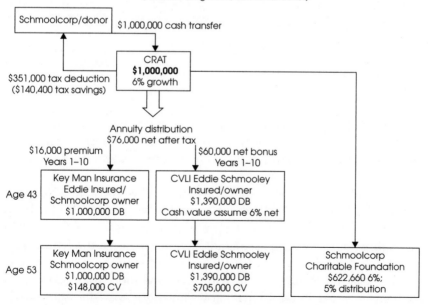

Schmoolcorp Funded Charitably Leveraged Key Executive Bonus Plan With Cost Recovery
(Assumes 6% growth; 40% tax bracket)

Figure 16.4   Progress at the End of the CRAT Term

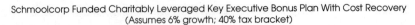

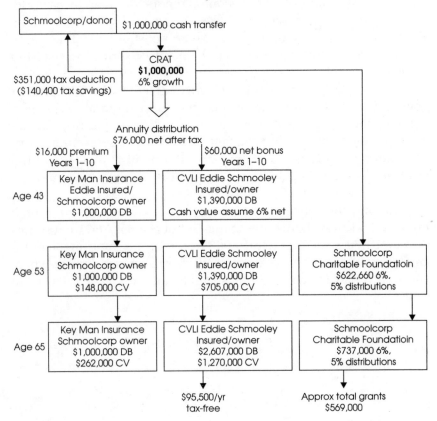

Figure 16.5   Impact at Age 65

of which are supplied by the employer. I know that this case is all in the family, but if it wasn't, don't you think an employee would think twice before walking away from the employer. I mean that's a lot of cash to leave on the table.

From the employer's side, providing this substantial benefit package to a key person has a remarkable impact on the business and society. Schmoolcorp put up a $1,000,000 gift to a CRAT and in exchange received a $351,000 tax deduction—up front. The transfer to CRAT *completely funded* the benefits to the Key Executive (Eddie) that I just showed you, while creating more than $2,000,000 for charity. And it wasn't just any charity; it was the Schmooley Charitable Foundation and the creation and generation of the

Schmooley family charitable legacy. If all that wasn't enough, when the key executive dies, the company gets all their money back—tax-free! (See Figure 16.6.)

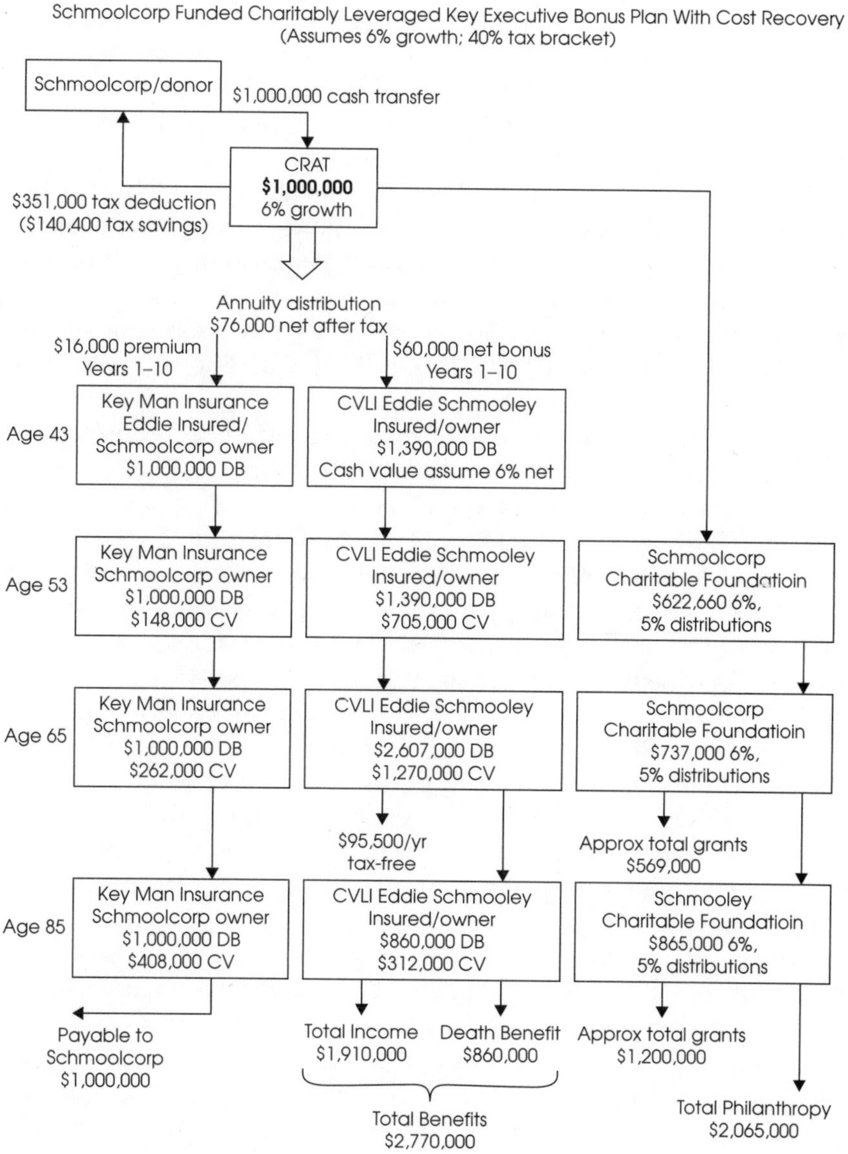

Schmoolcorp Funded Charitably Leveraged Key Executive Bonus Plan With Cost Recovery
(Assumes 6% growth; 40% tax bracket)

Figure 16.6 The Power of Charitable Leverage in a Business Situation

Making Sure Your Company Gets Its Money Back

It is hard to imagine that a single transfer of $1,000,000, accompanied by a $351,000 (35 percent) tax deduction could generate more than $2,700,000 of cash benefits and $2,000,000 more for charity. It's even harder to comprehend that a company could do all that and then get the $1,000,000 back! But then, that is the power of charitable leverage. And it wasn't like we played fast and loose with the projections. I think you agree that I used more than reasonable assumptions in this and all the other war stories.

I want to emphasize that I used $1,000,000 in the Schmoolcorp example to make the math easier to follow—it is by no means an entry level. I suggest to you that an employer-sponsored program will function at the $100,000 level. If you want to think a little further outside the box, your business could build a series of smaller CRATs, say $50,000 to $100,000 each. Each CRAT would run for its own 10-year period while the individual annuity payments fund the same CVLI policy on the same key executive (or a series of policies on a bunch of key people). The same charitable foundation could be the beneficiary of all of them! Hey, we're business owners, be creative. If you want to do this type of benefit planning, you can.

There are a lot of us small business owners out there. We provide most of the jobs and we create most of the wealth. We fuel the economy, and in return we get damn little thanks and almost no breaks. Speaking for me as a small business with fewer than 10 employees, I'm fine with no thanks and no breaks as long as I'm left alone to run my company. But that is not how it works. As government gets bigger and grabs more power we increasingly become the capitalist enemy. A raging government that teaches its people to depend on it for all their needs, also needs to be fed in return. It gets nourishment through more regulation on businesses and ultimately more taxes—there is no other way. More government regulation and oversight caused by congress's overreaction to localized acts of greed is a covert form of tax used in the War on Wealth, and we all pay for it, the business owner *and* the consumer. One needs only to look at the compliance nightmare created by Sarbanes-Oxley for an example of a congress gone wild. Who do you think paid for the cost of the new regulations? If you guessed the U.S. consumer, you'd be right. Some call the legislative measures—bailouts included—taken by congress in response to the economic meltdown of 2008 a knee-jerk reaction; I call it a reaction by a bunch of jerks.

The War on Wealth is fought against America's businesses through overt and covert operations. The goal is the same, to make accidental philanthropists out of us all. One way a business can fight back is through the use of charitable leverage to fund special incentives for our best and brightest people. It's your call; *you* choose where *your* money goes or congress will do it for you. I like it better when I get to choose. I like it ever *better* when I get to choose and by doing so, my company gets all its money back.

CHAPTER 17

Can Charitable Leverage Save Your IRA?

I've been rich and I've been poor—and believe me, rich is better.

—Sophie Tucker

I need to tell you at the start that this chapter is not for everyone. It is intended only for those members of the targeted classes who have accumulated a substantial sum in their retirement plans but do not think they'll use all of it for their retirement. If it's your desire to pass the remainder of your retirement accounts to your children it is okay to continue, otherwise you can stop reading now. Close the book and walk away before somebody gets hurt. If, however, you fit the profile, you may continue with caution, for you are about to enter dangerous territory for the following reasons:

- Your head may explode. I don't mean a like "pop," or "poof." I'm talking fly off your shoulders like a bottle rocket. Never to be seen again.
- Your blood pressure may increase to the point where your face resembles the bulb in a thermometer resulting in item one above.

- If you survive items one and two, and I'm allowed to work a little charitable leverage magic, you may experience such a state of euphoria that item one might still happen, but at least the missile will be smiling.

In the pages that follow, We discuss the destruction of your retirement accumulations through multiple WMD in the War on Wealth resulting in accidental philanthropy. Then I show you how to rescue your wealth through a *version* of charitable leverage. I snuck in the word "version" because this is the one situation where the "same chassis–different players" axiom does not apply. Don't worry; you won't need to learn anything new. I stick with our reliable 10-year CRAT, but I pair it this one time with a different type of CVLI policy.

Before you begin reading, you may want to go all the way back to Chapter 1 and reread the section on how your IRA is taxed ("But Wait, There's One More Tax"). I use the same calculations in this chapter. Also, all the assumptions I used in every other chapter remain the same except for one, I shortened the life expectancy of our subjects to age 80.

The best way for me to present this concept to you is through one final war story. When you read the story don't get too hung up on the numbers. They can be divided or multiplied. The important thing is to get the whole picture of how charitable leverage can once again defeat the forces of accidental philanthropy.

Paging Dr. Sherman, Paging Dr. Sherman, Your *IRA* Is in Cardiac Arrest

Dr. William Ditmars Sherman is a thoracic surgeon who has accumulated an estate in excess of $9,000,000 while working like a dog in the O.R. He and his wife Ruth are both age 60, born only a couple of days apart, and in excellent health. They have three children, who will someday inherit their wealth. In addition to his other investments, Dr. Sherman has accumulated $2,000,000 in qualified retirement accounts (for the purpose of this exercise, we lump them together and call it an IRA). It is this IRA that is the subject of our focus.

Though Dr. Sherman has enjoyed tax-deferred growth in his IRA, the reality is that he will not need it to supplement his retirement income. It will become part of his estate to be transferred to his wife upon his death, and then to the children upon hers. Here is where the problem lies. The IRA will suffer tremendous shrinkage upon transfer due to a combination of Federal Estate Tax and Federal Income Tax on "income in respect of a decedent (IRD)."

Dr. Sherman has met with his financial and tax advisors to address his concerns about transferring the IRA to the children. They showed him two scenarios that illustrate the potential IRA tax devastation.

1. Transfer today or in this year: Assumes the unlikely case that both Dr. and Mrs. Sherman die this year and the IRA transfers to their children.
2. Transfer in 20 years: Assumes the more likely case where the IRA continues to grow for the next 20 years and is then transferred upon death of the surviving spouse.

In both situations we are assuming that the surviving spouse has the full unified credit remaining for federal estate tax purposes, which would eliminate tax on $3,500,000 each. Since the Sherman estate is more than $9,000,000, the entire IRA is subject to federal estate and income tax.

Transfer Today or in this Year

It really doesn't matter what year "this year" is. It represents both Bill and Ruth getting hit by the proverbial bus today, thus requiring the estate transfer to their children this year. The following is an excerpt from IRS Publication 559 for Survivors, Executors, and Administrators on how to handle the tax due on "Inherited IRAs."

> If a beneficiary receives a lump-sum distribution from a traditional IRA he or she inherited, all or some of it may be taxable. The distribution is taxable in the year received as income in respect of a decedent up to the decedent's taxable balance. This is the decedent's balance at the time of death, including unrealized appreciation and income accrued to date of death, minus any basis (nondeductible contributions). . . . (The beneficiary) may take a deduction for any federal estate taxes that were paid on that portion.

Huh? Leave it to the IRS to give you instructions like that. So I'll interpret for you. Based on the size of the Sherman estate, the full

$2,000,000 IRA would be subject to federal estate tax. The portion of the estate tax attributable to the IRA is paid first. The heirs do not pay income tax on the portion of the IRA that is withdrawn to pay the estate tax. I guess that's the IRS's version of helping you out. Anything above the estate tax would be taxed as ordinary income in the beneficiary's tax bracket. In this case, all the tax brackets are assumed to be 40 percent. Here's the skinny:

Federal estate tax of the IRA	$900,000
Remaining value of the IRA	$1,100,000
Ordinary income tax due	$440,000
Total tax burden on the transfer of the Shermans' $2,000,000 IRA	$1,340,000

In other words, the government would receive 67 percent of the IRA, while the kids get a whopping $660,000, just 33 percent. (See Figure 17.1 for a graphical depiction of this IRA transfer.) That's not a misprint. The government gets more than twice what the kids get. How's that for fair and balanced.

Estate Transfer 20 Years from Now

Twenty years from now, old Bill and Ruth are each age 80. Knowing that I need to show an example of what happens to their IRA at their death, they simultaneously spontaneously combust. That, of course, leaves quite a mess to clean up—and I'm just talking about the estate.

We assume that the IRA will grow at net 6 percent for the next 20 years. At age 80 the value is $6,414,270. You need to work with me here. We know that there would have been forced minimum required distributions starting at age 70½; so at a pure 6 percent growth the net value at death would be lower. Using the same calculation process that was used in the "today" example, here's the skinny:

Federal estate tax of the IRA	**$2,886,420**
Remaining value of the IRA	**$3,525,850**
Ordinary income tax due	**$1,411,140**
Total tax burden on the transfer of the Shermans' $6,414,270 IRA	**$4,298,560**

Wow! That is an enormous amount of accidental philanthropy.

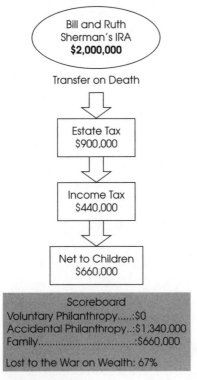

Bill and Ruth Sherman's IRA **2009**
(Distribution to the children upon the death of the second parent;
assumes an estate in excess of $9,000,000)

Bill and Ruth
Sherman's IRA
$2,000,000

Transfer on Death

Estate Tax
$900,000

Income Tax
$440,000

Net to Children
$660,000

Scoreboard
Voluntary Philanthropy......:$0
Accidental Philanthropy..:$1,340,000
Family...................................:$660,000

Lost to the War on Wealth: 67%

Figure 17.1   IRA Transfer this Year

Once again 67 percent of the IRA is lost to the War on Wealth. While only 33 percent or $2,116,710 is distributed to the children. Here's an even more disturbing thought. The value of the IRA in 2009 was $2,000,000. The kids inherit a little more than $2,000,000 20 years later. (See Figure 17.2 for a graphical depiction of this IRA transfer.) That means that just about *all of the growth for 20 years was paid to the IRS!*

A Solution That Is Not Without Its Problems

Dr. Sherman's advisors, noting the results above, suggest that he may be better off biting the bullet now, withdraw the IRA funds, pay the tax, and reinvest elsewhere. He could even transfer the net proceeds to a trust for his children and avoid future estate tax. Unfortunately,

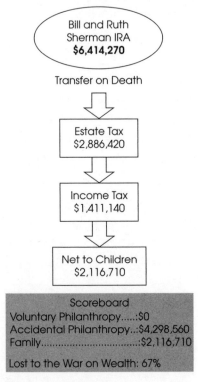

Bill and Ruth Sherman's IRA **2029**
(Distribution to the children upon the death of the second parent;
assumes an estate in excess of $15,000,000)

Figure 17.2 IRA Transfer, 20 Years Later

that too has a sizable tax cost. In a 40 percent tax bracket the IRA of $2,000,000 would lose about $800,000 to taxes. Dr. Sherman would net $1,200,000 from the withdrawal.

Let's assume Bill and Ruth use $600,000 each of their gift tax credit and transfer the remaining $1,200,000 to a trust for their children and grandchildren. Keeping the same assumptions for growth and taxes, the trust invests the funds at a net return of 6 percent for the next 20 years. The future value to the children would be $3,843,560. (See Figure 17.3.)

It seems that the advisors are correct in their thinking as this approach would generate $1,531,850 more net dollars to the family than keeping the proceeds locked in the IRA. The estate tax in 20 years does not come into play because the IRA was

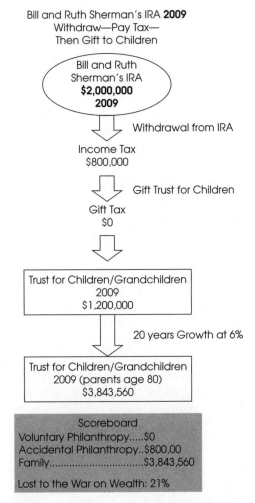

Bill and Ruth Sherman's IRA **2009**
Withdraw—Pay Tax—
Then Gift to Children

Bill and Ruth
Sherman's IRA
$2,000,000
2009

Withdrawal from IRA

Income Tax
$800,000

Gift Trust for Children

Gift Tax
$0

Trust for Children/Grandchildren
2009
$1,200,000

20 years Growth at 6%

Trust for Children/Grandchildren
2009 (parents age 80)
$3,843,560

Scoreboard
Voluntary Philanthropy.....$0
Accidental Philanthropy..$800,00
Family..............................$3,843,560

Lost to the War on Wealth: 21%

Figure 17.3   Withdraw, Pay Tax, and Transfer to Children

transferred out of the estate 20 years earlier. I should note, however, that the overall estate tax on the balance of the Sherman estate would unfortunately *increase* because the combined unified credits would have been reduced by the $1,200,000 gift. The free pass-through of assets would be reduced from $7,000,000 to $5,800,000. Don't look at me, I didn't make the rules.

The bottom line of this approach is that it leaves more net cash to the children and that satisfies the advisors. But they're not the ones who'll need to write a check for $800,000 to the IRS this year.

A Solution That Uses the Power of Charitable Leverage

Can a charitably leveraged plan actually help Dr. and Mrs. Sherman beat the accidental philanthropy they face? That depends on their desire to leave a charitable legacy and their ability to do math. Bill and Ruth have an established record of charitable intent through their support various local charities, the hospital, and both of their colleges. The idea that they could provide more money to their children by creating ongoing support of their philanthropic endeavors appeals to them. I believe this sets the stage nicely for unleashing the power of charitable leverage.

What follows is what I call *The Charitably Leveraged IRA Rescue Strategy.* Obviously I use "IRA" as a catchall for qualified retirement accounts. Remember, I'm going change our one-chassis design slightly so kindly pay attention.

Step 1: Dr. and Mrs. Sherman establish the same 10-year term Charitable Remainder Annuity Trust that you've grown to love. However, I want to push the tax deduction from the CRAT to the maximum, so the first variation from our routine is that the annuity distribution rate will be 5 percent. The CRAT charitable beneficiary will be the Sherman Family Donor Advised Fund established under the local Community Foundation umbrella. The Donor Advised Fund will receive the CRAT balance at the end of the 10-year term.

Step 2: Dr. Sherman withdraws the $2,000,000 from the IRA and gifts it to the CRAT. The withdrawal of the IRA creates $2,000,000 of taxable income subject to the same income taxes as shown in the withdraw-pay tax—and transfer example in Figure 17.3. However, the gift to the CRAT generates a charitable income tax deduction that may be used to reduce the overall tax. Based upon a 4 percent Applicable Federal Rate (AFR), if anyone transfers $2,000,000 to a 10-year term CRAT with a 5 percent annuity rate, the deduction will be $1,188,910. In the Shermans' tax bracket of 40 percent, the tax savings of the deduction is $475,565. (See Figure 17.4.)

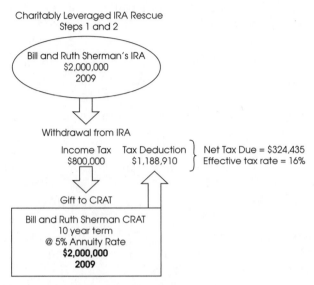

Figure 17.4 Withdraw and Gift to CRAT

The impact of steps 1 and 2 is that the tax due on the IRA distribution is reduced by the tax savings from the deduction. The tax is reduced from $800,000 to $325,435, a drop in the effective tax rate from 40 percent to 16 percent!

Please note that for simplicity sake I have assumed that the Shermans pay the tax due on the IRA distribution from other funds so that I can use the full $2,000,000 as that CRAT principal. If they pay the tax directly from the IRA withdrawal then the net payment to the CRAT would be less, the tax deduction would be less and we'd all wind up with headaches. The "pay with other money" approach makes things a whole lot easier to follow.

Step 3: The CRAT will generate $100,000 per year to Dr. and Mrs. Sherman for the next 10 years regardless of how the funds are invested. Assuming the trust earns 5 percent over the 10-year period, the charitable gift passing to the Sherman Family Donor Advised Fund at the end of the 10th year will be $2,000,000. Since the CRAT is funded with cash type assets, I will assume that the trustee invests in tax-free bonds and bond funds with very little taxable income. Under the four-tier accounting rules the net distribution after taxes is projected to be $95,000 per year.

Step 4: Here comes the second *huge* departure from every other charitably leveraged strategy you've read about so far. Instead of using the CRAT cash flow to purchase a minimum death benefit CVLI policy for the accumulation of cash, Dr. and Mrs. Sherman are going to use the cash flow to buy the maximum amount of death benefit they can, without any regard to cash value accumulation. The ideal policy to purchase is a "2nd to Die" CVLI policy because it will provide the maximum death benefit for the premium dollar. Why the change? It's really very logical; the use of life insurance in an IRA rescue strategy is for the replacement of the IRA that has been given to the CRAT. The death benefit of the policy will multiply the value of the IRA and distribute it to an irrevocable life insurance trust (ILIT) for the children and grandchildren in form of tax-free cash. How cool is that?

- The annual premium the Shermans will pay for the policy is targeted to $95,000 for 10 years to match the distribution from the CRAT.

- By backing into the premium payment, the face amount of the policy is $6,600,000, which represents a guaranteed death benefit based on the couple's combined health status as preferred nonsmokers (the face amount is actually a little greater and I rounded it down for illustrative purposes). I used a typical off the shelf guaranteed second to die policy that you can find from many top-rated insurance companies.

- The annual premiums paid to the ILIT are treated as gifts. Bill and Ruth are each allowed to gift $12,000 per person without gift tax each year. Therefore, based on the three children as beneficiaries of the ILIT, $72,000 of the premium gifts is free and the $23,000 would be washed by filing a gift tax return and using a little gift tax credit. In short there will be no gift taxes.

Impact of steps 3 and 4 is that the cash flow from the CRAT completely funds the insurance policy. At the death of the surviving spouse, when the *original IRA was scheduled to transfer to the children, $6,600,000 will be paid to them, free of income tax, inheritance tax, and estate tax. That is a sizable improvement over the $2.1 million and $3.8 million distributions that would have been available using the first two planning scenarios.*

But There Is More to This IRA Rescue— A Charitable Legacy

The CRAT serves a greater purpose than just to fund the insurance policy each year; it promotes a philanthropic legacy that will last generations. It will take the dollars earmarked for redistribution and give them a new direction with a profound impact on society.

The CRAT was funded with $2,000,000 from the Bill's IRA. If the CRAT earns 5 percent and distributes 5 percent each year for the 10-year run, the remainder payable to the Sherman Family Fund will be $2,000,000. That's math that even I can do. The Sherman Family Fund continues the Sherman Legacy by distributing more than $100,000 in new gifts each year (assuming a 5 percent distribution and 1 percent net fund growth). By the time our story ends at their age 80, Bill and Ruth's charitable fund would have distributed over $1,000,000 to various local charities, the hospital, and both of their colleges, with the original $2,000,000 still in the tank. As their children and grandchildren move into leadership roles with the fund, the Sherman Family name will forever be coupled with their good deeds. (See Figure 17.5.)

Is the Bottom Line the Only Moral of the Story?

Before I give you my two cents worth about the question above, let's take a look at Table 17.1 that shows the bottom line to this unique story about the transfer of the Shermans' IRA to their children and grandchildren.

The charitably leveraged strategy will provide the following results:

- Reduces the income tax on the IRA distribution from $800,000 to $324,825
- Increases the children's inheritance from $3,843,560 to $6,600,000
- Creates a charitable legacy of $3,256,000

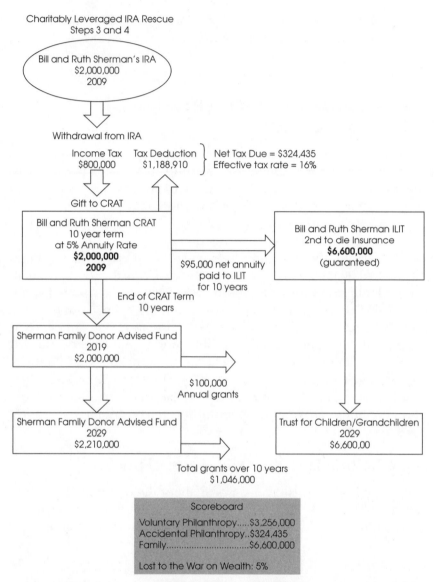

Figure 17.5 Transfer to Children with a Charitable Legacy on the Side

It may look to you like it's not much of contest, and you're right, it's not even close *as long as you share the desire to create a charitable legacy*. There are other methods that you could employ to reduce the tax on transfer of an unused IRA at death, which are discussed below. None of them will reduce the tax as dramatically

Table 17.1   The Tax Upon Transferon Dr. and Mrs. Sherman's $2,000,000 IRA (Assuming 6% growth for 20 years; estate tax at 45% and income tax at 40%)

	Current Plan	Withdraw-pay tax-transfer to trust for children in 2009	Charitably Leveraged IRA Rescue
Taxable IRA Value in 20 years (2029)	$6,414,270	$0	$0
Total Taxes Due	$4,298,560 (paid in the 20th year)	$800,000 (paid this year)	$324,435 (paid this year)
Net to Children	$2,116,710	$3,843,560	$6,600,000
Net to Charity	$0	$0	$3,256,000
Total Net Benefits to Family and Charity	$2,116,710	$3,843,560	$9,556,000 (reflects tax paid this year)
Percentage of IRA lost to the War on Wealth	67%	21%	3%

Presented for educational purposes only. See text for details and assumptions.

as a charitably leveraged plan or obviously create the philanthropic legacy, but they might actually produce more money overall to your children.

Stretch IRA: One such technique is called a stretch IRA. Simply put, the Shermans would name their children as the IRA beneficiary at death. From that point the children would be allowed to stretch the IRA distributions over the rest of their lives. The impact would be that the Sherman IRA would grow during that 20-year period leading up to their death (less the required minimum distributions) and the income payments would be stretched over the lives of their children/beneficiaries. The combination of tax deferral and stretched income will probably provide the children with more overall income, but, of course, they will also pay a lot more tax, they'll just do it over time. In addition, there are a ton of rules regarding this technique so a qualified tax professional must be consulted. This is a gross over-simplification of the process, but you may want to look into it if you're on the fence regarding a charitable gift.

Second to die insurance: Also, the Shermans could just buy the second to die insurance policy with funds outside of the IRA, and let the IRA ride until their death. We've seen that the value of IRA at that point would be worth $6,414,270 but the taxes due would be $4,297,560. Bill could pay the $95,000 annual insurance premium out of pocket and use the $6,600,000 to pay the $4,297,560 tax tally. The kids would wind up with the full $6,414,270 from the IRA and the balance of the insurance proceeds ($2,302,440). Even factoring the $950,000 Bill paid out pocket, the kids would net $7,766,710. Wow, this method wins! It beats charitable leverage by $1.1 million. Really? This method still contributed more than $4,000,000 to accidental philanthropy and not a penny to the real charities. But the kids do get more.

You see that's my point; there will always be multiple methods to transfer wealth. It comes down to what feels right for your wallet and your soul. My personal preference is to reduce the real dollars going to government and give them to charity instead, but that's me. Remember, charitable leverage does not need to be an all or nothing deal. You could do this technique with a portion of your IRA, or even phase it in over a few years. My hope is that folks who read this might see the power of the charitable leverage alternative and at least consider it.

When it comes to the billions of dollars of accumulated wealth in qualified retirement plans that will be transferred from one generation to the next, the WMD are ready and aimed. What if there was nothing for them to hit?

Epilogue

Well there you have it, a completed journey through the wonderful world of charitable leverage. I've tried to keep things fairly simple. I mean the concept of physical leverage may be science, but it's not rocket science. I have found that the simpler things are, the more effective they are, and the more we're apt to use them. If you can work a wrench, you can understand this program.

The strategy concerning charitable leverage, while not for everybody, is remarkably simple and produces some amazing results. We can build alternative methods for the accumulation of wealth without tax, while fueling our favorite charities with dollars that might otherwise be lost to the whims of congress. We can use this simple technique in supplemental retirement plans, grandparent gifting plans, and employer-sponsored key executive deferred income plans—all built on the exact same chassis. We can also tweak the chassis a little and create a magnificent approach to rescue our retirement plans from the clutches of Uncle Sam.

Now it's up to you to crunch some numbers on your own and then meet with your financial advisors to get some professional guidance. But I need to give you a tip. If the advisors start talking about how things are done traditionally, tell them you *blew up* that paradigm and set them straight about the new paradigms. If they just can't get their head around the concept of charitable leverage, get a new advisor. Ultimately it is your money, and you control it.

And isn't that what this War on Wealth is all about, control? How you will exercise control over the money you earn and who benefits from it. My battle-plan is really very simple. The government can't control what they can't take. Charitable leverage substitutes voluntary philanthropy for accidental philanthropy. Our assets become insulated from taxation, but it accomplishes so much more. Through charitable leverage we gain the opportunity to speak to future generations about who we were, what was important to us. We get to raise the bar a little higher for them.

The War on Wealth is here. The Weapons of Mass Destruction are taxes. The objective is the redistribution of wealth, namely yours. The targets are America's best, brightest, youngest, and oldest. As government gets bigger and grabs more power, it will intervene in every aspect of our lives. Ultimately the war on wealth will create many casualties: success, capitalism, free markets, free choice. There is more at stake than our money. At stake is America's soul. How important is your freedom? Are you ready to join the fight?

About the Author

Daniel G. Nigito, CFP® is the Chairman and CEO of Market Street Financial Advisors, LLC and its subsidiary, Market Street Philanthropic Advisors, Inc. The combined mission of the two companies is to *"provide wealth management for people who want to add meaning to their money."* To fulfill his vision, Dan specializes in using charitable remainder trusts and family foundations to provide strategies for wealth accumulation, preservation, and transfer for private clients and their families. His programs have saved families millions in tax dollars and created millions more for charities across the United States. 2009 marks Dan's 31st year in the financial services industry.

He is the author of two books: *Avoiding the Estate Tax Trap* (Contemporary Books, 1992) and *Don't Die Until You Read This! The 7-Step Program for Creating and Preserving Your Financial Legacy* (American Books, 2001). In addition, he has published numerous articles on estate planning and has been the subject of features in the *Wall Street Journal, New York Post, Morning Call and Express Times* among other newspapers. His witty banter and concise presentation of complex ideas make him a welcome guest of radio and TV talk shows. He is a much sought after platform speaker on the national level.

Dan is the creator of the CLEAR Plan™ (Charitably Leveraged Estate Accumulation & Retirement Plan) marketed nationally through a network of independent financial advisors. CLEAR™ Plan is the nation's first interactive software based financial planning program that focuses on using charitable remainder trusts to solve common estate and retirement concerns.

He received his BA in English and Journalism from Moravian College, Bethlehem, PA in 1978. He achieved the Certified Financial Planner® (CFP®) designation from the College for Financial Planning, Denver CO in 1984.

Dan lives in Bethlehem, PA where he spends his time listening obediently to his wife, Shelley, while doling out money to their five children and four grandchildren. His bulldog, Gracie, asks for nothing.

For more information visit www.nigito.com.

Index